The Social Psychology
of Procedural Justice

CRITICAL ISSUES IN SOCIAL JUSTICE

Series Editor: **MELVIN J. LERNER**
University of Waterloo
Waterloo, Ontario, Canada

CHILDREN'S COMPETENCE TO CONSENT
Edited by Gary B. Melton, Gerald P. Koocher, and Michael J. Saks

DEVELOPMENT AND MAINTENANCE OF PROSOCIAL BEHAVIOR
International Perspectives on Positive Morality
Edited by Ervin Staub, Daniel Bar-Tal, Jerzy Karylowski,
and Janus Reykowski

JUSTICE
Views from the Social Sciences
Edited by Ronald L. Cohen

JUSTICE AND THE CRITIQUE OF PURE PSYCHOLOGY
Edward E. Sampson

JUSTICE IN SOCIAL RELATIONS
Edited by Hans-Werner Bierhoff, Ronald L. Cohen, and
Jerald Greenberg

THE JUSTICE MOTIVE IN SOCIAL BEHAVIOR
Adapting to Times of Scarcity and Change
Edited by Melvin J. Lerner and Sally C. Lerner

SCHOOL DESEGREGATION RESEARCH
New Directions in Situational Analysis
Edited by Jeffrey Prager, Douglas Longshore, and Melvin Seeman

THE SENSE OF INJUSTICE
Social Psychological Perspectives
Edited by Robert G. Folger

THE SOCIAL PSYCHOLOGY OF PROCEDURAL JUSTICE
E. Allan Lind and Tom R. Tyler

A Continuation Order Plan is available for this series. A continuation order will bring
delivery of each new volume immediately upon publication. Volumes are billed only
upon actual shipment. For further information please contact the publisher.

The Social Psychology
of Procedural Justice

E. Allan Lind

Institute for Civil Justice
The RAND Corporation
Santa Monica, California

and

Tom R. Tyler

Northwestern University
Evanston, Illinois
and The American Bar Foundation
Chicago, Illinois

Plenum Press • *New York and London*

Library of Congress Cataloging in Publication Data

Lind, E. Allan (Edgar Allan), 1948–
   The social psychology of procedural justice.

   (Critical issues in social justice)
   Includes bibliographical references and index.
   1. Justice, Administration of. 2. Social contract. 3. Social psychology. I. Tyler, Tom
R. II. Title. III. Series.
K240.L56   1988   340′.115   87-38473
ISBN 0-306-42726-5

© 1988 Plenum Press, New York
A Division of Plenum Publishing Corporation
233 Spring Street, New York, N.Y. 10013

Printed in the United States of America

Preface

We dedicate this book to John Thibaut. He was mentor and personal friend to one of us, and his work had a profound intellectual influence on both of us. We were both strongly influenced by Thibaut's insightful articulation of the importance to psychology of the concept of procedural justice and by his empirical work with Laurens Walker demonstrating the role of procedural justice in reactions to legal institutions. The great importance we accord the Thibaut and Walker work is evident throughout this volume. If any one person can be said to have created an entire field of inquiry, John Thibaut created the psychological study of procedural justice. (To honor Thibaut thus in no sense reduces our recognition of the contributions of his co-worker, Laurens Walker, in the creation of the field. We are as certain that Walker would endorse our statement as we are that Thibaut, with characteristic modesty, would demur from it.)

Even to praise Thibaut in this fashion falls short of recognizing all of his contributions to procedural justice. Not only did he initiate the psychological study of the topic, he also built much of the intellectual foundation upon which the study of procedural justice rests. Thibaut's work with Harold Kelley (1959; Kelley & Thibaut, 1978) created a social psychological theory of interdependence that, among many other applications, serves as the basis for one of the major models of the psychology of procedural justice. His work with Claude Faucheux and Charles Gruder (Thibaut, 1968; Thibaut & Faucheux, 1965; Thibaut & Gruder, 1969) on the role of contractual norms in the resolution of conflict both illustrated the utility of the Thibaut and Kelley model and presaged one of the most important themes of procedural justice—that all parties to a relationship can benefit from social contracts that limit and channel egoistic inclinations. As we shall see in Chapter 2, this idea is an important feature of the Thibaut and Walker work on procedural justice, which viewed procedures as social contracts to regulate conflict for general benefit. Even after he moved on to topics other than procedural justice, Thibaut's interests in the psychology of conflict and the psychological foundation of social institutions led to work closely linked to many important issues in procedural justice. His research with Chester Insko and others (e.g., Insko *et al.*, 1980) on the emergence of leadership norms and on the psychology of group identity and intergroup conflict addressed topics that are likely to be important in future research and theory on procedural justice.

Thibaut's death was a great sadness and an enormous loss to our field. We are fortunate, however, that a scientist of his caliber shared our interests and devoted so much of his intellect, time, and energy to understanding procedural justice. We who study the field, and all who benefit from its applications, owe much to John Thibaut.

We would like to acknowledge here the support and encouragement of many other scientists. The completion of this book owes much to the early and continuous encouragement of Melvin Lerner. Many of our fellow procedural justice researchers, individuals whose works will be cited frequently throughout this book, have encouraged us in this enterprise. Laurens Walker has encouraged us in our research and in our work on this book. Robert Folger, Jerald Greenberg, and Blair Sheppard have also offered much encouragement and have been constant allies as we tried to carry the message of procedural justice to audiences inside and outside psychology.

We would also like to acknowledge the support that the field in general and our own research in particular has received from the Law and Social Sciences Program of the National Science Foundation. The Director of the Program, Felice Levine, has been instrumental in encouraging our work in procedural justice and in engendering an active and vibrant field of procedural justice research. Without the support of the Law and Social Sciences Program, beginning with its funding of the original Thibaut and Walker project, there might well be no coherent field of procedural justice research. Without Felice Levine's encouragement in particular the field would be far less advanced than it is now.

Allan Lind's work in procedural justice has been supported by the National Science Foundation, the Institute for Civil Justice at the RAND Corporation, RAND's Behavioral Sciences Department, and the University of Illinois Research Board. At the University of Illinois, thanks are due to the faculty and students of the Department of Psychology, and especially the members of the Social, Organizational, and Individual Differences Division. At RAND, Barbara Williams, Deborah Hensler, Gus Shubert, David Kanouse, Kevin McCarthy, and Richard Darilek have especially been instrumental in creating a climate of encouragement and support that contributed substantially to this book. Direct support for Lind's work in completing the book has been supplied by the RAND Behavioral Sciences Department. Special thanks are due two of Lind's ICJ colleagues, Deborah Hensler and Bill Felstiner, who offered both their encouragement for this enterprise and, even more important, the stimulus for thought that comes from shared interests.

Tom Tyler would like to thank the American Bar Foundation and its former director John Heinz for support and encouragement in both his research on procedural justice and his efforts to complete this book. ABF project directors Lori Andrews, Jonathan Casper, Janet Gilboy, Wayne Kerstetter, Robert Nelson, Raymond Solomon, and Eric Steele also provided helpful comments on the research described here. The Northwestern University Center for Urban Affairs and Policy Research, directed by Margaret Gordon, provided a congenial environment within which much of Tyler's contribution was written. Special thanks are due to Christopher Jencks, Dan Lewis, Jane Mansbridge, and Wesley Skogan for helpful suggestions.

A number of people read and commented on an earlier draft of this book: Robert Bies, Jeanne Brett, Ronald Cohen, Jerald Greenberg, Eugene Griffin, Valerie Hans, Larry Heuer, Gina Ke, Robert Kidder, Kwok Leung, Mack O'Barr, and Judith Resnik. Their suggestions resulted in substantial improvement in the manuscript, and we are very grateful indeed for their help and their interest.

Contents

Chapter 1. Introduction 1

Outcomes and Process 1
Scope of the Present Book 2
Organization of the Book 5

Chapter 2. Early Research in Procedural Justice 7

Early Research on Procedure and Psychology 7
Distributive Fairness and Equity 10
The Work of Thibaut and Walker 12
When Do People Turn to Third Parties? 13
Adversary and Inquisitorial Systems of Justice 17
Procedural Justice as Fairness 30
Procedural Justice and the Distribution of Control in
Decision Making 34
The Thibaut and Walker Theory of Procedure 36
Description of the Theory 36
Comment and Critique 39

Chapter 3. Research Methods in Procedural Justice Research ... 41

Research Designs 41
Laboratory Experiments 41
Scenario Studies 46
Field Experiments 48
Field Studies 50
Correlational Designs 51
Convergence of Findings in Procedural Justice Research 57

Chapter 4. Procedural Justice in Law I: Legal Attitudes and
Behavior   61

Procedural Concerns in Law   62
Consequences of Procedural Fairness Judgments   63
Consequences of the Experience of Procedural Justice   64
Procedural Preferences   83

Chapter 5. Procedural Justice in Law II: Sources and
Implications of Procedural Justice Judgments   93

Sources of Procedural Fairness Judgments   93
Control over Process and Decision   94
Expression and Consideration of Arguments   101
Other Procedural Fairness Standards   107
Outcome Effects on Procedural Fairness   110
Other Desiderata of Legal Procedures   112
Accuracy of Evidence and Decisions   113
Issues of Current Debate   118
Policy Implications of Procedural Justice: The Case of Court-
Annexed Arbitration   124

Chapter 6. The Generality of Procedural Justice   129

Leventhal's Theory of Procedural Justice   130
A Theory of Procedural Justice Judgments   131
Comments and Critique   134
Context, Culture, and the Generality of Procedural Justice
Concepts   135
Studies of Context and Procedural Justice   136
Studies of Culture and Procedural Justice   141

Chapter 7. Procedural Justice in the Political Arena   147

Consequences of Judgments about the Fairness of
Government   149
The Basis of Public Reactions to Government Policies and
Authorities   151
Influences on Policy Evaluations   155
Influences on Incumbent and System Evaluations   160
Implications   162
Procedural Justice and Political Behavior   166
What Is Procedural Justice in Politics?   170
Voice   170
A Theory of Fair Political Process   172

Chapter 8. Procedural Justice in Organizations **173**

Procedures in Organizations 173
Procedures and Fairness in Organizational Psychology 175
   Equity and Motivation 175
   Participation and Satisfaction 176
Consequences of Procedural Justice in Organizations 177
   Organizational Attitudes 177
   Distributive Fairness and Outcome Satisfaction 179
   Compliance with Organizational Rules and Decisions 187
   Procedural Justice and Performance 188
Antecedents of Procedural Justice in Organization 191
   Control and Expression 191
   Other Fairness Standards 197
Designing Organizational Procedures 200

Chapter 9. Conclusions and Hypotheses **203**

The Validity of Procedural Justice Phenomena 203
   Methodological Concerns 203
   Substantive Concerns 206
Generalizations of Procedural Justice 208
   New Relations 208
   New Arenas 211
The Meaning of Procedural Justice 215
   Process and Decision Control 215
   New Determinants of Procedural Justice 216
Implications of the Procedural Justice Literature 217
   Implications for the Social Sciences 217
   Applications 218

Chapter 10. Two Models of Procedural Justice **221**

The Self-Interest Model 222
   Description of the Model 222
   Predictions from the Model 226
   Strengths and Limitations of the Model 228
A Group Value Model 230
   Procedures as Elements of Groups and Societies 231
   Predictions from the Model 237
   Strengths and Limitations of the Model 239
Reconciliation of the Two Models 240
Implications of Procedural Justice for Social Psychology 241

Appendix 243

References 249

Author Index 261

Subject Index 265

Chapter 1

Introduction

OUTCOMES AND PROCESS

In social psychology, as in the behavioral and social sciences more generally, people have often been viewed as evaluating social experiences, relationships, and institutions on the basis of the outcomes they receive. Theorists have differed in precisely how they think outcomes are linked to evaluations, but a general focus on outcomes characterizes some of the most widely accepted explanations of social behavior. Economists and public choice theorists (e.g., Laver, 1981) have focused on the absolute favorability of outcomes. Some psychologists have focused on the level of outcomes relative to expectations (e.g., Thibaut & Kelley, 1959), others have been concerned with outcomes relative to norms of fair distribution (e.g., Adams, 1965; Walster, Walster, & Berscheid, 1978). Although these approaches differ in many ways, they all assume that people judge their social experiences in terms of the outcomes they receive and that attitudes and behavior can be explained by these outcome-based judgments.

This book presents a field of social psychology that offers a different image of the person. It views people as more interested in issues of process than issues of outcome, and it addresses the way in which their evaluations of experiences and relationships are influenced by the *form* of social interaction. There are many dimensions of social process that might be important in determining reactions to experiences; we focus on the one dimension that has dominated psychological research on the topic: judgments that procedures and social processes are just and fair.

To many social scientists, the suggestion that people care about *how* allocations are made seems counterintuitive. The presumption that outcomes drive evaluations of social experiences is strong in all the social sciences, and it conforms to widely held lay views of "human nature." There is a tension between outcome-based and process-based models of

1

the person that manifests itself repeatedly in procedural justice research. For example, much procedural justice research has been designed to test whether procedures actually invoke fairness judgments independent of the outcome the procedure yields. Even after procedural effects on fairness judgments had been found to occur independently of outcomes, questions arose about whether the fairness judgments resulted from expectations that certain outcomes usually accompany certain procedures. Much of this book is devoted to exploring these issues in a variety of settings and to pursuing the theoretical and applied implications of evidence that process judgments are important determinants of attitudes and behavior.

An illustration will help show why one would want to study procedures and processes and why there is any need at all for process-based models of attitude and behavior. Some of the most intuitively compelling examples of the importance of process are situations in which a person receives favorable outcomes in a social situation but is nonetheless dissatisfied. Such dissatisfaction is difficult to understand if it is assumed that people are concerned only about outcomes but is often easily explained if it is assumed that people are concerned about process. Consider an example from some recent research on reactions to traffic court in the city of Chicago (Tyler, 1987c). Judges in that court often take the view that showing up for court and losing a day's pay at work is punishment enough for a traffic offense. As a result, those who arrive in court often have their case dismissed without any hearing. From a defendant's perspective this is a good outcome—the defendant pays no fine, does not go to jail, and has no violation record. However, interviews with traffic court defendants suggest that despite these favorable outcomes they often leave the court dissatisfied. For example, one woman showed up for court with photographs that she felt showed that a sign warning her not to make an illegal turn was not clearly visible. After her case was dismissed (a victory!) she was angry and expressed considerable dissatisfaction with the court (as well as making several unflattering remarks about the judge). Outcome-based models might find the woman's dissatisfaction difficult to explain, but process-based models would have little trouble in accounting for her reaction: the woman felt angry because the outcome she received was not arrived at using a procedure that met her standards of proper judicial process.

SCOPE OF THE PRESENT BOOK

This book reviews current theory and research on procedural justice and explores its implications for legal, political, interpersonal, and work-related settings. The study of procedural justice is one part of the more general study of the social psychology of justice. Like other areas of justice research, procedural justice begins with the hypothesis that there is a class of psychological reactions to adherence to or violation of norms that prescribe certain patterns of treatment or certain patterns of alloca- tion (cf. Lerner, 1986). Such reactions have long been known to exert a powerful influence on human cognitions and behavior.[1] The norms that form the basis of the justice response can be divided into two categories, those dealing with social outcomes and those dealing with social pro- cess, that is, with proper behavior and treatment of people. Justice judg- ments based on norms of social process are the topic of this book.

There are several distinctions that are relevant to the scope and organization of the book. The first of these is the distinction between outcome-based and process-based explanations of reactions to social experiences, which we discussed above. A related distinction concerns whether a particular justice judgment is based on norms about proper outcomes or norms about proper procedures—as just noted, we are concerned here with the latter, with *procedural* justice. Another crucial distinction is that between justice as a subjective, psychological re- sponse and justice as an objective state of affairs. Our major concern is with subjective justice, although, as we will see in a moment, one can- not ignore the possibility that subjective judgments of justice might be inaccurate.

The justice of social processes, procedures, and outcomes can be discussed with reference to either subjective or objective standards. Thus, one can study what it is that makes some procedures *seem* to be more fair than others, or one can study whether there are features of some procedures that make them more accurate or that make their deci- sions more just according to some objective standard. *Objective procedural justice* concerns the capacity of a procedure to conform to normative standards of justice, to make either the decisions themselves or the decision-making process more fair by, for example, reducing some clearly unacceptable bias or prejudice. *Subjective procedural justice* con- cerns the capacity of each procedure to enhance the fairness judgments

---

[1]In Anglo-American societies we frequently use the term *fairness* to describe a social situa- tion in which norms of entitlement or propriety are fulfilled, and we will use the terms procedural *justice* and procedural *fairness* interchangeably in this book to describe such situations. In doing so, however, we do not mean to imply that cultures that lack concepts easily translatable as "fairness" lack procedural justice effects. We believe that whether violation of an entitlement is labeled "unfair" or "inappropriate" or "impolite," the psy- chological consequences are much the same. In support of our contention that the justice response is universal, we document in Chapter 6 a number of studies that show general- ization of procedural justice effects across nations and across cultures.

of those who encounter procedures. The effort to apply some objective rule to establish fairness has occupied the attention of philosophers, political scientists, and lawyers for centuries. Since the time of Plato and Aristotle, philosophers have devoted attention to choosing standards against which social justice might be measured, and the questions they have raised continue to provoke debate among such contemporary philosophers as Rawls and Nozick.

This book is concerned for the most part with subjective justice. For recent reviews of social psychological studies of objective procedural justice the reader is referred to Kassin and Wrightsman (1985), Kerr and Bray (1982), Hans and Vidmar (1986), and Kaplan (1986). We will discuss issues of objective justice only when, as in the initial work on procedural justice by Thibaut and Walker, those issues are intertwined with efforts to study feelings about fair process.

But in the interest of avoiding misunderstanding, we entreat the reader to remember throughout the book that our major interest is in subjective justice. In order to avoid awkwardness of expression, we often write about procedural justice being high or low when what we mean is that those involved feel that the process was fair or unfair. We recognize, though, that people's feelings that they were or were not fairly treated can sometimes be erroneous in terms of objective standards of justice. Indeed, we will refer frequently to the problem of "false consciousness" of procedural justice, by which we mean that people believe a given procedure to be structured and enacted fairly when in fact, by objective standards, it is not.

An example of the potential conflict between psychological and objective approaches to the study of justice is suggested by Marxist theories that articulate the concept of "false consciousness." According to these theories, powerful members of society have created a set of political and cultural rules that benefit them but harm other members of society. To legitimize these rules, particular norms of distributive and procedural justice are articulated to suggest that the existing social system is fair. New members of society grow up accepting these norms and, as a result, view the existing social system as "fair." Although people may, therefore, feel fairly treated, this feeling of subjective fairness is regarded as "false consciousness" in that it is in conflict with the true self-interest of the disadvantaged. These theories of society provide the important insight that people's feelings about fairness should not be uncritically accepted as the key input into normative evaluations of institutions.

Conflicts between subjective and objective standards of fairness can also occur on a more mundane level. The research we will describe in later chapters shows that people usually feel more fairly treated when they have had an opportunity to express their point of view about their situation. In small claims court cases this means that all parties to a case would like to have an opportunity to tell their story, taking as much time as they feel they need to articulate the issues that matter to them. But judges must often limit such opportunities for expression because of judicial concerns with efficiency and legal propriety. They must be sensitive to the caseload they must handle, and this may prompt them to limit litigants' opportunities to speak. Judges are also knowledgeable about the law and may restrict litigants' opportunities to present information that is legally irrelevant or inappropriate. In these situations, the judge is acting to maximize objective justice and legal efficiency, but his or her actions may clash with the experience of subjective justice on the part of the litigant.

Finally we note that the scope of the book and the scope of procedural justice judgments as a psychological phenomenon extend beyond decision-making procedures. Most procedural justice studies and almost all procedural justice theory to date have concerned reactions to formal or informal procedures for making outcome allocations and resolving social conflicts. In this context, procedural justice concerns the way that decisions are made rather than the nature of those decisions themselves or their implications for the outcomes received by different people. But, as we note later in the book, in Chapters 5, 9, and 10, there is recent evidence showing that the definition of procedural justice with reference only to social decision-making procedures places artificial restrictions on procedural justice phenomena. Recent studies have shown that judgments of procedural justice arise in contexts in which no real decision is made and that procedural judgments are stimulated by factors such as respect or politeness, which have nothing really to do with decision making. These findings show that procedural justice judgments are stimulated by a general concern with process entitlements, which may be triggered outside the social decision-making contexts that have been to date the focus of most research in the area.

ORGANIZATION OF THE BOOK

We regard the publication of the Thibaut and Walker book *Procedural Justice: A Psychological Analysis* in 1975 as a seminal event in the emergence of the social psychology of procedural justice. Although the study of process has a long history within social psychology, it was Thibaut and Walker who combined the study of process with an interest in the psychology of justice to initiate the study of procedural justice. The 1975 book introduced procedural justice to a wide audience and presented the original research through which Thibaut and Walker established the value of the psychological investigation of the concept. We begin this book with a discussion of the original Thibaut and Walker work (Chapter 2).

The Thibaut and Walker research, and criticisms of their use of laboratory methods, raised a number of questions about how procedural justice should be studied. Chapter 3 addresses these methodological issues. There we consider the rationale for the laboratory methods used in the early studies of procedural justice, and we discuss the wider variety of research methods used in more recent research on procedural justice.

The original research on procedural justice focused on dispute resolution in law. Legal forums have remained the most common settings for procedural justice research, and Chapters 4 and 5 review work in this area. Chapter 4 deals with the consequences of the perception of procedural justice for such issues as satisfaction with legal experiences, evaluations of legal authorities and institutions, and compliance with laws. Chapter 5 examines the factors that affect procedural justice judgments and explores the policy implications of our growing knowledge of procedural justice in law.

Since the social psychology of justice is fundamentally concerned with social allocation rather than with dispute resolution, the bulk of early procedural justice research was peripheral to the traditional concerns of many psychologists interested in justice judgments. More recent work has broadened the base of procedural justice research. Chapter 6 discusses work of this type, describing cross-situational and cross-cultural studies of procedural justice, as well as the theoretical work of Gerald Leventhal, which encouraged a view of procedural justice as an element of all social allocation settings.

Procedural justice concepts have been applied successfully in research on the political arena and work organizations. We describe research in these two areas in Chapters 7 and 8, respectively.

Having explored the psychology of procedural justice in a variety of settings, we describe findings common across areas in Chapter 9. There we present the general conclusions that seem to be justified on the basis of our current knowledge of procedural justice, and we advance a number of hypotheses for future research.

In Chapter 10, we close the book with a consideration of the implication of current research for theory in procedural justice. We discuss two general models of the person and the manner in which each model accounts for some of the basic findings of procedural justice.

Early Research in Procedural Justice

The systematic study of the psychology of social decision-making procedures began with the work of John Thibaut, Laurens Walker, and their colleagues in the early 1970s. Thibaut and Walker in their 1975 book and in an earlier article with Stephen LaTour and Pauline Houlden (Thibaut, Walker, LaTour, & Houlden, 1974) first used the term *procedural justice* to refer to social psychological consequences of procedural variation, with particular emphasis on procedural effects on fairness judgments.[1] Prior to that time, the study of justice as a topic in psychology had been concerned largely with distributive justice, that is, with fairness-oriented responses to outcomes rather than procedures. Our goal in this chapter is to describe the origins of procedural justice research.

EARLY RESEARCH ON PROCEDURE AND PSYCHOLOGY

Although origin of the study of procedural justice is associated most strongly with the work of Thibaut and Walker, a number of social psychologists had earlier conducted research on procedural issues. In fact, this earlier work addressed some of the same topics now studied under the rubric of procedural justice. The relation of this previous literature to current procedural justice theory and research was perhaps best conveyed by social psychologist James Davis' comment that, like Molière's character Monsieur Jourdain who discovered one day that he had been speaking prose for more than forty years, Davis felt upon reading the Thibaut and Walker work that he had been doing procedural justice research for quite some time. By focusing research and theoretical analy-

---

[1]Several other well-known social psychologists contributed to the early acceptance of procedural justice, e.g., Deutsch (1975); Lerner & Whitehead (1980); Leventhal (1976, 1980).

ses on procedure *per se* and by positing a connection between process and justice, Thibaut and Walker identified a concept—procedural justice—that permitted them to draw on the work of these earlier researchers and provided an organizing principle for later research.

Many studies of leadership behavior and its consequences are conceptually quite similar to procedural justice research. The classic studies by Lewin, Lippitt, and White (1939; White & Lippitt, 1960) are an early example. Lewin *et al.* varied what they termed the "social climate" introduced by adult counselors in boys' recreational groups. Three social climates were studied: an "autocratic" climate, which involved extensive counselor control over decisions about the organization of the group and the tasks it undertook; a "democratic" climate, which involved counselor encouragement of voting on these issues; and a "laissez faire" climate, which involved minimal counselor involvement in decisions. One could argue that these "climates" were really procedures for group decision making, which varied in terms of the extent to which the adult leader controlled the decisions. The Lewin, Lippitt, and White studies showed that the autocratic climate produced the most task-oriented behavior (that is, the most time devoted to work), but that the democratic climate produced friendlier and more cohesive groups without much decrement in performance. From the perspective of procedural justice research these studies are noteworthy as very early demonstrations that variation in decision-making procedures does affect the behavior and attitudes of those subject to the procedure.

Another example of procedural effects in leadership research can be found in the work of Hollander and Julian on the legitimacy of elected and appointed leaders (see Hollander, 1985). Their studies showed that elected leaders are less vulnerable to rejection by the group than are appointed leaders. Although this difference is not interpreted by Hollander and Julian as being due to the procedural justice of the elective and appointive processes, their findings are in line with the procedural justice literature. Thibaut and Walker, for example, found that decisions are more likely to be accepted when the procedure used to generate the decision allows participation by those affected. One especially noteworthy feature of the Hollander and Julian findings is that it is similar to a frequent finding in procedural justice research: that evaluations of leaders are strongly affected by the perceived fairness of procedures associated with the leader. Later chapters will consider at some length the relations among characteristics of procedures, procedural justice, and leadership.

Many studies of group structure and performance have used manipulations and measures similar to those studied by procedural justice researchers. For example, early studies of communication networks share with more recent procedural justice studies a concern with the attitudinal and behavioral consequences of variations in the availability of potential communication channels. Several experiments on procedural justice in the law have examined the effects of various prescribed and proscribed patterns of communication among disputants and judges (e.g., Lind, Erickson, Friedland, & Dickenberger, 1978; Thibaut, Walker, LaTour, & Houlden, 1974), a topic that recalls the classic communication network studies (e.g., Bavelas, 1950; Leavitt, 1951; Shaw, 1954). Research on communication networks typically placed subjects in more or less central positions in a variety of networks, where positions and networks were defined in terms of which subjects could or could not communicate with each other. In general, communication network research has shown that subjects report greater satisfaction with the group when they are in more central positions or more open networks; that is, subjects are more satisfied when they are allowed to communicate with more members of the group. As will be seen below, when we describe work on a procedural feature known as "process control" or "voice," this finding presaged one of the most reliable findings in research on procedural justice: that people react more favorably to procedures that give them considerable freedom in communicating their views and arguments. However, as Folger, Rosenfield, Grove, and Corkran (1979) have noted, prior to procedural justice research on process control and voice *per se* it was not clear whether the satisfaction differences seen in communication network research were due solely to variation in communication procedures. Because of the way in which communication network research was done, the studies could not determine whether network effects on satisfaction were a direct result of the procedural variation or whether they arose from differences in the level of performance or the quality of outcomes experienced by members of the group.

Finally, there is a body of research that developed at about the same time as the Thibaut and Walker work, but largely independent of it, that studied the consequences of jury procedures on verdicts. An excellent example of this work is the research on group processes in jury decision making conducted by James Davis and his students (see, e.g., Davis, 1980). Davis has investigated the relation between jurors' individual judgments about the guilt or innocence of a criminal defendant and the final verdict of mock juries. He has developed "social decision schemes," mathematical models relating distributions of individual juror judgments to the probability of each possible group verdict, and he has used the social decision schemes that were most often observed in mock juries to analyze the likely effects of procedural variation. His research and analyses have focused on issues of objective procedural justice such as the effects on verdicts of various jury sizes and various decision rules. This work has demonstrated that procedural variations do indeed affect social decisions, and together with the work already described it shows the value of using theories and methods from social psychology in the analysis of procedures.

The various areas of investigation described above had two important effects on the development of procedural justice as an area of scientific endeavor. First, they showed that variation in social decision-making procedures affects variables of interest in social, organizational, and political psychology. Knowing that procedural variation affects the satisfaction and behavior of those subject to a procedure made the focus on procedural variables initiated by Thibaut and Walker a reasonable step. The systemization of knowledge on procedural effects had to await the focus of attention on procedures *per se*, but when this shift of focus occurred there was research other than that of the Thibaut and Walker group to be included in theories of procedural justice. To state it differently, because of this previous research the Thibaut and Walker focus on process *per se* and their assertion that there was a link between procedures and fairness were ideas that were revolutionary without being radical. A second important consequence of the previous research was that it demonstrated that issues very much like those that arose in the study of procedural justice could be investigated using the laboratory methods popular in social psychology. We will have more to say on this second point in the next chapter.

DISTRIBUTIVE FAIRNESS AND EQUITY

There is another body of theory and research that helped set the stage for the study of procedural justice. By the time the Thibaut and Walker group began working on procedural justice, several theorists had suggested that *distributive justice* was an important factor in social behavior (Adams, 1963, 1965; Blau, 1968; Homans, 1961). The most influential of these theories for early work in procedural justice was Adams' equity theory.

Adams argued that social behavior is affected profoundly by beliefs that the allocation of benefits and costs within a group should be *equitable*, that is, that outcomes should be proportional to the contributions of group members. He suggests that equity is such a fundamental norm that when the allocation of outcomes does not meet the standard of proportionality individuals in the group will experience "inequity distress," a motivational state that prompts actions to restore equity. One of the most remarkable features of equity theory was its prediction that even those benefiting from inequity would feel inequity distress and would act to restore equity one way or another. Adams admitted that the direction of the inequity would be a major factor in determining how one went about restoring inequity, so that those advantaged by inequity would choose, if they had a choice, a means of restoring equity that would not diminish their outcomes. However, Adams' theory predicts that, if it is the only way to achieve a sense of equity, people advantaged by inequity will forego that advantage in the interest of fairness. As we will see below, procedural justice research has shown similar effects for procedural fairness judgments.

By the early 1970s, when the Thibaut and Walker work began, there was a growing body of research supporting and extending Adams' theory. The idea that fairness is a major social concern played an important role in the development of procedural justice, of course. Also important was the idea, prompted directly by Adams' theory and indirectly by the results of some cognitive dissonance studies (cf. Festinger, 1957), that actions and attitudes sometimes fly in the face of apparent outcome advantage. As we will see later in this chapter, one of the most important discoveries of procedural justice research has a similar message: that even those receiving poor outcomes from a procedure will react more favorably if the procedure is fair.

About the time Thibaut and Walker were doing most of their early work on procedural justice the study of distributive justice was expanding rapidly. It was becoming increasingly apparent that Adams' equity rule (i.e., that outcomes should be proportional to contributions) was only one of several rules of distributive fairness. Other fairness rules that are now known to have substantial influence on social behavior involve norms of equality and norms of need-based allocation. New theories have emerged that link distributive fairness concerns to a variety of social contexts and phenomena (e.g., Lerner, 1970, 1974; Leventhal, 1976; Walster, Berscheid, & Walster, 1973). In this context, the development of procedural justice can be viewed as one of two lines of research on the psychology of justice, both of which emerged as topics of considerable activity in the 1970s. As we will see at the conclusion of this chapter, by 1978, when Thibaut and Walker published their most extensive theoretical work on procedural justice, distributive justice was sufficiently well-developed for them to offer the normative suggestion that procedures for resolving outcome disputes should be judged in terms of the likelihood that they would achieve equitable decisions.

The importance of distributive justice concepts was also suggested by the literature on relative deprivation (Merton & Rossi, 1957). That literature suggested that individuals' reactions to their experiences could not be predicted by knowledge of the absolute quality of those experiences. The theory of relative deprivation proposes that individuals judge their situation not in absolute terms, but by comparing it to the situation of those around them. Individuals could encounter a favorable situation in objective terms and still feel dissatisfied, or they could be reasonably happy in conditions that seem objectively to be quite poor. The theory of relative deprivation has had a widespread impact on social science thinking about discontent. It has been particularly influential in writing about why people engage in acts of civil disorder, such as rioting, and in acts of political violence (Moore, 1978; Muller, 1979).

Theories of relative deprivation are important to the psychology of justice because research on political and social discontent stimulated by that theory has suggested that people's comparisons with others are heavily dependent on their views about justice. For individuals to feel deprived when they lack some resource, it is necessary for them to feel that they deserve that resource. Analyses of such judgments of deservedness required the use of concepts of fairness and justice (see Crosby, 1976, 1982; Folger, 1986b). Hence, as was true with the equity literature, the relative deprivation literature contributed to a climate in which the study of subjective fairness judgments was recognized as important.

THE WORK OF THIBAUT AND WALKER

Thibaut and Walker summarize their initial research project in *Procedural Justice: A Psychological Analysis (1975)*. The book has three sections, each addressing a different concern with respect to procedure and dispute resolution. The first section explores the question of when disputants will turn to a third party to help them resolve their conflict. Psychological theories of social exchange are used to develop several hypotheses that are tested in experiments on the relationship between various dispute characteristics and the form of third-party intervention needed or preferred. In this section of the Thibaut and Walker book the range of dispute-resolution procedures under consideration includes bargaining, a variety of non-binding third-party procedures (for example, mediation and moot procedures), and binding arbitration and adjudication.

The second section addresses both psychological and legal issues. The focus is on dispute-resolution procedures that involve binding decisions by a third party: that is, arbitration and adjudication. This section reports studies that explore the effects of idealized adversary and inquisitorial legal procedures on two aspects of procedural justice: objective justice and subjective justice. Both objective justice and subjective justice are studied from a psychological perspective; in both instances the major interest is the effect of procedural variation on social perception, social judgment, and behavior. The legal issues addressed in this section of the Thibaut and Walker book are those surrounding the use of two well-known constellations of courtroom procedure, the Anglo-American adversary system and the European inquisitorial system.

The third section of the book deals with broad questions concerning the psychological and cultural underpinnings of preferences for various adjudication procedures. The relation between perceived fairness and procedural preferences is explored, and the proposition is advanced that fairness is the preeminent determinant of disputant preferences for conflict-resolution procedures. Thibaut and Walker then elaborate their theoretical position as they seek to explain the procedural justice effects reported in the book. Their analysis emphasizes the level of disputant control over the adjudication process, and the basic ideas that they advance remain today some of the major topics of discussion, debate, and research in procedural justice. In the remainder of this chapter we present a summary of their research and theory. Subsequent work on procedural justice has been profoundly influenced by their work, and only with an appreciation of their contribution can one understand the current state of knowledge.

WHEN DO PEOPLE TURN TO THIRD PARTIES?

According to social exchange explanations of social behavior, people are motivated by the desire to maximize their gain in interactions with others (Thibaut & Kelley, 1959). In line with this motivation, people seek to obtain and maintain control over decisions that might affect their outcomes. At the same time, however, people recognize that the maintenance of social relationships and the resolution of disputes sometimes require that control over decisions be relinquished to a third party. Two of the studies reported by Thibaut and Walker (1975) concern the conditions under which there is a real or perceived need for third-party intervention in disputes and the forms of third-party intervention that appear best to meet the desires of disputants.

Thibaut and Walker (1975, chapter 3; see also Erickson, Holmes, Frey, Walker, & Thibaut, 1974; Walker & Thibaut, 1971) conducted a study that examined the need for binding third-party intervention in disputes. The research focused on whether disputes could be resolved by mediation, a procedure in which an impartial third party offers suggestions for resolving the dispute but is not allowed either to dictate or to veto any particular settlement. This study was an important first step toward work on binding third-party procedures because if some substantial class of disputes could not be resolved by mediation, it would suggest that the study of procedural justice must include research on more intrusive third-party procedures, such as adjudication, that involve the imposition of a binding third-party decision.

On the basis of social exchange theory and research on the social psychology of bargaining, Thibaut and Walker hypothesized that mediation would be less successful in resolving disputes in which the outcomes of the two sides were strongly "noncorrespondent," that is, disputes in which interests are so directly and severely opposed that there was little opportunity for mutual benefit from a negotiated settlement (see Thibaut & Kelley, 1959, for more on the concept of correspondence of outcomes).

In a laboratory study, law students and young lawyers taking a bar review course participated in a simulation of mediation procedures modeled on those used in pretrial settlement conferences. Half of the subjects attempted to negotiate a settlement for a dispute in which the potential outcomes of the two sides were only mildly noncorrespondent; the remaining subjects attempted to negotiate a settlement for a dispute in which the outcomes of the two sides were severely noncorrespondent. The results of the experiment supported the hypothesis. When outcomes were mildly noncorrespondent fully two-thirds of the disputes were settled, but when outcomes were severely noncorrespondent only one-third of the disputes were settled. In other words, when the dispute was characterized by severe noncorrespondence of outcomes, as are many real-world disputes, mediation was usually insufficient to produce resolution of the conflict and more intrusive third-party intervention was needed.

In a later study, Thibaut, Walker, and their colleagues examined several factors that might influence the desirability of certain types of third-party intervention (LaTour, Houlden, Walker, & Thibaut, 1976; Thibaut & Walker, 1975, chapter 2). They considered the effects of three factors—the need to resolve the dispute quickly, the degree of outcome correspondence, and the extent to which a clear standard existed for resolving the dispute—in determining which of several procedures should be used. The study examined reactions to four third-party dispute-resolution procedures: mediation (wherein a third party may only suggest how the dispute might be resolved), moot (wherein both disputants and the third party must all agree on the resolution), arbitration (wherein the third party resolves the dispute by binding judgment but only after the disputants have had a chance to explain their positions), and autocratic adjudication (wherein the third party resolves the dispute by binding judgment without explicit provision for information input by the disputants).[2] These four third-party procedures were compared to bargaining without the assistance of a third party. The five procedures represent five points on a continuum of third-party control over the dispute-resolution process; bargaining, with no third-party involvement, constituted the low end of this continuum, followed in order by mediation, moot, arbitration, and autocratic adjudication. The study used a rather complicated approach in which undergraduate subjects were placed in the role of disputants in each time pressure, outcome correspondence, and standard availability condition and asked to rate the importance of various desiderata of an ideal procedure. A separate sample of law students rated the five procedures on the extent to which each procedure fulfilled each desideratum. A multidimensional weighting scheme was used to compute how well each procedure met the desires of the disputants in each condition. Because of the peculiar methodological approach, there is some reason to question what exactly the study tells us about the psychology of procedural justice. The results should certainly not be interpreted as indicating straightforward disputant preferences as do studies in which disputant preferences are measured directly. At best, the results tell us which procedures disputants *should* prefer, if the law students were correct in their assessment of the extent to which each procedure met the various criteria. But the experimental method may well be overrationalizing the preference phenomena; disputants may not actually exhibit the preferences they "should" in this sense.

The overall results of the study showed that the arbitration procedure best met the disputants' desires for a dispute-resolution procedure, followed by moot, mediation, bargaining, and autocratic adjudication, in that order. The results suggest that disputants desire some third-party control in dispute-resolution procedures but that they generally reject the high level of third-party control that characterizes the autocratic procedure. This overall ordering was affected by each of the three factors manipulated in the experiment. Under severe time pressure, presence of a standard, or severe noncorrespondence of outcomes, ideal procedures are more likely to involve high levels of third-party control. In addition, some combinations of the three factors produced results that were not what one would expect from the effects of each factor alone. For example, the strongest movement toward acceptance of high levels of third-party control over the dispute-resolution process

[2]In this study, as in most studies of procedural justice, the terms used by the researchers to describe the procedures in their reports were not used in the materials given to the subjects. The stimulus materials contain only neutrally worded descriptions of the procedures, and did not use such emotion-charged terms as *autocratic, inquisitorial,* or *adversary.*

was seen under conditions of severe time pressure, presence of a standard, and *mild* noncorrespondence of outcomes. Thibaut and Walker summarize their findings eloquently:

> [A]utocratic procedures are likely to be sought by men in hurried pursuit of common goals who agree on a standard (a credo or an ideological canon) that can be quickly applied to resolve differences in belief. Equally responsive to third-party control are those who unequipped with a standard must quickly resolve unmanageable conflict. Contrariwise, those least inclined to delegate control to third parties are persons who are at leisure to develop through full discussion a surrogate standard for settling their differences about ways to achieve their common goals. (Thibaut & Walker, 1975, p. 16)

These two studies had a profound impact on the development of procedural justice research as a field of psychological study. Following the direction that Thibaut and Walker took after conducting these two studies, procedural justice research focused for quite some time on binding procedures and high levels of conflict. Only relatively recently, beginning with the work of such scholars as Houlden (1980) and Brett and Goldberg (1983), have nonbinding dispute resolution procedures been studied. The net result is that we know much more about the procedural justice of binding procedures than the procedural justice of nonbinding procedures.[3]

The two studies described in this section strongly influenced the research agenda of the Thibaut and Walker group. Thibaut and Walker used the results of the first study, which showed that two-thirds of severe disputes were not resolved by their mediation procedure, to justify their focus on binding, adjudicative procedures in most of their later research. The curvilinear relation between third-party control and desirability, observed in the study just described, emphasized the need to understand why some third-party control seems to be desired but too much seems to be disdained. This in turn contributed to a focus on the study of the consequences of binding procedures that differ in third-party control; and most often this involved the comparison of two legal procedures that resemble the autocratic and arbitration procedures studied in this experiment—the inquisitorial and adversary procedures.

---

[3]One topic suggested by the results of the second study described above has been neglected by procedural justice researchers. The study found that high third-party control is more acceptable when the dispute involves individuals with common interests, under time pressure, and possessing a standard. In other words, parties appear to be willing to give the third party substantial control over the conflict not only when the dispute is very difficult but also when it is very easy to resolve. Thibaut and Walker, in their more recent theoretical statement (1978; see the last section of this chapter), made use of this finding of acceptance of third-party-controlled inquisitorial hearing procedures when standards and common interests are present. However, there has been little empirical investigation of procedural justice in "easy" disputes.

ADVERSARY AND INQUISITORIAL SYSTEMS OF JUSTICE

Having decided to focus on binding dispute resolution procedures such as arbitration or adjudication, Thibaut and Walker turned to the question of which particular binding procedure might be best. The universe of procedures that they consider is not extensive; they focus on inquisitorial and adversary adjudicatory procedures and variations of these two basic procedures.[4] The concern with third-party control, which was introduced in the study just described, is much in evidence in the decision to study these two procedures. In the pure inquisitorial procedure both the decision that resolves the dispute and the process of investigation that precedes the decision are under the control of the third party. In contrast, in the adversary procedure the decision is in the hands of the third party, but the disputants and their lawyers control the investigatory, information-development process.

The implications of adoption of an adversary or inquisitorial procedure pervade the legal process from the filing of a lawsuit or indictment to the final appeal, but a basic sense of the difference between the two procedures can be gained by comparing an American criminal trial, structured according to the adversary procedure, to a French criminal trial, structured according to the inquisitorial procedure. In the American trial, most of the evidence is produced through the questioning of witnesses by the attorneys for the prosecution and defense. Each attorney asks questions designed to elicit information favorable to the side of the case he or she represents. The judge is largely passive, ruling on objections when the attorneys raise them but participating only infrequently in the questioning of witnesses. Each attorney is given extensive opportunities to present arguments favorable to his or her side of the case. When both sides have concluded their presentations, the judge or jury renders a verdict. In contrast, in a French trial, most of the evidence is available to the judge or judges at the beginning of the trial, having been discovered by an investigating judge and included in a *dossier* that seeks to present all information relevant to the case. In a French trial witnesses are questioned almost exclusively by the judge. In the French trial, it is up to the judge, not to the attorneys for the two sides, to decide when enough evidence has been heard.

In considering the research reported in the second section of the Thibaut and Walker book and described below, it is important to keep in mind that the procedural variations included in the studies involved manipulations of who had (or appeared to have) control over the at-

---

[4]As noted below, another limitation on the procedures examined by the Thibaut and Walker work was that they were idealized, "pure" versions of each procedure. There was no attempt to sample the many real variations that exist for these procedures.

torneys and manipulations of whether there were separate presentations of the evidence favoring the two sides of the case. There was never
any direct manipulation of the behavioral style of the attorneys. Thus
the experimental manipulations did not include elements that might
reflect traditional notions of combative adversary trials or bureaucratic
inquisitorial trials. Indeed, in the interest of achieving rigorous experimental control, in the experiments dealing with the psychology of disputants and decision makers the behavior of the attorneys was held
constant across the various procedures. What was varied was the control and power relations specified by the procedures or the format used
in the presentation of evidence.

Thibaut and Walker describe the aspects of adversary and inquisitorial procedure that they studied as "pure forms," meaning that
they contain only those features that characterize the procedure in an
idealized perfect enactment of the procedure. They justified this approach in two ways. First, the early research was conducted with no
certainty that procedures affected either objective or subjective justice,
and the use of pure forms of each procedure provided a strong test of
the consequences of the procedures. Second, Thibaut and Walker note
that much procedural debate in law deals with idealized versions of the
procedures. Only by investigating the psychological consequences of
similarly idealized versions of the procedures could the research speak
directly to issues in this debate.

This focus on structural aspects of the adversary–inquisitorial procedure may have lead to a somewhat more flattering picture of the
adversary procedure than would have been the case if stylistic features
commonly thought to accompany adversary trials had been included in
the studies. On a basic level, however, the structural focus can be seen
to be quite proper. Initial studies in procedural justice research had to
focus on procedures, after all, and procedures are usually designed and
described in structural terms. Further, the stylistic features that accompany various procedures might well be viewed as a result of the procedure, not as elements of the procedures themselves. As it turned out,
the early emphasis on structural issues was fortunate. As research results accumulated, it became evident that structural manipulations have
simpler effects than do stylistic manipulations (see, e.g., Lind, 1974;
Thibaut & Walker, 1975, pp. 97–101), making structural variables a more
productive target for early research on procedural justice.

Objective Consequences of Procedures

The Thibaut and Walker group conducted several experiments that
examined the relative merits of adversary and inquisitorial procedures

with respect to objective criteria of justice. As we noted in Chapter 1, one dimension on which procedures can be compared is the objective quality of their products. For example, one might compare procedures in terms of their accuracy, looking at the frequency with which each procedure convicts the guilty and acquits the innocent. Our primary topic in this book is research on subjective, not objective, justice. The review of early work on objective justice, which occupies the next few pages, is included for two reasons. First, these studies illustrate that it is often more difficult to study objective justice than subjective justice. Second, these studies are important to the normative theory of procedure that Thibaut and Walker advanced in 1978, and that theory influenced later work on subjective justice. Hence we discuss objective justice here, although it is not our major concern.

There are two major difficulties in evaluating procedures in terms of objective criteria. First, one must find some way to establish a standard for measuring the extent to which a procedure meets a given objective criterion. Second, one must decide which objective criteria are important and what trade-offs should be made among various desiderata of procedures.[5] The first difficulty is illustrated by the problem of measuring accuracy: how is one to know which defendants are truly guilty or innocent?[6] The second difficulty arises when one procedure is found to be best on one justice criterion and another procedure is found to be best on another justice criterion: how does one decide which criterion should be used to select the procedure? These two difficulties often preclude definitive conclusions about the objective merit of a procedure.

Thibaut, Walker, and their students compared the adversary and inquisitorial systems on three factors relevant to objective justice. They studied the capacity of the two procedures to minimize pretrial bias, minimize order effects in evidence presentation, and maximize the amount and accuracy of information reaching the decision maker. They were able to overcome the problem of establishing an objective standard for judging the effects of the procedures by using prescaled stimuli that allowed them to assess, within the context of each particular experi-

[5]Davis (1980, pp. 198–208; Davis, Spitzer, Nagao, & Stasser, 1978) has raised similar concerns in an analysis of some of the problems that arise in deciding what constitutes bias in jury decision making. The reader is referred to his work for a discussion that explores these problems in considerable detail.

[6]In their laboratory studies of subjective justice, Thibaut and Walker did in fact "manipulate" guilt or innocence by controlling the information subjects received about wrongdoing on the part of a member of their group. This is one advantage of the early use of laboratory methods in procedural justice research. Had the early research used field methods, many of the effects reported in this chapter would never have been discovered. We return to this issue in Chapter 3.

ment, the accuracy and biases of the procedures under study. In addition, by studying phenomena in which there was little question concerning the desirability of particular effects, they were able to produce results that were amenable to relatively straightforward interpretation. For example, the two studies described next used case materials that were selected (on the basis of a previous scaling study) so as to produce a test case that was nearly perfectly balanced with respect to the evidence—half the evidence indicated unlawful action on the part of the defendant and half indicated lawful action. This allowed the researchers to interpret as bias any deviation from the scale midpoint on ratings of the guilt of the defendant. Value trade-off issues did not arise in these two studies because each study examined only one criterion of objective justice. Only in the third study described below did the issue of value trade-offs and choice among various justice criteria arise. We will discuss this problem further when we have described the experiment in which it arose.

Few would doubt that the objective fairness of a procedure is enhanced if the procedure reduces the effects of bias or prejudice arising from factors irrelevant to the decision at hand. One form that such bias can take is deciding one case in terms of expectations derived from cases unrelated to the case on trial. For example, an obvious injustice would take place if a procedure facilitated the conviction of a defendant in a criminal case because of an expectation on the part of the judge or jury that most people charged with this type of crime were in fact guilty. One of the experiments conducted by Thibaut and Walker (1975, chapter 6; Thibaut, Walker, & Lind, 1972) tested the capacity of adversary and inquisitorial trial procedures to reduce the effects of a prior expectancy bias in legal decision making. In this laboratory experiment some subjects were exposed to a series of cases designed to lead them to have a prior expectancy bias, while others were given no such experience. All of the subjects then heard evidence in a test case and reached a decision. If one of the procedures under study was successful in eliminating the effects of the bias, the decisions of biased and unbiased subjects would be similar. If the procedure was unsuccessful in eliminating the bias, the biased subjects would differ from the unbiased subjects in that they would make decisions in line with their bias.

The subjects in the experiment were undergraduate students. The experiment induced a prior expectancy bias in half of the subjects by having them decide six legal cases in which the behavior of the defendant was similar to that of the defendant in the seventh, test case. The defendants in five of the six biasing cases had acted in a manner that was clearly unlawful. All of the subjects in the experiment, those exposed to the biasing experience and those not exposed, were then presented with evidence in the test case and asked to judge the lawfulness of that defendant's action. The test case was constructed so that the evidence favoring the conclusion that the defendant's behavior was lawful was balanced equally with evidence favoring the conclusion that his action was unlawful. Thus, any expectancy bias would appear as judgments below the midpoint (0) on the lawfulness scale. In order to test which of the two legal procedures was more effective in combating expectancy bias, half of the subjects saw the evidence in the test case presented by one attorney, as in the inquisitorial procedure, while the other half saw the evidence presented by two attorneys, as in the adversary procedure.

Figure 2-1 shows the mean final judgments of biased and unbiased subjects who received adversary and inquisitorial presentations. As can be seen from the figure, the effect of prior expectancy bias was weaker in the adversary procedure conditions than in the inquisitorial procedure conditions. Thus the adversary procedure was more effective in combating expectancy bias. Thibaut and Walker (1975, chapter 6; Lind, Thibaut, & Walker, 1976) report a positive replication of this study using French undergraduate students as subjects.

A second type of bias that can lessen the objective fairness of an adjudication procedure comes from irrelevant features of the hearing process itself. Most of us would agree that it would not be fair for a defendant to be viewed less favorably because of some irrelevant aspect of courtroom procedure, such as which side was permitted to present evidence first. Similarly, we would prefer that the outcome of a case not

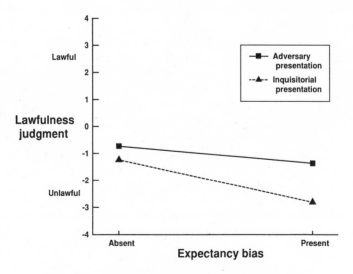

FIGURE 2-1. Adversary presentation and expectancy bias.

depend too much on purely tactical features of the lawyers' presenta-tions. Thibaut and Walker (1975, chapter 7; Walker, Thibaut, & An-dreoli, 1972) conducted an experiment that investigated the effects of gross procedural differences in the order of evidence presentation (pros-ecution–defense versus defense–prosecution) and the effects of finer, tactical differences (weak–strong versus strong–weak) in the ordering of evidence within these gross orders. This experiment used a method very much like that employed in the prior expectancy bias experiment, but in this study only unbiased subjects and only adversary presentations were used. As in the study just described, the evidence included in the attorneys' presentation was selected on the basis of a previous scaling study so that the judgment that best reflected the evidence would be a rating at the midpoint of the rating scale assessing the judged lawfulness of the defendant's actions.

The results of the study showed that the condition that came closest to producing an unbiased result in the case was the combination of prosecution-first, defense-second in the gross ordering and weak-to-strong ordering of facts within each side's presentation. Thibaut and Walker point out that this order is precisely what one would expect to occur at an adversary trial in which the gross order is dictated by estab-lished procedure and the fine ordering reflects each side's informed efforts to win the case. They argue that the adversary procedure is desirable because it can be expected to minimize order effects through the working of informed self-interest.

A third aspect of objective fairness that received attention from the Thibaut and Walker research group concerns the accuracy of the infor-mation collected by attorneys and transmitted to the legal decision maker, the judge or jury. It seems reasonable to assume that one wants the information reaching the decision maker to be both complete and unbiased.[7] One of the first studies conducted by the Thibaut and Walker group examined the consequences of various role specifications on the investigation of a dispute and the transmission of information to the decision maker (Lind, 1975; Lind, Thibaut, & Walker, 1973; Thibaut & Walker, 1975, chapter 5). The study tested an assertion advanced by advocates of adversary procedures who argued that attorneys in adver-sary justice systems are more diligent in their investigation of a case than are attorneys in inquisitorial systems.

---

[7]This assumption may not always be warranted; there are certainly some instances in which one would choose to have incomplete or biased information in the interest of achieving some other criterion of justice. Note that legal principles such as those involved in the Fifth Amendment to the U.S. Constitution and the "exclusionary rule" in American law mandate foregoing completeness and accuracy of information under some circum-stances in the interest of higher goals.

It had been argued that this greater diligence results in more and better information reaching the legal decision maker in adversary trials than in inquisitorial trials. The issue under study is somewhat complex, and a fictional illustration may help. The essence of the assertion tested in the experiment can be illustrated with reference to a popular film, *The Verdict*. In the film, a down-and-out attorney named Frank Galvin is representing a young woman who has been in a coma for years as the result of the negligent actions of a pair of doctors. In the beginning of the film Galvin is portrayed as an alcoholic who uses a variety of cynical ploys to get clients with a minimum of effort. But in the course of the film, he becomes increasingly involved in the malpractice case and ultimately uncovers a critical piece of evidence largely by virtue of his perseverance and diligence in fulfilling his role as an advocate for his side of the case.

In the film, the result of Galvin's diligence in fulfilling his adversary role is the discovery of a piece of evidence that would not otherwise have reached the jury. Galvin's opponent, played in the film by James Mason, is diligent in a less desirable fashion. He is quite ready to suppress the truth and to use unethical means to thwart Galvin's efforts. If we contrast these two images of the consequences of the adversary attorney roles, we see some of the basic questions that the experiment sought to address. On one hand, there is the question of whether the adversary role, because it aligns attorney and client interests, would provoke a deeper search for information than would a nonpartisan, inquisitorial role. On the other hand, there is the question of whether the adversary role would lead to biasing of the information so that the array of evidence ultimately reaching the judge or jury would not fairly represent the actual facts in the case.

In the experiment the subjects, who were law students, were given either the role of an adversary attorney (they were told that they should try to obtain a favorable outcome for one of the disputants in the case and that their payment in the experiment would depend on how well they discharged this duty) or the role of a inquisitorial attorney (they were told that they should try to assist the judge in making the best decision and that their payment would depend on how well they discharged this duty). Regardless of their role, the subjects were led to believe that there was another law student working on the case and that there were undergraduate students involved in the experiment as decision makers and disputants. The outcomes of the disputants were said to depend on the actions of the law students. In addition to the manipulation of the subject's role, there was a second manipulation, which involved giving some of the law students evidence that was evenly balanced with respect to the two sides of the case and giving others

TABLE 2-1. Information Gathered by Attorneys
in Adversary and Inquisitorial Roles

| | Attorney role assignment | |
Initial fact environment	Adversary	Inquisitorial
50%–50% (Case balanced)	21.0	22.6
75%–25% (Case favors attorney)	18.2	23.0
25%–75% (Case disfavors attorney)	26.0	20.2

Note. Values are mean numbers of facts discovered. This table is based on
Table 1 in Lind, Thibaut, and Walker (1973). Parenthetical notes in labels of
fact environments indicate whether distribution favored or disfavored attorney if he was assigned the adversary role.

evidence that favored one disputant or the other.[8] Adversary attorneys
were confronted with cases in which 25%, 50%, or 75% of the evidence was
favorable to their client.

The subjects had to invest their own resources in the investigation
of the case. Facts had to be bought from the experimenter, and the cost
of the facts was subtracted from the law students' own monetary payment for the experiment. The subjects could buy as many facts as they
wished. When they ceased buying facts they had to select which of the
facts were to be transmitted to the decision maker. The major dependent
variables in the study were the number of facts purchased by subjects in
the various conditions and the extent of bias in the facts presented by
pairs of attorneys whose role assignments matched the adversary and
inquisitorial procedures. Table 2-1 shows the results with respect to the
number of facts gathered. The investigations of individual adversary
role attorneys were more extensive than those of inquisitorial role attorneys only when the case was unfavorable to the adversary attorney's
client; otherwise adversary and inquisitorial attorneys gathered about
the same number of facts.

It was possible to compare the facts presented by pairs of attorneys
to the overall distribution of facts initially supplied to the pair. When the
facts presented by pairs of opposing adversary attorneys were compared
to the facts presented by pairs of inquisitorial attorneys, a somewhat
complex pattern of bias was seen. Regardless of the nature of the case,
inquisitorial pairs presented unbiased distributions of facts. Adversary
pairs investigating balanced cases also presented facts that were in total
unbiased; the bias in each attorney's presentation was offset by the bias

[8]A third manipulation concerned the purported role of a second law student participating
as an attorney in each experimental session. This manipulation did not qualify any of the
effects described here.

in his opponent's presentation. However, when the case was unbalanced, adversary pairs of attorneys presented distributions of facts that consistently overrepresented the proportion of facts favorable to the disputant with the fewest favorable facts. When adversary pairs encountered unbalanced cases, the distribution of the evidence presented was 36%–64%, rather than the 25%–75% distribution that actually existed in these cases. Adversary and inquisitorial pairs presented about the same total amount of unique information to the decision maker.

One interpretation of the results of this study might be that the inquisitorial procedure leads to better information gathering and presentation. The claimed advantage of the adversary system—that it leads to more diligent investigation—was confirmed in only one condition. Further, the balanced investigation by favored and disfavored adversary attorneys resulted in a complex pattern of bias in the presentations of adversary pairs. The inquisitorial pairs, on the other hand, generated as much information as did the adversary pairs and did so with accurate presentations under all conditions. However, some additional considerations raise questions about this interpretation of the experiment.

Consider the problem of choice of criteria that we mentioned in our discussion at the beginning of this section. As long as immediate accuracy in the information reaching the decision maker is the only criterion being considered, there is no problem in interpreting the experiment along the lines advanced in the preceding paragraph. But is this always what we want from a legal procedure? There are certainly instances, in the law and elsewhere, wherein procedures are deliberately made inaccurate because one desires to be especially careful to avoid certain errors. In the law, the "reasonable doubt" decision rule in criminal trials deliberately allows those who are probably, but not certainly, guilty to go free in order to avoid convicting those who are not guilty. In scientific research, one sees similar deliberate use of inaccuracy. For example, the use of the ".05" alpha level in inferential statistics deliberately accepts the substantial likelihood that some real effects will not be detected in order to minimize the likelihood that spurious effects will enter the literature. One could argue, as did Thibaut, Walker, and Lind, that the inaccuracy in adversary presentations could be a positive, rather than a negative, feature.[9] A conditional bias in favor of the party disadvantaged by the evidence could have at least two benefits. First, it would

---

[9]There is an apparent inconsistency between counting prior expectancy bias as an unquestionably negative feature in prior studies and counting information transmission bias as a possibly positive feature in this study. The inconsistency disappears in a later theoretical analysis of this study, the Thibaut and Walker theory of procedure (1978) which treats any type of bias as antithetical to accuracy in decision making. The information transmission bias could lead to frivolous lawsuits, as we note in Chapter 4.

assure that a full investigation would be conducted even if the initial evidence seemed, erroneously, to indicate an "open-and-shut case." Second, a conditional bias of this sort would make it more difficult for the party who is most likely to lose the case to complain that he or she had not received adequate consideration by the decision maker. Other researchers have found this line of reasoning less than persuasive, and more recently Thibaut and Walker (1978) have offered a theory that includes a different interpretation of the implications of the results of this study. We will discuss that theory at the end of this chapter.

Subjective Consequences of Procedures

In addition to studying the effects of procedures on objective criteria of justice, Thibaut, Walker, and their colleagues examined how procedural factors affect people's perceptions of the fairness of dispute resolution events and outcomes. Here their concern was with whether disputants and neutral observers *believe* that procedures and outcomes are fair, rather than whether the procedures or outcomes were fair in some objective sense. One of the most striking discoveries of the Thibaut and Walker research group was the finding that satisfaction and perceived fairness are affected substantially by factors other than whether the individual in question has won or lost the dispute. Once it had been found, in the studies described below, that variations in procedure resulted in across-the-board raising or lowering of the satisfaction of both winners and losers, an important potential application of procedural justice research was evident. This finding showed that it is possible, by judicious choice and design of procedures, to enhance the quality of social life without increasing the external outcomes available for distribution under the procedures. One of the great contributions of Thibaut and Walker is that they saw so clearly and so early that knowledge of the psychology of procedural justice might have critical importance in a world where resource constraints dictate that routes to satisfaction depend on something other than favorable outcomes.[10]

Thibaut and Walker advance another reason for concern with the effects of procedures on the feelings of litigants. Disputes often occur in the context of mutually profitable, ongoing social exchanges, and one must consider the feelings of those involved in the dispute in any attempt to assure that the resolution does not disrupt the original relationship. In the words of Thibaut and Walker, subjective justice is "crucial because one of the major aims of the legal process is to resolve conflicts

---

[10]The work of Thibaut and Walker emphasized beneficial applications of procedural justice. Later work, especially that of Ronald Cohen (1985) has pointed out that procedural justice can be abused.

in such a way as to bind up the social fabric and encourage the continuation of productive exchange between individuals" (1975, p. 67). Especially critical in this regard are the feelings of the litigant who loses an adjudication—it is the loser who, one would imagine, is most likely to distrust the procedure and the outcome and whose reactions pose the greatest obstacle to making the dispute resolution work as it is intended. If procedures exist that can enhance the satisfaction of even those who lose a case, it would certainly be important to know what those procedures are and how they function to enhance satisfaction.

One of the early experiments of the Thibaut and Walker group tested whether procedural variation alone could cause changes in the perceived fairness of and satisfaction with adjudicatory procedures and outcomes. As noted earlier, research on social climates and communication networks had shown that satisfaction differences often accompanied other effects of procedural variation. A study by Walker, LaTour, Lind, and Thibaut (1974; Thibaut & Walker, 1975, chapter 8) sought to determine whether variation in adjudication procedures affected the fairness judgments of disputants. To provide an unambiguous test, performance and outcome were controlled and only the independent and direct effect of procedure could influence subjects' reactions.

This experiment set out to investigate the effects of adversary and inquisitorial procedures on the fairness judgments of disputants in a laboratory adjudication. The study did this by creating an experimental situation that placed subjects in apparent conflict over an alleged rule violation and that resolved the conflict using either an adversary or an inquisitorial hearing procedure. The subjects, who believed that they were taking part in a simulation of a business competition, were told that their team had been charged with stealing ideas from an opposing team and that a hearing would be held to resolve the dispute and determine which team would be given the cash prize at stake in the competition. (The rule violation charge involved alleged misconduct by another member of the subject's team, who was in fact an experimental confederate.) In the adversary procedure conditions, evidence was presented at the hearing by two lawyers selected by the disputing subjects. Each lawyer was said to have been directed to present the most favorable case he could for the disputant he represented, and each lawyer's outcomes were supposedly tied to a favorable outcome for his client through the use of a contingent fee arrangement. In the inquisitorial procedure conditions, all of the evidence at the hearing was presented by a single lawyer selected by the judge. This lawyer was said to have been directed to present both sides' evidence, and his outcomes were said to be independent of the outcome of the trial.

Several steps were taken to control variables that might have produced indirect satisfaction or fairness effects. Performance prior to the initiation of the dispute resolution procedure was controlled by having the experimental confederate produce a constant product. Performance at the hearing itself was controlled by having the same evidence and arguments presented regardless of the procedure used. The effects of the outcome of the dispute resolution hearing were separated from those of the procedure by manipulating outcome as an independent variable in the experiment—half of the subjects in each procedure condition received a favorable verdict and half received an unfavorable verdict. The subjects' beliefs about the accuracy of the charge of rule violation were also manipulated by giving evidence to some subjects that the charge was true, evidence that the charge was not true to others, and to the rest no evidence at all.

Major dependent variables in the study were subjects' ratings of the fairness of the hearing, their ratings of the fairness of the hearing procedure, and their ratings of the fairness of the verdict. Other rating scales assessed the subjects' satisfaction with the verdict and the procedure. The ratings were made soon after the subject had been informed of the verdict.

Table 2-2 shows the mean ratings of the fairness of the procedure by subjects in each of the procedure and outcome combinations. In general the data showed strong main effects for both the procedure and the outcome manipulations. Most important for the study of procedural justice, fairness and satisfaction were higher in the adversary procedure conditions than in the nonadversary conditions, and this difference was not limited by interactions involving either the outcome or belief manip-

TABLE 2-2. Fairness of Procedure and Satisfaction with Verdict Ratings of Disputants in Adversary and Inquisitorial Hearings

	Hearing procedure	
Outcome of hearing	Adversary	Inquisitorial
Fairness of procedure		
Disputant's team found innocent	8.10	6.51
Disputant's team found guilty	4.51	3.08
Satisfaction with verdict		
Disputant's team found innocent	8.71	7.94
Disputant's team found guilty	2.69	1.92

Note. Values are unweighted marginal means for ratings on a nine-point rating scale. Higher values indicate perceptions of greater fairness or satisfaction. From Walker et al. (1974, p. 304).

ulations. The subjects did rate the procedure as more fair when they won than when they lost, but this outcome effect was independent of the procedure effect.

The manner in which procedural justice judgments can differ markedly even in the face of similar outcomes is illustrated dramatically when one considers the procedural fairness ratings of subjects who knew their team to be innocent of the charged offense but who were found guilty. Subjects in this situation who experienced the inquisitorial procedure showed very low ratings (1.13 on the nine-point rating scale), whereas subjects in this situation who experienced the adversary procedure showed ratings almost at the midpoint of the scale (4.13).

The results of the study just described were important not only because they provided the first unambiguous demonstration of attitudinal effects of procedural variation and thereby did much to establish the study of procedural justice as a topic of inquiry, but also because they illuminated some notable limitations of two major social psychological theories. Theories of social behavior based on "social exchange" theory (e.g., Thibaut & Kelley, 1959) and equity theory (Adams, 1965) view outcomes as the major determinant of satisfaction and perceived fairness. The findings just reported supported this notion only in part. The outcome effects were what one would expect from these theories, but the independent effects of the procedure manipulation showed that outcomes are not the whole story. The experiment demonstrated that the method of reaching a decision, as well as the outcomes resulting from the decision, is important in determining fairness and satisfaction.

It is this finding, that the use of a fair procedure can increase the satisfaction of all concerned *without any increase in the real outcomes available for distribution*, that is probably the most striking discovery of the Thibaut and Walker group. As we noted above, this phenomenon provides an answer to a problem that Thibaut frequently posed in this fashion in discussions with his students: Given a world with constant, or even shrinking, physical resources, how might psychological and social processes be used to increase satisfaction and reduce conflict? Apparently, one answer to the question is that satisfaction can be enhanced through the redesign of the social decision-making procedures of society.

The basic findings of the Walker *et al.* (1974) study have been replicated and extended. LaTour (1978; Thibaut & Walker, 1975, chapter 9) repeated the study with a more finely differentiated manipulation of factors that distinguish adversary and inquisitorial procedures. He included the inquisitorial and adversary conditions described above as well as two intermediate conditions. In a "dual investigator" condition two judge-appointed lawyers whose outcomes did not depend on the outcome of the case each investigated and presented different sides of the case. In an "assigned adversary" condition two judge-selected lawyers who would be paid on a contingent fee basis investigated and presented each side of the case. LaTour found that ratings of procedural fairness and satisfaction with the procedure increased in more or less equal steps from the inquisitorial to the dual investigator to the assigned adversary to the full adversary conditions. Satisfaction with the verdict showed a similar effect for subjects found guilty, but this measure showed little procedure effect at all for subjects found innocent.[11] LaTour also collected data from observer subjects and found that their judgments were affected only by the more "structural" portion of the procedure variable (the variation between the single-investigator inquisitorial condition and the double-investigator condition). LaTour's study is also noteworthy because it contributed to the development of the idea that the critical psychological element leading to higher fairness ratings for adversary procedures is that these procedures give disputants more "process control"—more opportunity to express their views and to present their evidence. LaTour conducted a series of covariance analyses that suggested that, for participants at least, the enhancement of procedural fairness was due to the perception that the more adversarial procedures allowed more opportunity for both parties to present evidence.

PROCEDURAL JUSTICE AS FAIRNESS

Having established through the experiments just described that procedures can differ substantially in the procedural fairness judgments they engender, Thibaut and Walker set out to investigate the importance of procedural fairness in determining other subjective reactions to procedures. There was already a strong intellectual foundation for supposing that fairness was a major factor in determining how people evaluate dispute resolution experiences in general and dispute resolution procedures in particular. As noted above, at the time Thibaut and Walker wrote their 1975 book a decade of research based on equity theory had shown that distributive fairness judgments are ubiquitous and influential determinants of satisfaction with conflict resolution and allocations. In addition, the philosopher John Rawls (1971) had advanced a normative theory of societal justice that was based on the analysis of social structures and procedures from the perspective of an individual "behind the veil of ignorance." Rawls argued that social justice results from

[11]This may have been due to a "ceiling effect"—all the subjects gave such high ratings when found innocent that little variation was possible among the four procedures. We will have more to say in Chapters 4 and 8 about whether fair procedures always enhance satisfaction and distributive fairness.

fairness in the basic structure and procedures of society. He defined fair procedures or social structures to be those that would be agreed to or endorsed by an individual who was informed of the structure or procedure in question and who knew that he or she would occupy some position in society but who did not know what that position would be. Thus for Rawls the question of whether, for example, slavery is a fair institution would depend on whether one would expect it to be endorsed by people who knew they would have to live in a slaveholding society but who did not know whether they would be slaves or slave owners. Because we would not expect people "behind the veil of ignorance" to endorse slavery, we conclude that it is an unfair, and therefore unacceptable, institution.

Rawls' theorizing suggested that it was reasonable to ask whether procedural fairness might be the primary factor in disputant preferences for procedures and that an experimental condition based on the concept of the veil of ignorance might be an interesting way of studying the issue. In an experiment based on these ideas, the Thibaut and Walker group studied disputant preferences and other subjective reactions to five dispute resolution procedures (Thibaut & Walker, 1975, chapter 11; Thibaut, Walker, LaTour, & Houlden, 1974). The five procedures included in the experiment were bargaining (consensual dispute resolution without a third party),[12] pure inquisitorial adjudication (adjudication with the third party acting as both investigator and judge), single-investigator adjudication (adjudication with a single investigator who was to work for the adjudicator in developing information and evidence), double-investigator adjudication (adjudication with two investigators who were to be appointed by the adjudicator but each of whom was to be assigned to work with one disputant to develop and present that disputant's side of the case), and pure adversary adjudication (a binding third-party decision procedure with two investigators selected by the disputants and responsible for developing and presenting the case of the disputant).

The subjects in the experiment were told that they would be asked to role-play one of the disputants in a legal case and that they would receive $5 if the case was resolved in a fashion that favored their role over the opposing disputant. The case was constructed so that one of the disputants was strongly favored by the evidence. The subjects were assigned to one of three experimental conditions: some were told that they would be assigned to the role of the disputant favored by the

---

[12]The bargaining procedure used in this experiment was not typical of bargaining as a method of dispute resolution. In order to hold constant the type of outcome that could be produced by each procedure, the bargaining procedure, like the adjudication procedures, was constrained to all-or-nothing outcomes.

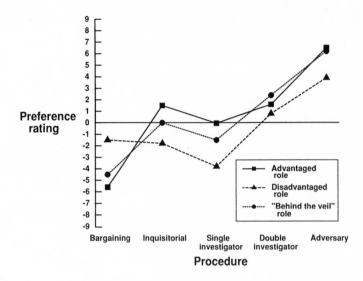

FIGURE 2-2. Preference ratings: Disputant role study.

evidence, some were told that they would be assigned to the role of the disputant disfavored by the evidence, and some were not told which disputant they would be in the forthcoming dispute resolution procedure. The last of these three conditions was designed to create an experimental analogue of the position of being "behind the veil of ignorance" in Rawls' analysis.

The subjects in the experiment were given descriptions of the five procedures under study and were asked to rate their preference for using each procedure as well as their perceptions of each procedure on a variety of dimensions. Figure 2-2 shows the results for the preference ratings, which are noteworthy in two respects. First, subjects in all three roles showed greatest preference for the pure adversary procedure. Second, although the role assignment of the subjects did have some effects on preference ratings, these effects were not sufficiently strong to overcome the general preference for the adversary procedure.

Because each subject rated each of the five procedures on a variety of dimensions, it was possible to examine the extent to which the ratings on a given dimension tracked the subject's preference ratings, in order to see which features of the procedures were most closely related to the preferences.[13] There was a consistent and strong relation between pref-

[13]These analyses used what were in essence simple correlations computed within each subject, across the several procedures rated by each subject. The index suffers from the limitation of any simple correlation in a multivariate context: it cannot show how much of the relationship between the variables is due to other variables. To do this a between-subjects, multiple regression approach is needed.

erence ratings and perceptions of procedural fairness in all three role conditions. The fact that procedural fairness was so closely related to preferences vindicated the attention that Thibaut and Walker were devoting to the psychological processes involved in procedural fairness judgments. A second strongly related rating dimension for subjects who knew what their role assignment would be was the extent to which the procedure was seen as favoring their role. For subjects "behind the veil of ignorance," who did not know their role condition, the second most strongly related dimension was the extent to which the procedure resulted in less control by the judge and the third most strongly related dimension was the extent to which the procedure favored the party disadvantaged by the evidence.

Thibaut and Walker recognized that it was possible that the preference for adversary procedures observed in the experiment just described was due to the use of American undergraduates as subjects in the experiment. The legal system of the United States, like the legal systems of most nations that have taken their legal principles from British law, is based on the use of adversary procedures. One could argue that the findings of the Thibaut *et al.* experiment were seen simply because subjects preferred the dispute resolution procedure that was most familiar to them on the basis of popular knowledge of legal dispute resolution. To test this possibility, a second preference study was conducted (Thibaut & Walker, Chapter 8; Lind *et al.*, 1978), using subjects in the United States and three Western European nations, Great Britain, France, and West Germany. France and West Germany use legal procedures that combine elements of the pure inquisitorial and single-investigator procedures. The research used what is termed a "scenario study" method (see Chapter 3) in which respondents were asked to imagine themselves as a disputant in a dispute over an injury-causing action. Half of the respondents at each site were asked to imagine themselves as the person accused of having done someone injury; the other respondents were asked to imagine themselves as the person accusing someone else of having done them injury. All of the respondents received descriptions of the pure inquisitorial, single-investigator, double-investigator, and pure adversary adjudication procedures used in the original "veil of ignorance" experiment. After reading the descriptions of the procedures, the respondents were asked to rate their preference for using each procedure and their perceptions of the procedures on several dimensions.

The preference ratings are shown in Figure 2-3. Respondents in all four nations, including those whose national legal system is based on nonadversary procedures, preferred the pure adversary adjudication procedure. The cross-national study also led to similar conclusions with respect to the extent to which the various perceptual dimensions were

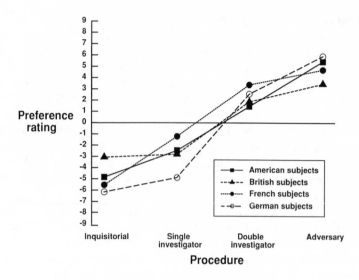

FIGURE 2-3. Preference ratings: Cross-national study.

related to the preference ratings. In three of the four nations fairness was the perceptual dimension most closely related to procedural preferences; in the fourth nation (France) fairness was the second most closely related dimension. We will return to the issue of cross-cultural differences and similarities in procedural justice in Chapter 6. For the moment it is sufficient to note, as did Thibaut and Walker, that at least in Western societies fairness is a major, and very likely *the* major, determinant of procedural preferences.

PROCEDURAL JUSTICE AND THE DISTRIBUTION OF CONTROL IN DECISION MAKING

Establishing that adversary procedures are preferred over inquisitorial procedures and that this preference is to a considerable extent due to the greater perceived fairness of adversary procedures leads to the next logical question. What is it about adversary procedures that leads disputants to see such procedures as fairer than other ways of conducting an adjudication? Thibaut and Walker suggest that the answer to this question lies in the differences between the two procedures in the distribution of control in decision-making.

Thibaut and Walker note that in the two studies described in the last section it was found that subjects had no difficulty discriminating between procedures in terms of the distribution of control among the various individuals involved in the adjudication. Table 2-3 shows mean ratings of the overall amount of third-party control in the four procedures studied in the cross-national study. The rating scales were constructed so that ratings of about "8" indicated the right amount of third-party control. The ratings show not only that the subjects in each country did differentiate the procedures along a dimension of third-party control but also that all of the procedures except the pure adversary procedure were seen as having "too much" third-party control. Thibaut and Walker also note that when they examined the relationship between subjects' fairness ratings and their perceptions of third-party and disputant control, there was a consistent positive relationship between disputant control and procedural fairness and a consistent negative relationship between third-party control and procedural fairness. Again, the implication is that disputants prefer that most of the control over the conflict resolution be vested in them rather than in the role of the third-party. Some third-party control is often necessary and apparently acceptable to disputants. They are willing to give the third-party control over the decision itself, so long as they retain control over the process—that is, over the definition of the issues and the collection and presentation of evidence at the hearing.

Thibaut and Walker, in the closing chapter of their 1975 book and in later publications (Houlden, LaTour, Walker, & Thibaut, 1978; Thibaut & Walker, 1978), discriminate between control over the verdict or judgment in an adjudication, "decision control," and control over the presentation of evidence and arguments, "process control." Thibaut and Walker contend that procedures that vest process control in those affected by the outcome of the procedure are viewed as more fair than are procedures that vest process control in the decision maker. The reason adversary procedures are seen as more fair than inquisitorial procedures is that they conform to the distribution of process control that disputants prefer.

Thibaut and Walker argue that the balanced contentiousness per-

TABLE 2-3. Ratings of Third-Party Control in Four Dispute Resolution Procedures: Cross-National Study

Dispute resolution procedure	Nationality of subjects			
	American	British	French	German
Pure inquisitorial	13.10	12.44	13.21	12.20
Single investigator	11.63	9.44	10.42	10.10
Double investigator	10.11	9.00	10.05	9.43
Pure adversary	8.71	8.34	8.49	8.93

Note. Values are mean control ratings reported by Thibaut and Walker (1975, Table 12–1, p. 120). Scale values ranged from 1 ("Too little") to 15 ("Too much"), with a midpoint value of 8 indicating neither too little nor too much.

mitted by disputant process control will promote objective justice as well as subjective justice. They point to the findings on the reduction of prior expectancy and order effect bias as indications that adversary procedures are superior on both objective grounds. As we describe in the next section, in a later theoretical analysis Thibaut and Walker (1978) modify this position and argue that procedures high in disputant process control are desirable for some types of disputes but not for others. In all instances, however, Thibaut and Walker contend that the distribution of control is a major issue in the psychology of procedure. This view has shaped much subsequent procedural justice research and theory. The focus of research and theory on issues related to process and decision control is one of the most important contributions of the Thibaut and Walker work, nearly as important as their identification of procedural justice as a fruitful area of investigation and their discovery that procedural variation can be used to effect overall increases in perceived fairness and satisfaction.

THE THIBAUT AND WALKER THEORY OF PROCEDURE

DESCRIPTION OF THE THEORY

Thibaut and Walker (1978) used the research described above to generate a theory of procedural justice that extended and superseded the theoretical statements in their 1975 book. The 1978 theory focuses on dispute resolution procedures in general and on legal procedures in particular, but many of the explanations and prescriptions that it offers shed light on the working of social decision-making procedures in other contexts. The theory is a *prescriptive* theory of procedural justice, concerned most with achieving an integration of social psychological knowledge that could guide decisions about when various procedures might have the best overall results for conflict resolution. It is important to remember that the theory is concerned with objective and subjective factors that might affect the design and use of procedures. Less attention is devoted in the 1978 statement than in the 1975 book to the psychological explanation of specific procedural justice phenomena, although the 1978 statement does contain many interesting and enlightening ideas about the psychology of procedural justice.

Thibaut and Walker begin their theory by drawing a distinction between disputes that involve conflicting beliefs about objective truth and disputes that involve the distribution of outcomes. They argue that in the former class of disputes, the principal criterion of successful dispute resolution is the accuracy or correctness of decisions resulting from the procedure; in the latter class of disputes, the principal criterion for successful dispute resolution is the fairness of decisions. Thibaut and Walker point to pure scientific disputes as an example of the first type of dispute. Disputes of this type are termed "cognitive conflicts" (see the work of Hammond and his associates for research on this type of conflict, e.g., Hammond & Adelman, 1976). In scientific disputes the parties are in a situation of nearly complete agreement with respect to their desires or interests; this agreement arises by virtue of socialization to the scientific ethic of disinterested search for knowledge. All concerned want the decision-making procedure to yield the correct answer, and there is little motivation for any of the disputants to prefer one answer over another for reasons other than its accuracy. There exist standards in science for determining which of several rival hypotheses is most likely to be true, and the resolution of a given dispute requires only the application of these standards in an atmosphere of unbiased investigation and logical analysis. A critical feature of procedures for resolving these disputes is that the procedure must allow as complete and as unbiased an investigation as possible. There is little need for concern with the satisfaction of the disputing parties or with fairness in the sense of distributive justice: as long as the disputing scientists hold to their norm of disinterestedness they must accept whatever resolution is dictated by the application of the standard for determining the truth.[14]

In contrast, disputes over the distribution of outcomes, according to Thibaut and Walker, are best resolved when the distribution meets societal definitions of fairness. The disputants in these disputes have strongly conflicting interests: any outcome that satisfies one disputant is likely to be opposed by the other disputant. The only standards that exist for resolving such disputes are general distributional prescriptions such as that which forms the basis of equity theory (Adams, 1965; Walster et al., 1973): that outcomes from a relationship should be in constant proportion to inputs across all members of the relationship. The procedures that are used to resolve disputes of this sort should promote equitable resolutions of the dispute; there is often either no objective standard or a variety of objective standards, each favoring a different party. Thibaut and Walker place most civil and criminal disputes in this category. Disputes of this type are termed "conflicts of interests," because they involve parties who are interested in obtaining incompatible outcomes.

Thibaut and Walker note that the consideration of individual circumstances is especially important in producing equitable decisions, because equity norms require that outcomes be apportioned in terms of

[14]Some have questioned the ability of scientists to be disinterested and neutral.

inputs to the situation, and these inputs include the individual circumstances of each party. For this reason, Thibaut and Walker suggest that the achievement of procedural justice in conflicts of interests is best accomplished using procedures that vest process control in the parties to the dispute. They argue that disputant process control places control over the development of information for the decision in the hands of those most likely to have access to individualized information relevant to the decision. The disputants were, after all, the people most involved in the situation being assessed.

Research on social cognition processes (e.g., Hansen & Lowe, 1976; Jones & Nisbett, 1971; Storms, 1973) has suggested that uninvolved decision makers are likely to overlook information on the individual circumstances that might account for behavior. Uninvolved decision makers tend, often wrongly, to explain events in terms of the characteristics of the people involved. When process control is placed in the hands of the decision maker, this cognitive bias might result in a decision that overlooks individual circumstances. Thus, when process control is placed in the hands of those subject to the decision, Thibaut and Walker argue, individualized information is more likely to be produced and considered.

In an analysis of procedures available for the adjudication of disputes,[15] Thibaut and Walker note that those procedures that are most fair, such as high disputant process-control adversary procedures, also appear to produce substantial inaccuracy and bias in information gathering, as evidenced by the information gathering and presentation study described earlier in this chapter. It appears to be impossible to find a procedure that simultaneously maximizes fairness and accuracy. This observation leads Thibaut and Walker to argue that it is necessary to use different procedures for each of the two main categories of disputes. For disputes in which cognitive conflicts predominate and in which accurate decision making is the major criterion, inquisitorial procedures should be used because such procedures maximize accuracy and minimize bias in information gathering.[16] For disputes dominated by conflicts of interests, procedures high in disputant process control should be used because these procedures, although biased in their information gathering, assure the consideration of individual circumstances that is required to maximize fairness. Finally, Thibaut and Walker recommend that disputes involving both cognitive and outcome conflict use a two-stage adjudication process that consists of a low disputant process-control

[15]Thibaut and Walker focus on adjudicatory procedures because, they argue, in high-conflict situations a binding procedure is necessary to resolve the dispute.

[16]But this recommendation ignores the weakness of inquisitorial procedures in countering prior expectancy bias.

procedure to resolve the cognitive conflict and then a high disputant process-control procedure to resolve the conflict of interests.

COMMENT AND CRITIQUE

The Thibaut and Walker theory is important for our understanding of procedural justice both because it prompted and shaped much subsequent research in procedural justice and because it introduced the idea that no single procedure can maximize all criteria. As we review in Chapters 4 and 5 more recent research on procedural justice in law, some limitations of the theory will become evident. There is some value in mentioning these limitations here, however, while the theory is fresh in our minds.

The first limitation of the Thibaut and Walker theory is that it is not really intended to be a theory of subjective justice. As we noted earlier in this chapter, the theory is an attempt to prescribe which procedures are best in certain given circumstances, rather than an attempt to describe how people evaluate the fairness of procedures. To be sure, one component of the theory is a consideration of which procedures are most likely to be seen as fair, but because this is not the sole concern of the theory, we should take care not to read the Thibaut and Walker suggestions about which procedures are *best* to mean which procedures will be *preferred*.

A more serious limitation of the theory is that even when it is speaking to the issue of procedural fairness the theory evaluates procedures in terms of the outcomes they produce. Thibaut and Walker focused on process control as a major determinant of the fairness of procedures because they believed that control over the evidence and arguments presented at trial lead to greater consideration of individualized arguments, and that this in turn leads to fairer outcomes. Hence procedural fairness is defined in terms of outcome fairness.

Although the Thibaut and Walker argument was congruent with the research available at the time the theory was published, more recent research shows that the last part of the argument—the link between individualized arguments and fair outcomes—does not reflect the whole picture with respect to the psychology of process control. In Chapter 4 we will discuss evidence that procedural fairness is a major cause of distributive fairness, rather than the reverse, and in Chapter 5 we will describe a number of studies showing that process control enhances procedural fairness because it promotes opportunities for expression, whether or not it promotes fairer outcomes. In general, the gist of work since the publication of the Thibaut and Walker theory has been that procedure and process *per se* are more important and outcomes are less important than the theory indicates. In this sense, bold as the Thibaut and Walker statement was at the time it was published, it was less bold than it should have been concerning the importance of procedure.

Notwithstanding these limitations, there is no doubt that the theory should be credited with producing a substantial increase in the level of sophistication of procedural justice research and with motivating much of the subsequent work in the area. The attention that the theory gave to process control had an especially profound influence. As we will see in later chapters, studies of the sources of the procedural justice experience have devoted more attention to process control than to any other factor.

Chapter 3

Research Methods in Procedural Justice

RESEARCH DESIGNS

The study of procedural justice phenomena has used a variety of research methods: laboratory experiments, scenario studies, field experiments, field studies, and surveys. In this chapter we will discuss each of these methods and consider their strengths and weaknesses. Especially in recent years, procedural justice research has used many different research methods. The diversity of methods allows research to compensate for the weaknesses inherent in any one method with the strengths of other methods. Where the findings of studies using different methods converge we can be certain that the phenomena discovered are not artifacts of any particular research method. Such convergence of findings from different research methods has occurred with respect to some of the most important discoveries of procedural justice research.

LABORATORY EXPERIMENTS

The earliest procedural justice studies (e.g., Lind *et al.*, 1973; Thibaut *et al.*, 1972; Walker *et al.*, 1974) used laboratory experimental methods, as have many later studies in the area. Because questions have been raised about the validity of laboratory experiments in procedural justice research (e.g., Damaska, 1975; Hayden & Anderson, 1979), we will pay particular attention to the rationale for and proper uses of this research method. We do so because we believe that previous criticisms of the use of laboratory methods in procedural justice have not always been correct in identifying the weaknesses and strengths of such methods. Proper interpretation of the implications of the numerous labora-

41

tory experiments on procedural justice requires an understanding of the logic and practice of these studies.

The methodological strengths of laboratory experiments derive from the high level of control that a researcher is able to exert over the manipulation and measurement of variables and over the context within which a phenomenon occurs. This high level of control allows the researcher to eliminate at the start many complications that would make a field study on the same topic difficult or impossible to interpret. In procedural justice research this feature of laboratory experiments has been used to good advantage. Early procedural justice studies sought to test whether variation in procedure *per se* produced differences in attitudes or behavior, the control afforded by laboratory methods was crucial. For example, in the Walker *et al.* (1974) experiment on perceived fairness and satisfaction with procedures (described in Chapter 2), it was critical that the researchers eliminate or control extraneous factors that might produce differences in perceived fairness and satisfaction. The laboratory setting allowed the pretrial and posttrial experiences of the subjects to be held constant, except for those that were intentionally manipulated. The laboratory setting also allowed the researchers to expose the subjects to independent manipulations of the outcome of the dispute, the subject's beliefs about the justification for the accusation being tried, and the trial procedure, so that any differences seen between the two procedures could be attributed unambiguously to the procedure variable and not to either of the other two manipulations.

Without the level of control possible in laboratory experiments, it would have been much more difficult to show clearly that procedural variation alone could affect perceived fairness. In a field experiment or a field study, different procedures can produce outcomes that are at least slightly different, and it is very difficult to demonstrate conclusively that these outcome differences do not cause the differences in fairness judgments. There are, to be sure, a number of statistical techniques that could be used to attempt to remove the effects of different outcomes, but none of these techniques can match the control of the situation that is possible in the laboratory.

We do not mean to imply that laboratory experiments are always the best method for research on topics such as procedural justice. Rather, we want to show why the Thibaut and Walker group chose these methods and what benefits (and costs) resulted from that choice. As we describe other methods later in this chapter, we will point out advantages that they have over laboratory methods for addressing some procedural justice issues.

The Thibaut and Walker research was guided by the idea that laboratory experiments are most effective when the goal of the research is to test theories in a deductive fashion or to study situations that rarely or never arise in natural settings. The first of these uses of experiments is best understood in the context of the philosophy of science of Karl Popper (1959). Popper notes that advance in any scientific discipline comes from advance in scientific theory. Theory is advanced and improved by the testing of hypotheses deduced from theory, specifically by disconfirmation of theories through the disconfirmation of relations predicted from the theory. When disconfirmations are found, new theory must be developed to replace the old. The new theory must explain the findings that disconfirmed the old theory as well as other findings in the area. The development of theory is viewed as the major goal of science and research is viewed as an enterprise to develop theory by disconfirming theoretical predictions. (Confirmation of theoretical predictions is less useful than disconfirmation, because of the logical principle that confirmation of the consequent of a deductive relation—in this case confirmation of the relation predicted by the theory—does not confirm the antecedent—the theory itself.) Another point in the Popperian argument is that scientific theories must be complete; that is, theories must specify all limitations on the phenomena they address. The theory should include sufficient specification of the phenomena to permit a researcher to determine whether a given laboratory situation is an appropriate test of the theory. A high level of specification is also necessary if a scientific theory is to be usefully applied; without specification of the limits of theory-predicted relations it is not possible to determine whether a phenomenon can be applied in a given situation.

From a Popperian perspective, laboratory experiments are entirely appropriate for testing theory *provided that the relation deduced from the theory can be reproduced in the laboratory, given the limitations on the phenomena explicit in the theory.* In other words, the logic of laboratory methods does not require that they accurately or completely duplicate "real settings." If the test situation in the laboratory includes those elements that are required by the theory for the appearance of a particular effect, the laboratory experiment constitutes a valid test of the theory. This means that the most frequent criticism of laboratory experiments—that they do not adequately simulate real-life situations—is spurious. The view derived from Popperian philosophy of science is that the theory being tested should specify the elements of "real-life" situations that are important to the theory so that these elements can be taken into account in tests and applications of the theory. If the elements in question can be reproduced in the laboratory, the test is valid and informative whether it simulates the real world or not. Those who argue that it is not possible to generalize laboratory findings to nonlaboratory settings are best answered with the statement that it is the theory, not specific findings, that is generalized and applied across a variety of settings.[1]

Consider the Lind *et al.* (1973) experiment on gathering and presentation of evidence under adversary and inquisitorial legal procedures. The experiment was conducted to test a fairly coherent legal theory describing the purported advantages of adversary procedures. The theory does not suggest that there are any limitations on when one can expect these advantages, nor is any limitation generally assumed to exist, as evidenced by application of the theory to justify legal decisions calling for greater use of adversary procedures in settings other than the traditional court setting in which it was developed.[2]

Lind and Walker argue that the information gathering and presentation experiment included all of the elements necessary to test two major assertions of the legal theory: that adversary attorneys are more diligent in their investigation of case facts than are inquisitorial attorneys and that the evidence adversary attorneys presented to the decision maker would be more complete and balanced. The experimental situation involved legal representatives (law students) who thought that the facts they discovered would be presented to a decision maker whose decision would have real, if relatively minor, financial consequences for the parties to a dispute. As described in the preceding chapter, the experiment manipulated the outcome contingencies of the attorneys to place some in an adversary role and others in an inquisitorial role. A second manipulation varied the extent to which the case favored one disputant over another. The results of the study disconfirmed the theory, showing that adversary attorneys were more diligent only when the case was unfavorable to their client and that, unless the case was balanced, the evidence reaching the judge from adversary attorneys was more biased than the presentations of inquisitorial attorneys. These findings contributed to the development of a new theory of procedure (Thibaut & Walker, 1978; see Chapter 2), which offers prescriptions concerning the situations in which adversary and inquisitorial procedures should be used.

According to the Popperian perspective, it makes little sense to

---

[1]Even in the case of studies that are conducted in real-world settings, generalization of findings without theory is problematic because there is no certainty that phenomena observed in one setting can be expected to occur in another apparently similar, but always somewhat different, setting.

[2]See, e.g., *Mathews v. Eldridge*, 424 U.S. 319 (1976); *North Georgia Finishing, Inc., v. Di-Chem, Inc.*, 419 U.S. 601 (1975); *Mitchell v. W. T. Grant Company*, 416 U.S. 600 (1974); *Fuentes v. Shevin*, 407 U.S. 67 (1972); *Goldberg v. Kelly*, 397 U.S. 254 (1970); *Sniadach v. Family Finance Corp.*, 395 U.S. 337 (1969).

criticize this study on the basis of general differences between the setting and subjects used in the experiment and the settings and attorney populations usually encountered in actual legal cases. We can illustrate the Popperian response to such criticisms with reference to criticisms that the study used law students rather than practicing attorneys and that the minor amounts of money involved in the experimental case and in the payment of the subjects were unlike those involved in actual legal cases. Such criticisms are answered by pointing out that the legal justification of adversary procedures did not state that the purported advantages of adversary procedures occur only when counsel are experienced or substantial amounts are in controversy. Rather, the theoretical advantages of adversary procedures were presented as being the result of fundamental aspects of human motivation. Absent some explicit mention in the theory that these factors were limiting factors on the presumed advantages of the procedure, the subject population and the type of dispute used in the experiment were entirely appropriate for a test of the theory.

This is not to say that counsel experience and the amount in controversy are not *possible* limitations on phenomena related to diligence of discovery and quality of presentation in adjudication procedures. The Popperian line of argument says only that, unless there is a theoretical justification, criticism based on any possible limitation is not particularly useful. If a new theory were proposed that included the limitations mentioned above and that provided a credible rationale for the existence of these limitations, a different study would be needed to test the new theory. But there is little scientific merit in criticism on the basis simply of differences between the laboratory test situation and the situation presumed to be most common in natural settings. It would be better for the critic to advance an alternative theory that offers sufficient specification to allow competitive tests and disconfirmation of one theory or the other.

Before we close our discussion of laboratory experiments, however, we should note another strength of this method. Laboratory experiments are also extremely useful in investigating situations of theoretical interest that rarely or never arise in natural settings (Henshel, 1980). If a useful or interesting phenomenon can be expected to occur only in circumstances that do not regularly arise in natural settings, a well-conceived laboratory experiment may be the only way to test its existence. If the phenomenon does occur in the laboratory, it may be possible to construct real-world situations that make practical use of the phenomenon. Physics offers many examples of such uses of "unnatural" phenomena. For example, sustained chain reactions in the fission of heavy elements seldom occur naturally in terrestrial settings, but the laboratory investigation of this phenomenon led to the development of nuclear reactors.

Interesting situations can be created and studied in the laboratory, and innovative procedures can receive their first test in an experimental simulation. Organizational innovation is often resisted because of fears concerning the innovation's consequences. Laboratory findings can sometimes answer such concerns sufficiently to permit real-world testing of the innovation.

There are, to be sure, some things that laboratory experiments do not do well. For example, the laboratory experiment is often a poor method for estimating the relative strength of relationships among variables in the real world. Suppose, for example, that we were to conduct a laboratory experiment on the effects of procedural justice and distributive justice on compliance with a decision. We could use the results to determine whether each type of justice might affect compliance, but we could not use the result to determine whether procedural justice exerts stronger effects on compliance than does distributive justice. This is true because the strength of the procedural and distributive justice effects would depend in part on the strength of the manipulations of each type of justice. Procedural justice might have stronger effects because it was manipulated more strongly and not because it is a stronger determinant of compliance.

Perhaps the most concise description of the proper use of laboratory experiments in procedural justice is to say that laboratory experiments are very useful when one wants to test whether a given effect *can* occur. When one wants to test whether a given effect *frequently* occurs or *how strong* the effect normally is, correlational studies are best.[3] The importance of using correlational studies to discover the usual strength of effects is illustrated by research on the potency of procedural justice in determining attitudes about outcomes and institutions. By and large, the effects seen in correlational studies conducted in field settings are substantially larger than the corresponding effects seen in experiments conducted in the laboratory (see Tyler & Caine, 1981). Thus, if we relied only on laboratory findings we would underestimate the strength of procedural justice effects.

SCENARIO STUDIES

Another popular research method, which might be viewed as a variant of the laboratory experiment, is what we term the "scenario study." This method involves the presentation of descriptions of pro-

---

[3]Laboratory experiments can be used to explore the effects of phenomena discovered with observational methods, a point explored in more detail in O'Barr and Lind (1981).

cedural scenarios, which respondents are asked to imagine happening to themselves or to others, and the assessment of attitudes and beliefs with respect to the scenarios. An example of a scenario study is the cross-national study of preferences for adjudication procedures described in Chapter 2. Subjects in that study were given written instructions that asked them to imagine themselves as either the plaintiff or the defendant in a dispute involving a disagreement about payment for damages resulting from an unspecified injury. They were asked further to imagine that they would have some say about the adjudication procedure to be used to resolve the dispute. Four adjudication procedures were described, and the respondents were asked to indicate the strength of their preference for using each procedure. The subjects were also asked to give their perceptions of each procedure on a variety of dimensions in order to determine which dimensions were most highly correlated with the preference ratings. The study was replicated in four countries in order to examine cultural differences in procedural preferences.

Scenario studies are most appropriately used to study topics related to subjective reactions to procedures, such as procedural preferences and attitudes. They are less useful in the study of objective consequences of procedural variation. This is because scenario studies ask people to imagine themselves in the situation in question, rather than studying the behavior of people actually experiencing the situation. It is more reasonable to ask what procedures one would prefer in a particular situation or what one's attitudes would be given certain circumstances than to ask how one would behave in a scenario, because people are especially inaccurate in predicting how they will behave in a new situation. Consider the information search and presentation experiment described in the previous section: it seems unlikely that the fairly complex results of the study would have been found if the situation had only been described to the subjects. Indeed, it is clear from the hypotheses tested in the experiment—and disconfirmed—that even the experienced attorneys who advanced the proposition that adversary procedures lead to better investigation did not realize that the nature of the case would affect the extent of investigation, nor was it intuitively obvious that this effect would result in biased information reaching the judge.

In general, the key to valid scenario studies is to design the study to deal with situations the respondents have experienced and understand. To ask people who have never been abroad, "How would you like living in Spain?" does not tell us much about the experience of living there. To ask people who have spent a good deal of time in Spain how they would like to live there under various circumstances tells us much more.

Because scenario studies ask people to imagine themselves in a situation whereas laboratory experiments, field studies, and many surveys examine reactions to real events, findings from scenario studies are more meaningful when they are confirmed with findings using other research methods. However, there are some circumstances in which scenario studies are very useful precisely because of their hypothetical nature. For example, they have been used to great advantage in research on cross-cultural variation in attitudes and preferences and in research on procedures that have been experienced frequently by the respondents. The cross-national study just described illustrates the first use. The scenario method was appropriate because the study examined the effects of cultural values on procedural preferences and the use of scenarios allowed these effects to be seen without "contamination" by extraneous effects from the particular circumstances that might arise in any real experience with the procedures in question. The study by Tyler and Caine (1981), involving reactions to college course-grading procedures, is an example of the second use. Because the subjects in the Tyler and Caine study were college students who had had considerable experience with various grading procedures, their procedural justice judgments and the effects of these judgments on their likely attitudes concerning potential courses and instructors can be presumed to be based on well-developed attitudes and attitudinal relations.

In several instances the same phenomena have been studied using laboratory experiments, scenario studies, and correlational designs. As we noted above, a frequent finding has been that procedural justice effects emerge more strongly in correlational studies than in laboratory experiments or scenario studies. As we explain in Chapter 10, this is not due to the methodology used in the study but to the greater importance that people attach to loyalty to real-world groups and organizations.

As will be seen in later chapters dealing with procedural justice in a variety of settings, it is becoming increasing clear that procedural justice judgments affect a variety of attitudes and behaviors, and that some of these variables affect each other. It appears that in natural settings there is considerable opportunity for procedural justice effects on different variables to reinforce and magnify each other. Laboratory experiments and scenario studies should probably be taken as establishing minimum effects that are often exceeded in natural settings.

Field Experiments

It is occasionally possible to bring the power of randomized experimental designs to bear on studies of procedural justice in natural settings. Randomized experimental designs are used routinely in laboratory experiments and scenario studies because random assignment of subjects to experimental conditions allows unambiguous interpretation of the results of a study. The field experiment combines the logical power of random assignment with a higher level of reality in the study's context.

One example of the use of a randomized experimental design is a study by Earley and Lind (1987) on reactions to task-assignment procedures. The study involved random assignment of workers at a telephone marketing facility to one of three procedures. One procedure allowed workers to choose their own task assignments; a second allowed workers to voice their preferences to a supervisor who then chose the task assignments; the third allowed neither choice nor the voicing of preferences. The study showed that the task-assignment procedure affected perceived fairness and performance.

Field experiments are being used with increasing frequency in procedural justice research. Now that a substantial body of research and theory based on other research methods has been generated, it is possible to design field experiments in such a way as to gain maximum information. Lind, Shapard, and Cecil (1981) note that field experiments are most useful when there is well-developed theory guiding the research, because a solid understanding of the likely processes involved in a field manipulation is necessary to guide design of the manipulation and measures. Field settings by their very nature often involve more complex processes both in the execution of the experiment and in the appearance of the phenomena under study, and the expense involved in field research is often substantially greater than that involved in laboratory and scenario studies. For these reasons, the best research of this sort is typically that which capitalizes as much as possible on knowledge generated using other methods.

Field experiments have a high level of realism, of course, but constraints in organizational or institutional settings often preclude the complex manipulations and control over extraneous variation that are possible in laboratory experiments. (See Cook & Campbell, 1979, for a discussion of the problems that can arise in field experiments.) When findings from field experiments parallel those of laboratory experiments or scenario studies, they provide convincing evidence of both the validity and the usefulness of phenomena discovered using research methods that are more constrained and artificial. In this regard, we should mention an attractive feature of the Earley and Lind research, which makes it an good example of the well-considered use of field experimentation. In addition to their field experiment, they ran a parallel study of the same phenomena in the laboratory. The results of both studies showed similar effects on procedural justice judgments. This convergence of findings rendered the results of both studies more meaningful: the field experiment, with its greater realism, made it clear that the results of the laboratory experiment were not artifacts of the setting; and the laboratory experiment, with its greater statistical power and control, provided greater information on the processes involved and showed that the results of the field experiment were not due to some peculiarity in the field setting studied.

FIELD STUDIES

It is not always possible to use randomized experimental designs in field settings; we use the term *field study* to refer to any study conducted in a natural setting without the use of randomized assignment to conditions. Such studies usually rely on comparisons based on differences arising from changes in procedures ("time-series" designs), on differences that exist between groups of individuals in the procedures they experience ("comparison group" designs), or on statistical analyses of the relation between procedures and behavior or attitudes ("regression discontinuity" and "correlational" designs; see Cook & Campbell, 1979, for a more detailed discussion of the strengths and weaknesses of particular designs.) Because the differences that generate the procedural comparison of interest may be accompanied by other differences that can confound the interpretation of the results, field studies are less rigorous than laboratory and field experiments. Nevertheless, field studies can provide substantial information about procedural justice processes if they are conducted on topics that have a good theoretical foundation or if they benefit from convergence of findings with other studies.

A field study of procedural justice is found in Lissak (1983). The study examined the fairness judgments of enlisted personnel in the Canadian Armed Forces regarding the procedure used to decide where people would be posted. It capitalized on a naturally occurring difference in personnel procedures to test the hypothesis that posting procedures allowing individualized input would generate higher procedural justice judgments. Lissak studied the procedural justice judgments of personnel in what are termed "regimental" units. These units are transferred as a whole and do not have individualized input or make individualized decisions about posting. He compared the procedural justice judgments of personnel in these units to those of personnel in nonregimental units, who are transferred as individuals and who are allowed to express preferences about where they are posted. Lissak found that the posting procedure was thought to be fairer by nonregimental than by regimental personnel, as he had predicted.

Some of the limitations of field studies are evident if one considers the difficulties that arise in interpreting the Lissak study. One interpretation is that greater input in the posting procedure led to greater perceived justice, but there are other possibilities that must be taken into account. For example, it might be the case that individuals in nonregimental units, because they were posted as individuals, received postings that better suited their preferences than did individuals in regimental units. Or it might be that other aspects of life in regimental or nonregimental units acted to increase or diminish all positive attitudes toward the service, including the sense that service procedures are fair. The point is that it is difficult to say for certain that greater input led to greater perceived justice; the results of the study are rendered ambiguous by alternative explanations that can account for the findings.[4]

One can eliminate some of the ambiguity of interpretation that plagues field studies by careful choice of the comparison groups to be used and by the use of statistical methods to eliminate some alternative explanations of the results of the study. However, in field studies, as in studies using the other methods we have described, convergence of results with the findings of studies using different methods is the best source of confidence in the validity of comparisons. Convergence of findings is especially helpful in field studies, where methodological problems are more severe than is the case in more rigorous designs.

CORRELATIONAL DESIGNS

Correlational designs involve the assessment of respondents' attitudes, beliefs, and behaviors at one point in time. Typically this assessment is made through self-report. In contrast to the other designs described above, there is no effort to manipulate events or procedures to generate contrasting situations that might be informative. Instead, people are asked about what they have experienced and what they think, believe, and are doing at the time of the interview. When those interviewed are a random sample of some population of interest, the correlational design is referred to as a survey. Surveys are useful for examining natural relations between variables. When theory exists to aid in the interpretation of survey findings, the major weakness of this method— difficulty in determining the causal sequences involved in the relations discovered—can be largely overcome and useful information can be obtained.

An example of survey research on procedural justice is a study by Tyler (1984). The study examined people's reactions to experiences in court. A sample of defendants who had appeared in court were interviewed by telephone about their experiences. Respondents were asked to discuss the details of their case, indicating the favorability of the outcome, their views about the fairness of the judge's decision, and their assessment of the fairness of the procedures used during the trial. They

---

[4]It should be noted that Lissak's study was more sophisticated than we make it sound here. He used additional methods to eliminate alternative hypotheses, and conducted additional studies to establish a convergence of findings.

were also asked to evaluate the judge and the court system and to indicate how well satisfied they were with the outcome of their case.

Using respondents' judgments about their cases, the study explored the role of procedural justice judgments in determining reactions to courtroom experiences. Although this question is essentially the same as one of the questions addressed in the laboratory-based research program of Thibaut and Walker, the use of a correlational methodology leads to a somewhat different approach to hypothesis testing.

In a correlational study the "independent" variables are typically

TABLE 3-1. The Relationship among Defendant Judgments

| Measure | Overall outcome level | | | Fairness | |
	Absolute	Relative to expectations	Relative to others	Outcome	Procedural
Outcome level					
Absolute	—				
Relative to expectations	.31***	—			
Relative to others	.22*	.40***	—		
Fairness					
Outcome	.41***	.61***	.24**	—	
Procedural	.34***	.51***	.21*	.77***	—
Respondents indicating outcome is very important					
Outcome level					
Absolute	—				
Relative to expectations	.19*	—			
Relative to others	.24*	.34***	—		
Fairness					
Outcome	.43***	.65***	.29**	—	
Procedural	.35***	.52***	.33***	.80***	—
Respondents indicating outcome is less important					
Outcome level					
Absolute	—				
Relative to expectations	.56***	—			
Relative to others	.23	.11	—		
Fairness					
Outcome	.34*	.50***	.15	—	
Procedural	.33*	.50***	.05	.73***	—

Note. All entries are Pearson correlations. Entries involving outcome level relative to others are the average correlation for the two indices of that construct.
*$p < .05$
**$p < .01$
***$p < .001$

not statistically independent. Because they had control over the entire situation constructed in their laboratory, Thibaut and Walker were able to separate procedural variations from the verdict their subjects received, allowing for tests of procedural justice hypotheses that logically ruled out the possibility that outcome differences might be involved. In a natural setting, outcome and procedural issues may be correlated and such a clear separation of outcome effects and procedure effects is not possible. As a result, it is necessary to use statistical methods that establish the independent contributions of correlated variables.

Table 3-1 shows the correlations, in Tyler's (1984) study, among respondents' judgments of various aspects of their case. As can be seen from the table, the judgments are not independent. Instead, outcome favorability is associated with judgments of outcome and procedural fairness. Similarly, outcome and procedural fairness are correlated with each other.

Given the relationship between the various independent variables of concern in the study, multiple regression techniques had to be employed in the analysis in order to distinguish the unique contribution of each independent variable to the dependent variable of interest. One such technique is the "usefulness analysis" shown in Table 3-2. In a usefulness analysis, one variable or set of variables is entered into a regression equation and the proportion of variance in the dependent variable explained is noted. In a second step, a second independent variable or set of independent variables is entered into the equation and the total proportion of variance explained is noted. The increment in variance explained between step 1 and step 2 represents the independent contribution—the usefulness—of the second variable in explaining variation in the dependent variable. The increment represents the *independent* contribution because all joint variance is included in the first step of the process.

The usefulness analysis in Table 3-2 shows that defendants' evaluation of the judge in their case and their assessments of the court system were more strongly influenced by their fairness judgments than by the level of outcomes that they received. In other words, Tyler's results show that citizens evaluate courtroom actors and institutions primarily in terms of fairness, not in terms of whether they won or lost their case.

Of course the fact that citizens care about fairness does not necessarily mean that they care about procedural fairness. It may be that they are concerned only about issues of distributive fairness, that is, whether the verdict seems to them to be fair. To separate out issues of distributive and procedural fairness a second type of analysis, also shown in Table 3-2, can be used. This analysis uses a multiple regression equation in which all independent variables are entered simultaneously. In such an analysis the relative magnitude of each independent variable is in-

TABLE 3-2. Outcome Concerns and Defendant Attitudes Toward Authorities

	Outcome satisfaction			Evaluation of the judge			Evaluation of the court		
	Beta (1)	B(SE) (2)	R² (3)	Beta (1)	B(SE) (2)	R² (3)	Beta (1)	B(SE) (2)	R² (3)
Outcome level									
Absolute	.02	.02(.07)	.13***	.03	.09(.28)	.12**	.02	.16(.10)	.03
Relative to expectations	.16	.25(.15)	—	.02	.10(.56)	—	−.01	−.02(.20)	—
Others—general	.21	.38(.15)*	—	.10	.67(.56)	—	.17	.26(.20)	—
Others—specific	.08	.19(.18)	.42***	.09	.82(.67)	.27***	.16	.33(.24)	.09*
Relative to expectations as a bloc	—			—			—		
Total for outcome level variables	—	—	.44***	—	—	.30***	—	—	.09*
Fairness									
Outcome	.48	.55(.14)***	.62***	.45	1.98(.52)***	.64***	.12	.12(.18)	.19***
Procedural	.18	.22(.13)	.47***	.41	1.92(.50)***	.61***	.38	.40(.18)*	.24***
Total for fairness variables	—	—	.63***	—	—	.70***	—	—	.24***
Total for all variables	—	—	.67***	—	—	.70***	—	—	.24***
Usefulness analysis									
Outcome variables beyond fairness			.04***			.00			.00
Fairness beyond outcome variables			.23***			.40***			.15***

Note. Entries in columns 1 and 2 are the standardized and unstandardized regression coefficients for an equation including all variables. Numbers in parentheses are the standard error of the regression coefficient. Entries in column 3 are the adjusted square of the multiple correlation coefficient for variables entered singly or as a group.

*p < .05
**p < .01
***p < .001

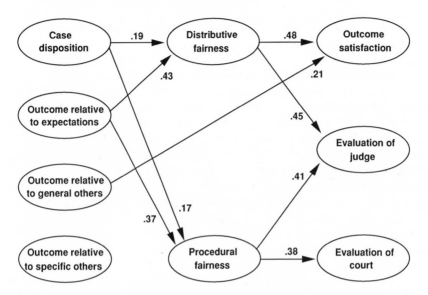

FIGURE 3-1. Direct and indirect outcome effects on evaluation.

dexed by its beta weight. The beta weight indicates the contribution of each independent variable removing any effects of other variables in the equation. An examination of the beta weights shown in Table 3-2 indicates that procedural justice is the major factor defendants consider when they are making evaluations of the court system, whereas evaluations of the judge are influenced by both procedural justice and distributive justice judgments.

An important limit of the regression analysis shown in Table 3-2 is that it indexes only the direct effects of the independent variables. Indirect effects are removed from the equation through statistical controls. Given the relationship between outcome favorability and fairness judgments, shown in Table 3-1, one plausible explanation is that outcome favorability exercises an indirect effect on evaluations of the judge and courts by virtue of its effects on judgments of fairness. This possibility can be tested by using a causal model that allows for indirect effects. The results of such modeling, shown in Figure 3-1, suggest that such effects do occur.[5]

[5]Figure 3-1 shows a causal path diagram in a form that will be used throughout the book. We use these diagrams to present the results of multiple regression and structural equation analyses. In these diagrams, variables or underlying factors (latent variables) are represented with ovals containing the name of the variable, and significant links between variables are represented with arrows. The numbers next to the arrows are standardized path coefficients, showing the relative strength of the link represented by the arrow. For the sake of clarity of presentation, we usually make no attempt to show the error terms or correlated errors that were included in the analyses in question.

A particularly useful feature of studies such as the Tyler survey is their capacity to test the relative contributions of several variables to variation in a belief or attitude. The capacity of multiple regression to test relative contributions depends on the quality of measurement of the variables. If the independent variables are measured with unequal reliability, these differences can lead to erroneous inferences about relative contributions. Fortunately, there exist other statistical techniques, such as structural equation modeling (Jöreskog & Sörbom, 1981), that correct for reliability differences. Because a survey measures natural variation in attitudes and characteristics, a clear picture of the natural relation between the variables can be obtained. (In contrast, as mentioned above, the variation of the manipulated factors in an experiment is responsive to the strength of the manipulation and can be either greater or less than the variation one would expect to find in natural settings. This can lead to greater or lesser effects than would occur naturally.) There is a need for both studies of natural variation, which show how relations currently exist in the real world, and studies of induced variation, which show how possible relations might be capitalized upon in applications designed to alter the real world. In the context of active theory development, both types of studies contribute to our understanding of the psychology of procedural justice.

A major problem in the interpretation of correlational studies is the possibility that the observed relationship between two variables is due to their relationship to some third variable. For example, in Tyler's study, general attitudes toward the courts held before the incident in question could have affected both the respondents' procedural justice judgments and their evaluations of the courts after the incident. This effect could have occurred independently of the respondent's experiences in the incident in question. That is, people who initially dislike the courts may come away from any encounter believing that the courts used unfair procedures, regardless of how the present case was handled. This problem can be solved in one of two ways: either by repeatedly interviewing the same people over time in order to relate changes in the dependent variable to changes that result from experience with the procedure (this approach is termed a "panel design") or by conducting additional research using laboratory experiments, scenario studies, or field experiments in order to determine independently the causal sequence involved in survey research findings. In procedural justice research both solutions have been used.

An example of a panel study controlling for prior evaluations of legal authorities is a recent study by Tyler (1987b). In this study, 804 residents of Chicago were asked about their views on legal authority on two occasions. During the one-year period between the first and second

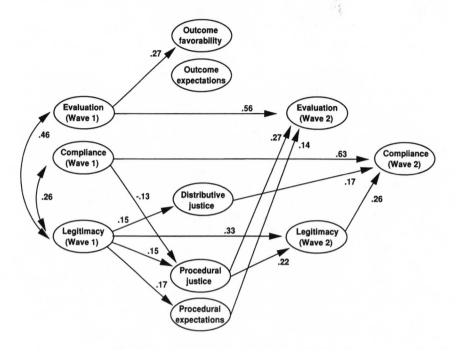

FIGURE 3-2. Prior views and procedural justice.

interviews, 329 of the panel residents had some personal experience with the police and courts. In addition to making other judgments, respondents rated the fairness of their treatment by those authorities. The results, shown in Figure 3-2, indicate that prior views do influence subsequent judgments of procedural fairness.

In closing this section, we should note that the combination of survey methods and open-ended questions has proved to be very useful in procedural justice studies. Some recent studies of procedural justice in organizations (Greenberg, 1986b; Sheppard & Lewicki, 1987) have asked people to describe incidents of fair or unfair treatment. Such studies are especially useful when researchers are interested in discovering the full range of issues that influence people's thinking about some question.

CONVERGENCE OF FINDINGS IN PROCEDURAL JUSTICE RESEARCH

Our discussion of methods has repeatedly argued that confidence in the results of a study using any research method is enhanced by convergence of the findings with those of studies using other methods. Several illustrations of such convergence of findings are available in procedural justice research; perhaps the most striking is the convergence of findings on the relation between process control and procedural justice judgments. We describe here five studies, each using one of the methods described above, that show the relation.

As noted in Chapter 2, the enhancement of perceived procedural justice by process control was first discovered in a laboratory experiment (Walker *et al.*, 1974). Undergraduate subjects were placed in a dispute in the course of an experiment that allegedly sought to simulate a business competition. In fact, the business competition was a cover story designed to lead the subjects to believe that they were in conflict with another subject in the experiment and to provide a rationale for using one of two adjudication procedures to resolve the dispute. One of the adjudication procedures, the adversary trial procedure, gave the subject an apparently high level of process control in the hearing used to resolve the dispute; the other, inquisitorial procedure, did not. Ratings taken after the hearing showed higher ratings of procedural justice for subjects who had experienced the high process-control procedure than for those who had experienced the low process-control procedure.

The Walker *et al.* (1974) experiment was conducted to test the assertions of legal scholars who contended that adversary legal procedures are desirable because, among other things, they result in greater perceived justice. Thus there was some theory to guide the research, and the use of the laboratory experimental method was appropriate. The results of the experiment were in line with the hypothesis. Because the study used the laboratory experimental method, there is little question about the causal relation between the procedural manipulation of process control and procedural justice judgments. The random assignment of subjects to conditions and the tight control over experimental events and situations that were possible in the laboratory make it clear that the variation in procedure caused the observed differences in procedural justice. What was less clear was whether the relation was limited by situational or subject population factors. Additional research using different methods resolved these ambiguities.

Lind *et al.* (1978), in a cross-national study described earlier in this chapter and in Chapter 2, used the scenario method to determine whether the results of the Walker *et al.* study were due to the familiarity of American undergraduates with legal procedures that give process control to the litigants. Their results provided encouraging convergence with those of the Walker *et al.* experiment, in that procedures with greater disputant process control led to increased procedural justice judgments even among subjects from nations that do not use legal procedures high in disputant process control. Additional support for the validity of the overall relation between process control and procedural justice is to be found in the results of a field experiment by Earley (1984). One of the conditions in Earley's experiment involved giving workers process control in the procedure used to decide their goals. Earley found that this condition enhanced procedural fairness judgments, confirming the relation between process control and procedural justice judgments in the context of a real-world social decision-making procedure that was quite different from the legal procedures examined in the previous studies. The field experiment lends additional weight to the conclusion that the laboratory and scenario findings are not due to any artifact of those methods.

Additional evidence for the effect of process control on procedural justice judgments is available in the Lissak field study of Canadian Forces posting procedures. As noted above, Lissak found that individuals who could offer comments and express preferences about their postings felt that the procedure was more fair. The Lissak findings further increase our confidence in the generality of the process control effect by showing the effect with a real-world procedure and with a previously untested subject population—military personnel. In turn, we are more confident that process control is in fact the cause of the differences that Lissak observed because the effect is so similar to those seen in experimental studies.

Still more evidence for the relation between process control and procedural justice judgments is available from two correlational studies by Tyler, Rasinski, and Spodick (1985). They examined the relation between procedural justice judgments and perceptions of process control for respondents who were questioned about their experiences with court procedures in one survey and about their experiences with college grading procedures in the other survey. The results were analyzed to determine whether there was some effect for process control over and above any effect for direct control over the legal or grading decisions. Both surveys showed a strong independent effect for perceptions of process control on judgments of procedural justice. These findings, by providing additional support for the process control–procedural justice relation in the context of additional real-world social decision-making procedures, give us more confidence in the results of the other studies mentioned in this section. The survey findings are rendered more conclusive because the Walker et al., Lind et al., and Earley studies, which used random assignment, support the contention that the direction of causality is from process control to procedural justice. There are other instances of convergence of findings in procedural justice research, but we will delay further discussion of this topic until Chapter 9, where we describe at some length the major themes that emerge from the past decade and a half of procedural justice research.

Chapter 4

Procedural Justice in Law I
Legal Attitudes and Behavior

It is no accident that the first systematic study of the psychology of procedural justice involved the application of psychological method and knowledge to legal issues: few areas of human endeavor place as much emphasis on procedure and process as does the law. As will be seen in later chapters, the procedures used in other social institutions provoke psychological responses similar to those seen in procedural justice research in legal settings; indeed, we contend that the same procedural concerns arise in almost any social environment. But these concerns are more obvious in the law than elsewhere. Because the essence of law is the regulation and regularization of social conduct, it is to be expected that the law would be preoccupied with its own regulation through procedure. This in turn makes the law a natural arena for discussions and analyses of the behavioral consequences of various procedures. Legal writing on procedure has over the centuries been much concerned with speculation about the reactions of litigants, lawyers, judges, and jurors to one procedural form or another. Given this centuries-old interest in how procedure affects the behavior of those involved with legal institutions, it is hardly surprising that the scientific study of the psychology of procedure should have begun with studies of legal procedures.

This is not to say that the psychological study of procedural justice in law has been without debate or criticism. Skepticism of procedural justice research by legal writers was evident immediately after the publication of the first procedural justice research (e.g., Damaska, 1975). The skepticism was based in part on misgivings about the laboratory methodology used in all of the early procedural justice research. As we noted in the preceding chapter, the use of laboratory methods was based on a well-considered approach to the study of procedural justice, and later research using other research methods has validated the major findings of the early laboratory studies. As methodological criticisms have been laid to rest, however, substantive debates have arisen about the implications and importance of procedural justice research. In the next chapter, where we consider the implications of procedural justice for policy making, we will point out several issues that continue to give rise to controversy.

In this chapter and the next we examine how procedural justice phenomena operate in legal settings. Because much procedural justice work in this area has focused on processing and resolving disputes, we also include in these chapters the literature on procedural justice processes in nonlegal dispute resolution contexts. Our fundamental concern here is with all of the procedures by which society disposes of disputes among its members and imposes its rules and standards. We do not limit ourselves strictly to formal legal processes, because we believe that dispute resolution procedures in noninstitutional settings show many of the same psychological processes that are seen, for example, in reactions to a civil trial. But because the language and history of the study of procedural justice in dispute resolution are tied closely to legal issues, we frequently concentrate on formal legal processes.

PROCEDURAL CONCERNS IN LAW

We have already noted that the law devotes much attention to the operation and implications of its decision-making procedures, a focus shared, of course, by work on the psychology of procedural justice. There are other similarities between legal and psychological approaches to the analysis of procedural issues. For example, in the law, as in the psychology of justice, a distinction is made between issues of distribution and issues of procedure. In the psychology of justice this distinction is conveyed by the terms *distributive justice* and *procedural justice*. In legal analysis, a distinction is made between *substantive law* and *procedural law*. A social psychologist uses the term distributive justice to refer to psychological reactions to the outcome of a dispute or an allocation; a legal theorist uses the term substantive law to refer to those rules of law that specify how one should conduct oneself in everyday affairs and how social outcomes are to be divided to resolve disputes and to punish wrongdoing, that is, to refer to the "rules governing rights and duties of men in their ordinary relations with each other or the body politic" (James, 1965). Procedural justice means to a psychologist the reactions of individuals to the norms and standards that govern social process, just as procedural law means to a lawyer the rules that order and structure the legal decision-making process, the "means whereby rights are maintained or redressed" (James, 1965). Indeed, the term procedural justice was used in law long before it came to have its special meaning in psychology and the other social sciences. We do not mean to imply that the terms that have arisen in psychology have exactly the same meaning or connotation as the corresponding terms in law. Rather, our interest here is to point out that, if they surmount each other's jargon, the psychologist and the legal scholar will find they share many basic concerns and recognize many similar distinctions.

Both psychology and law recognize that procedures can be evaluated either against objective criteria or in terms of the satisfaction, attitudes, and behavior the procedure provokes in disputants or citizens. In much the same way that psychological work on procedural justice can be divided into studies of objective consequences and studies of subjective consequences, legal analyses sometimes distinguish between objective fairness of a particular procedure and its likely effect on the feelings and beliefs of those who encounter it. The distinction in law between objective and subjective justice is most obvious in legal concern that procedures both *be fair* and *appear fair*. Among the objective criteria used in law for the evaluation of a procedure are the extent to which its outcomes meet standards of fairness and consistency, the accuracy of its decisions, and the cost and efficiency of the procedure. Subjective criteria in law, often subsumed under the heading of "psychological" consequences of procedures, include judgments of procedural fairness, disputant satisfaction, citizen approval and endorsement of institutions, and obedience or compliance with substantive rules, all of which are assumed to be affected by legal decision-making procedures. In this chapter we consider the consequences of subjective procedural justice for procedural preferences, for other legal attitudes, and for behavior. In the next chapter we discuss the sources of procedural justice judgments, and we consider how our knowledge of procedural justice can be integrated with our knowledge of objective justice of procedures and with other considerations as we apply procedural justice research to policy making.

CONSEQUENCES OF PROCEDURAL FAIRNESS JUDGMENTS

The interest that psychologists have shown in perceived fairness and other subjective reactions to legal procedures mirrors a longstanding interest in the law in these issues. A famous example of concern with litigant satisfaction is Roscoe Pound's critique of early twentieth-century justice, "The Causes of Popular Dissatisfaction with the Administration of Justice." There are several reasons for concern with subjective reactions to legal and dispute resolution procedures: (1) normative theories of justice (e.g., Rawls, 1971) view fairness as a desired quality in its own right; (2) the procedural preferences of litigants and citizens, which are closely linked to perceived fairness, are an issue to be considered in the design of any democratic institution; and (3) the experience of procedural justice or injustice may have serious consequences for such variables as citizen satisfaction, support for legal institutions, and compliance with laws and legal decisions.

Consequences of the Experience of Procedural Justice

Many citizen contacts with legal institutions are involuntary, and even those that are initiated voluntarily often involve the imposition of involuntary decisions and rulings. In this context it is not surprising that legal authorities are concerned about the risk of hostility on the part of those who come in contact with the law. One way to minimize such hostility is to use procedures that are viewed as fair. For example, Murphy and Tanenhaus (1969) suggest that people will continue to support the courts despite unfavorable decisions if they believe that the judicial process is impartial and just. Fair procedures can provide a "cushion of support" that protects the institution from the hostility that might otherwise accompany unpopular decisions. For example, Murphy and Tanenhaus contend that the ultimate acceptance of unpopular decisions of the Warren court was the result of a widespread fundamental belief in the fairness of the American judicial process.

On a more general level, one might look to procedural justice as an important factor not only in engendering favorable reactions to individual decisions but also in promoting citizens' satisfaction with their legal experiences and their perceptions of the legitimacy of law and legal authority. Legitimacy in turn is likely to be an important factor in compliance with legal rules and orders, a critical issue even in the nonvoluntary context of most legal dispute resolution. The importance of issues of legitimacy and compliance is evident when one considers such instances of general disobedience of legal authority as the failure of Prohibition or the current widespread use of marijuana and cocaine. Similarly, noncompliance with civil case judgments is frequently seen as a serious problem (McEwen & Maiman, 1984). Legitimacy and compliance are even more important in the case of nonbinding dispute resolution procedures, such as mediation, where voluntary compliance is necessary if the procedure is to be at all successful in resolving disputes.

As the preceding paragraphs suggest, there are several important classes of social attitudes and behavior that might be affected by perceptions of procedural fairness. Research to date has documented procedural justice effects on (1) evaluations of the performance of legal institutions and authorities, (2) evaluations of legal decisions and outcomes, (3) satisfaction with encounters with the legal system, (4) perceptions of legitimacy, (5) support for legal institutions, and (6) compliance with laws and judgments. We begin our review of research on the consequences of procedural justice with a study that examined the relationship between procedural fairness judgments and evaluations of courts and judges.

Evaluations of the Performance of Legal Institutions and Authorities

Tyler (1984) surveyed defendants in traffic and misdemeanor courts concerning their satisfaction with the outcome of their case, their evaluation of their judge, and their evaluations of the court system.[1] He also asked a variety of questions about the procedural and distributive fairness of the respondents' courtroom experience and about expectations concerning the outcome of the case and the outcomes that others were likely to receive. Respondents' answers to the fairness and expectation questions and their reports concerning the outcomes they actually received were analyzed using multiple regression procedures to determine the contribution of each of several factors to the respondents' attitudes about the outcome, the judge, and the court. The results of the regression analyses are shown in Table 4-1.

Tyler found that attitudes about the outcome, the judge, and the court were strongly related to fairness judgments. A usefulness analysis showed that the fairness measures accounted for significant variance over and above that explained by absolute and relative measures of outcome. The regression weights, which are shown in the table, revealed that procedural fairness was more important than distributive fairness in determining attitudes toward the court, that both types of fairness were important in determining attitudes toward the judge, and that distributive fairness was more important in determining satisfaction with the outcome.

A more recent study, also by Tyler (1987b) showed similar results. A random sample of Chicago residents were interviewed about their encounters with police and the courts. Table 4-3, presented in a later section, shows the results of this study. Again, a regression analysis was used to examine the direct effects of procedural fairness, distributive fairness, and nonfairness features of the encounter. Tyler found that both types of fairness had substantial effects on evaluations of the authorities involved. The two Tyler studies make it clear that high levels of

---

[1]This study is also described in Chapter 3; see that description for more details concerning its method and rationale.

TABLE 4-1. Fairness, Outcomes, and Defendant Attitudes toward Authorities

| | Dependent variable | | | | | |
| | Outcome satisfaction | | Evaluation of judge | | Evaluation of court | |
Predictor variable	Beta	R^2	Beta	R^2	Beta	R^2
Outcome level:						
Absolute	.02	.13**	.03	.12**	.02	.03
Relative to:						
Expectations	.16	—	.02	—	−.01	—
General others	.21*	—	.10	—	.17	—
Specific others	.08	—	.09	—	.16	—
All relative	—	.42**	—	.27**	—	.09*
All outcome level	—	.44**	—	.30**	—	.09*
Fairness:						
Procedural	.18	.47**	.41**	.61**	.38*	.24**
Distributive	.48**	.62**	.45**	.64**	.12	.19**
All fairness variables	—	.63**	—	.70**	—	.24**
Total for all variables	—	.67**	—	.70**	—	.24**

Note. Beta column reports standardized regression coefficients for an equation containing all variables. Entries in R^2 columnn are the adjusted square of the multiple correlation coefficient for variables entered singly or as a group. From Tyler (1984).
*$p < .05$
**$p < .01$

perceived procedural justice do indeed lead to more favorable evaluations of the performance of legal institutions and authorities.[2]

Evaluations of Legal Outcomes and Decisions

A number of studies have found evidence of either direct or indirect enhancement of evaluations of legal outcomes when procedures are viewed as fair. Let us first consider the studies that have suggested that procedural justice can enhance evaluations of outcomes through the enhancement of distributive justice judgments, which in turn lead to higher overall evaluations of the outcome.

Evidence suggesting that perceptions of distributive fairness are affected by perceptions of procedural fairness is seen as early as the first Thibaut and Walker study on perceived fairness and legal procedures (Walker *et al.*, 1974). In that study and in LaTour's later replication with four procedure conditions (LaTour, 1978), both of which are described in

[2]These findings are in close accord with the results of other studies of the effects of procedural justice on attitudes toward political institutions and authorities and on attitudes toward organizational leaders and organizations; we describe this research in Chapters 7 and 8.

Chapter 2, satisfaction and fairness ratings of the verdict showed procedure effects similar to, but somewhat weaker than, the procedure effects seen on procedural fairness measures. This is precisely the pattern of results that would be expected if the procedure manipulations in these studies had direct effects on procedural fairness judgments and the procedural fairness judgments in turn affected distributive fairness judgments. A more recent replication of the Walker *et al.* study using more varied and refined measures (Lind, Kurtz, Musante, Walker, & Thibaut, 1980) showed higher distributive fairness ratings and higher ratings of acceptance of the verdict under adversary than under inquisitorial procedures. These effects mirrored stronger effects of procedural variation on procedural fairness.[3]

For fair procedures to provide a "cushion of support" procedural justice must not only enhance outcome evaluations generally but must make negative outcomes in particular more palatable. There is a substantial body of research showing procedural justice enhancement of satisfaction with negative outcomes. In most of the studies cited, procedures high in procedural fairness produced perceptions of greater distributive fairness under both negative and positive outcome conditions. There have been occasional studies (e.g., LaTour, 1978) showing that the strength of the positive effects of fair procedures on outcome evaluations varies depending on whether the outcome in question is positive or negative, but these studies have always found that procedural justice most strongly affects distributive fairness judgments when outcomes are *negative*.

As noted in our discussion in Chapter 2 of the LaTour (1978) experiment, occasionally the distributive fairness ratings of winning disputants cluster around the top scale intervals regardless of the level of procedural fairness. In these circumstances, it is unclear whether the absence of any procedural justice effect is an artifact of the measurement instrument, that is, a "ceiling effect" caused by subjects' frequent use of the high extreme of the rating scales, or whether this pattern of findings is interpretable as a real phenomenon. Further research with more refined instruments is needed to resolve this question. It is clear, however,

[3]Most surveys show a moderately strong correlation between procedural and distributive fairness ratings, and there is evidence that the correlation is not solely the result of procedural fairness effects on distributive fairness. It is likely that procedural fairness judgments are affected by both the raw valence of the outcome and the distributive fairness judgments that the outcome engenders. Thus it appears that the strong correlation is due to reciprocal causality between procedural and distributive fairness and to similar effects on both by other variables. This, of course, does not lessen the importance of the relation discussed here—whatever other causal relations involved, it is still the case that judgments of procedural fairness do enhance judgments of distributive fairness and lead to greater satisfaction with the outcome in question.

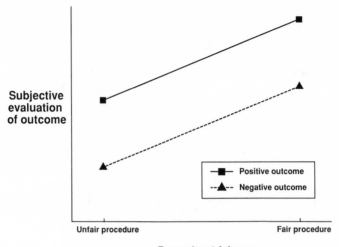

FIGURE 4-1a. Normal procedural justice effect.

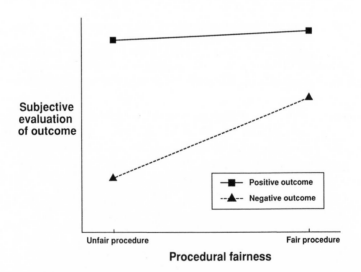

FIGURE 4-1b. Effect attenuated for positive outcomes.

that the enhancement of outcome satisfaction and the amelioration of discontent, which is the critical element of the cushion of support concept, is a ubiquitous phenomenon among losing disputants.

Figures 4-1a and 4-1b show the patterns of effects usually seen in laboratory experiments examining the effects of procedural fairness on ratings of distributive fairness or outcome satisfaction. The first figure shows the most common pattern of means for the effect—high levels of procedural fairness produce higher ratings of both positive and negative outcomes. The second figure shows the pattern of means seen in most studies that do not show across-the-board enhancement of outcome ratings—in these studies procedural fairness enhances outcome ratings only when the outcome is negative. Note that in both figures when outcomes are negative, higher outcome evaluations are seen with fair procedures; it is only when outcomes are positive that the effect is sometimes attenuated.[4]

There is also some evidence that judgments of procedural fairness have direct effects on satisfaction with legal outcomes, independent of any effect mediated by distributive fairness judgments. In a recent study of citizen reaction to experiences with police and courts, Tyler (1984) found that fairness exerted an independent effect on satisfaction with the outcome of the encounter (see Table 4-1). It appears that procedural fairness enhances satisfaction with legal outcomes not only because it makes the outcomes themselves seem more fair but also because it directly affects feelings about the outcome.

The effect of procedural justice on distributive justice is diminished when there is no direct involvement or participation in the procedure. Walker, Lind, and Thibaut (1979) studied the procedural and distributive fairness judgments of disputants who participated actively in the procedure, observers who had an outcome interest in the dispute but who did not participate actively, and observers who neither had an outcome interest in the dispute nor participated in the procedure. All three groups showed strong procedure effects on procedural fairness judgments, with adversary procedures being seen as fairer than inquisitorial procedures. However, only the disputant subjects showed any procedure-linked differences in their distributive fairness judg-

---

[4]Some procedural justice researchers (Cohen, 1985; Folger, 1977; Folger, Rosenfield, Grove, & Corkran, 1979) have suggested that allocation procedures, as opposed to dispute resolution procedures, occasionally show *less* satisfaction with negative outcomes under fair procedures than under unfair procedures, a response that Folger (1977) has termed a "frustration effect." We discuss this phenomenon further when we describe work on organizational procedures in Chapter 8, because the discussions of this effect have typically focused on reactions to procedures for determining how much a person should be paid for his or her performance on a task. Only one legal procedure study (Austin, Williams, Worchel, Wentzel, & Siegel, 1981) has shown this pattern of results, and that study involved a scenario method asking undergraduate subjects to rate how they *thought* a criminal defendant would rate the outcome. As we noted in Chapter 3, scenario methods are weak when the subject is not familiar with the situation being considered. Folger's work (Folger et al., 1979) suggests that the frustration effect may occur only when there is social support for feelings of inequitable treatment and when the decision maker has a vested interest in the outcome of the dispute.

ments. Walker *et al.* speculated that direct participation in the procedure in question is necessary to activate the causal link from procedural fairness to distributive fairness.

Overall Satisfaction

There is a growing body of research showing that the experience of procedural justice not only enhances evaluations of persons, institutions, and specific outcomes, but also leads to greater overall satisfaction with the legal experience and more positive affect with respect to an encounter with the justice system. Let us return to Tyler's (1987b) study, the results of which are shown in Table 4-2. As mentioned earlier, Tyler interviewed a random sample of Chicago residents about encounters with the police and courts, and then, for the 652 respondents who had had encounters with the legal system, examined the extent to which procedural fairness judgments, distributive fairness judgments, and nonfairness variables explained each of several potential consequences of the experience. Of interest to us here are the consequences for respondents' overall satisfaction with the outcome, for their overall satis-

TABLE 4-2. Fairness, Outcomes, and Satisfaction with Experience with Legal Authorities

Predictor variable	Dependent Variable					
	Outcome satisfaction		Treatment satisfaction		Affect	
	Beta	R^2	Beta	R^2	Beta	R^2
Nonfairness variables:						
Absolute outcomes	.00		.01		.02	
Relative outcomes	.18**		.13**		.09**	
Relative treatment	.01		.05		.05	
All nonfairness variables		.40		.38		.33
Fairness:						
Procedural	.31**		.55**		.45**	
Distributive	.39**		.18**		.24**	
All fairness variables		.60		.54		.55
Total for all variables		.61		.65		.55
Usefulness analysis						
Nonfairness beyond fairness		.01		.11		.01
Fairness beyond nonfairness		.21		.27		.22

Note. Beta column reports standardized regression coefficients for an equation containing all variables. Entries in R^2 column are the adjusted square of the multiple correlation coefficient for variables entered singly or as a group. From Tyler (1987c).
**$p < .01$

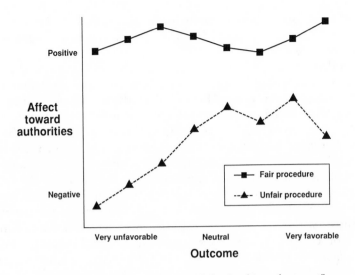

FIGURE 4-2. Procedural justice and the "cushion of support."

faction with their treatment, and for a measure of their general affect, which tapped their feelings of hostility and frustration as a result of the encounter.

Tyler found that fairness judgments were the strongest determinants of both types of satisfaction and of respondents' general affect toward the encounter. Further, for the measures of satisfaction with treatment and general affect, the regression weights showed that procedural fairness accounted for the lion's share of the fairness effect.

As we noted above, using fair procedures to make decisions is often viewed as particularly important for retaining the support of those who receive unfavorable outcomes (those who lose). For losers fair process is thought of as providing a cushion that allows a support for the authorities involved to remain high. That cushion is the belief that the decision-making procedure is a fair one. Tyler used his data to test whether this cushion of support actually exists. He divided respondents into groups based on the absolute favorability or unfavorability of the outcome that they had received in their dealings with the police or the courts. He then further divided respondents by whether they felt that the outcomes had resulted from a fair or an unfair procedure. Figure 4-2 shows the average affect that each group felt toward the authorities with whom they had dealt.

The data in Figure 4-2 show that the use of fair procedures does indeed provide a cushion for authorities when the outcomes they have provided are unfavorable. When fair procedures were used feelings about the authorities remain positive, irrespective of the favorability of outcomes. When unfair procedures were used negative outcomes lead to negative affect toward the authorities involved.

Another compelling example of the capacity of procedural fairness to cushion the dissatisfaction that might result from unfavorable outcomes is seen in the results of a field study by Adler, Hensler, and Nelson (1983), which examined litigant reactions to court-annexed arbitration procedures. Adler *et al.* grouped their respondents on the basis of whether they had won or lost at arbitration and on the basis of whether the respondent viewed the arbitration procedure as fair or unfair. Those who lost were less satisfied when they felt that the hearing was unfair (their mean satisfaction rating on a four point scale was 1.4) than when they thought the hearing was fair (mean satisfaction = 2.9). In contrast, winners showed no differences in satisfaction as a function of their procedural fairness judgments; those who thought the hearing was unfair were as satisfied (mean = 4.0) as were those who thought the hearing was fair (mean = 3.8). Figure 4-3 shows these results, which match the attenuated procedural justice effect described in the previous section.

Both of these studies show that fair procedures lead to greater general satisfaction with legal experiences. But we should consider whether there are limits to this effect. Do fair procedures always result in greater satisfaction with legal decisions? Two possible limits have been suggested. One limit on the effect may lie in the level of outcome involved.

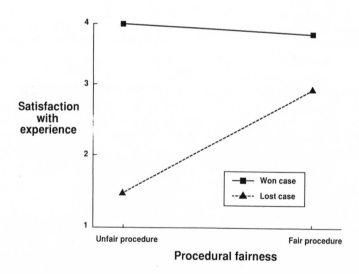

FIGURE 4–3. Procedural justice and satisfaction with court-annexed arbitration.

A criminal defendant facing twenty years in prison might not care much about issues of fairness; he might be concerned solely with the outcomes involved in his sentence (Heinz, 1985a, 1985b).[5] It *may* be the case that when outcomes as serious as personal freedom versus imprisonment are involved, procedural concerns are less potent factors psychologically than when less serious outcomes are at stake. The existence of such a limitation is unlikely, however, given the results of some recent studies on the relation between procedural justice and satisfaction among individuals evaluating encounters with the law. One of these studies is a survey of examining reactions to encounters with police and courts (Tyler, 1986b). Tyler found that procedural justice effects were strong even among those respondents who said that receiving favorable outcomes was very important to them.

Additional evidence that procedures continue to be important when the outcomes involved are substantial is provided by two recent studies of defendants accused of felonies. In both studies defendants in felony cases, in which substantial stakes such as long prison terms were involved, were interviewed about the disposition of their cases. The defendants were asked about the outcome of their case, as well as about the fairness of the case disposition process. These judgments were then used to predict defendant reactions to their experience. The first study involved interviews with 411 convicted felony defendants in three cities (Casper, Tyler, & Fisher, in press). The second study (Landis & Goodstein, 1986) is based on interviews with 619 convicted felons in two states.

The results of the Casper *et al.* study are shown in Figure 4-4a, those of the Landis and Goodstein study in Figure 4-4b. Both showed that defendants' evaluations of their experiences were heavily influenced by their assessments of whether their case was handled in a way that they regarded as fair. In contrast, the severity of their sentences did not have a direct effect on evaluations in either study. The only influence of outcomes was indirect. Individuals' judgments of process fairness were affected by outcomes and, through this influence, outcomes indirectly affected evaluations. Overall, however, the dominant finding of these studies was that defendants who had a substantial investment in their case and who were facing very serious outcomes were still heavily influenced by their assessments of procedural fairness.

[5]Heinz reports findings that appear to show few procedural justice differences between plea bargaining and trial and that suggest relatively weak effects of procedural justice judgments on other variables. Her measures of procedural justice judgments are weak, however, because her respondents were never asked directly about procedural fairness or about satisfaction with procedures. When the measurement of procedural justice judgments contains considerable error, of course, real effects may be obscured by the irrelevant variation resulting from the error. See the Appendix for a discussion of how procedural justice is usually measured.

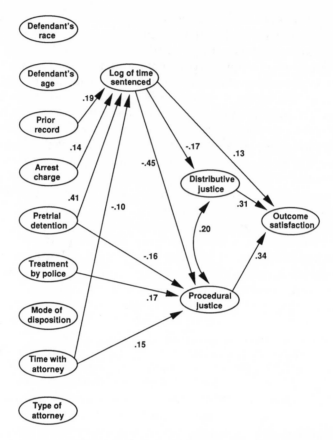

FIGURE 4-4a. Determinants of defendants' satisfaction: Casper, Tyler, and Fisher study (in press).

A second potential limit of the satisfaction effect is that some initial confidence in the procedural fairness of the forum in question might be necessary for the effect to appear. The Tyler (1987b) survey found that procedural justice effects are weakened but not absent when the individual in question does not expect to be treated fairly. This hypothesis is also suggested by research on allocation procedures by Folger *et al.* (1979) and by a study of trial procedures by Lind and Lissak (1985). Folger *et al.* found that, when subjects heard others support their own interpretation that a procedure's outcome was inequitable, they did not show any procedure-based enhancement of either procedural or distributive fairness; apparently the social reality of the negative comments subverted the capacity of a fair procedure to blunt the discontent engendered by a negative outcome. Lind and Lissak found that when there was a suggestion of corruption in the enactment of a procedure, percep-

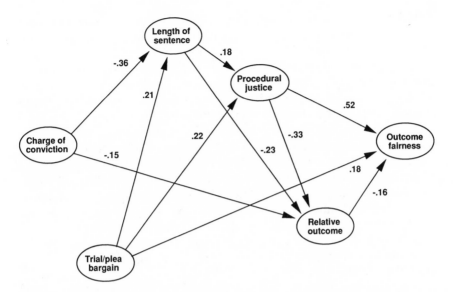

FIGURE 4–4b. Determinants of defendants' satisfaction: Landis and Goodstein study (1986).

tions of both procedural and distributive fairness were strongly affected by the outcome. One implication of both studies is that the satisfaction effect might be diminished when there are strong social or contextual reasons to believe that the procedure is not actually as fair as it appears to be.

Our discussion of these possible limitations does not mean that we believe the satisfaction effect to be a weak or rare phenomenon. In fact, we believe that the experience of procedural justice acts to increase satisfaction and to ameliorate discontent across a wide variety of legal situations. We do believe, however, that further research on possible limitations of the effect is needed.

The enhancement of satisfaction by procedural fairness is a remarkable phenomenon that suggests a host of potential beneficial applications of procedural justice research and, at the same time, raises some difficult questions. In essence, the existence of the effect means that we can increase the net satisfaction of all those who come in contact with the law by designing procedures so that they lead to judgments of greater procedural fairness. Because we now know that it is possible to produce a net gain in disputant satisfaction by proper procedural design, we have more reason than ever to study the relationship between the characteristics of a procedure and the judgment that the procedure is fair.

There are some important questions that accompany this new-found potential for enhancing disputant satisfaction. We now must consider, for example, how much importance policy makers should accord to such subjective variables as procedural fairness and disputant satisfaction. Given that certain procedures will increase disputant satisfaction and that others will decrease satisfaction, we have to face the possibility that the choices dictated by efforts to enhance satisfaction will run contrary to the choices dictated by other desiderata of the legal process. For example, our current knowledge emphasizes the trade-off posited in the Thibaut and Walker (1978) theory of procedure: we can design procedures to maximize either accuracy of information gathering or disputant satisfaction, but it may well be impossible to design a single procedure that does both. The knowledge of how to predict and assess the fairness and satisfaction consequences of various procedures brings with it the necessity of weighing these criteria against others.

There is also a serious ethical question. It is certainly possible for the unscrupulous to design procedures that *appear* fair and *feel* satisfying even though they are not at all fair by objective standards. The issue here is that raised by the Marxist concept of "false consciousness"—people might be led to believe that a procedure is fair through deceptive manipulation of the trappings of the procedure. Because procedural justice is linked to compliance with legal decisions, discussed below, there is an incentive for the state to make its legal procedures appear fair, whether they actually are fair or not. We have to worry more about such deceptions now that procedural justice research has provided information on how one can most effectively deceive the populace into believing that procedures are fair. We believe that such concerns must be addressed as we expand our knowledge and as the likelihood increases that our findings can be used for unethical purposes. Like all knowledge, our understanding of the psychology of procedural justice can be abused.[6]

Legitimacy and Compliance with Law

When we speak of such issues as legitimacy and overall support for legal institutions, we move from judgments about experiences with legal procedures to general political attitudes. To date, there has been only one study in the procedural justice tradition that has focused on general perceptions of legitimacy in legal settings. Tyler (1987b), in the study mentioned above, asked people about their perceptions of the legitimacy of legal authorities, as well as their judgments of distributive and

[6]It should be noted, however, that the Folger *et al.* (1979) study and the Lind and Lissak (1985) study suggest that those who attempt to deceptively manipulate procedural justice do so at the risk that their efforts will backfire if they are detected. We discuss this issue further in Chapter 8.

procedural fairness in encounters with police and the courts. He also asked for evaluations of the performance of the authorities and for self-reports about disobedience to laws. Table 4-3 shows the results of regression analyses linking evaluations of the authorities and perceived legitimacy to fairness and nonfairness variables describing the encounters with legal authorities. Three findings are especially noteworthy in the context of our present discussion of legitimacy and support. First, as is the case with evaluations of the performance of authorities and satisfaction with outcomes and treatment, perceived legitimacy was found to be more strongly influenced by fairness than nonfairness ratings. Second, as is the case with evaluation of the performance of authorities, the legitimacy measure is more strongly influenced by procedural fairness judgments than by distributive fairness judgments. Third, as one might expect from the more general nature of the concept, legitimacy appears to be less strongly affected by either fairness or nonfairness reactions to specific encounters than are evaluations of the performance of authorities or ratings of satisfaction. Tables 4-2 and 4-3 show that fairness judgments account for 60% of the variance in satisfaction with outcomes,

TABLE 4-3. Fairness, Outcomes, and Evaluation of the Performance and Legitimacy of Legal Authorities

| | Dependent variable | | | |
| | Performance of authorities | | Legitimacy and support | |
Predictor variable	Beta	R^2	Beta	R^2
Nonfairness variables:				
Absolute outcomes	.08		.02	
Relative outcomes	−.03		−.18*	
Relative treatment	−.07		.00	
All nonfairness variables		.16		.00
Fairness:				
Procedural	.41**		.20*	
Distributive	.22**		.10	
All fairness variables		.34		.04
Total for all variables		.34		.04
Usefulness analysis				
Nonfairness beyond fairness		.00		.00
Fairness beyond nonfairness		.18		.04

Note. Beta column reports standardized regression coefficients for an equation containing all variables. Entries in R^2 column are the adjusted square of the multiple correlation coefficient for variables entered singly or as a group. From Tyler (1986b).
*$p < .05$
**$p < .01$

54% of the variance in satisfaction with treatment, and 34% of the variance in evaluations of the performance of legal authorities. In contrast, as can be seen from Table 4-3, only 4% of the variance in perceived legitimacy is linked to fairness judgments.

A recent study by Tyler, Casper, and Fisher (1987) examined whether legitimacy is also process-based for those whose involvement with legal authorities is more substantial. Their analysis used the same sample of 411 defendants accused of felonies used in the study by Casper *et al.* (in press) described earlier. In this study, however, the concern was not satisfaction with one's trial experience, but instead the effects of the trial experience on general views about legal authorities and the law.

To examine generalization from trial experiences Tyler *et al.* (1987) used a panel design in which defendants were interviewed both prior to and following the disposition of their felony case. Several attitudes were of concern. The first was the respondent's view about legal authorities of the type they had dealt with: lawyers, prosecutors, and judges. Those defendants whose case was disposed of through plea bargaining (90%) were also asked to evaluate the plea-bargaining process. Finally, defendants were asked questions assessing their orientation toward the law and their attitude toward the government.

The results of the analysis are shown in Figure 4-5. In each case defendants' posttrial views were first predicted using their pretrial views. Their experience-based judgments were then added to the equation, and both were used to predict posttrial views. As the results in Figure 4-5 indicate, experience-based judgments always made a significant independent contribution to predictions of posttrial views. In other words, defendants' experiences shaped their views about the legal system, the law, and the government above and beyond their prior attitudes. As might be expected, views about the legal system were more strongly influenced by experience (average $R^2 = .17$) than were views about either law ($R^2 = .06$) or government ($R^2 = .09$).

Tyler *et al.* (1987) also examined what it is about experience that causes its impact on views about the legal system, law and government. They found that judgments of process fairness were consistently the major factor involved in generalizations from personal experience to system-level views. In other words, it is defendants' assessments of the fairness of the case disposition process that are the major influence on their views about the criminal justice system, the law, and the government. The severity of the sentence they receive has no independent impact on any of these variables except evaluations of the judge (who gives the sentence), and even in that case outcome effects are not as strong as are assessments of process fairness.

To go beyond the effects of procedural justice on attitudes about

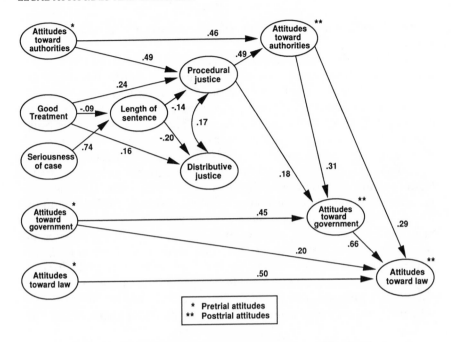

FIGURE 4-5. Causal paths linking legal experiences and legal attitudes.

institutions, authorities, and outcomes and say that procedural justice improves compliance with laws requires an additional step: not only must the legal or dispute resolution procedure be seen as fair and therefore legitimate, but behavior must be brought into line with these attitudes. Two studies, one conducted in the laboratory and one in the field, link obedience to laws to procedural justice judgments. The laboratory study, conducted by Friedland, Thibaut, and Walker (1973) examined the effects of three factors: the fairness of procedures for monitoring compliance with rules, the severity of penalties for noncompliance, and the extent to which the person with rule-making authority acted to exploit the workers whose compliance was under study. Friedland *et al.* found that compliance was indeed higher under fair surveillance procedures than under unfair procedures and that this procedure-linked difference in compliance was greater when the rule-making authority was actively exploiting the subject. (Exploitation resulted in substantially less compliance than did cooperation.) Further, the unfair procedure led subjects to be more efficient in using their noncompliance to obtain good outcomes for themselves—they became more clever lawbreakers, in essence. This effect was also stronger when the rule-making authority was behaving exploitatively. Both of these behavioral effects mirror those observed on ratings of the fairness and legitimacy of the procedure.

In the study described earlier Tyler (1987b) surveyed citizens and asked about their perceptions of the police and courts and their compliance with the law. He found that procedural fairness influenced evaluations of legal authorities and judged legitimacy and that these variables in turn affected obedience to laws. Figure 4-6 diagrams the causal relationships among procedural justice, perceived legitimacy, and compliance to laws. Two aspects of Tyler's findings are of particular interest here. First, the survey showed that procedural justice judgments arising from personal experiences with the law can indeed affect obedience to laws through their influence on perceived legitimacy. According to this finding, if a society's legal system used procedures that were judged to be unfair by a substantial proportion of its citizenry, one would expect to see an erosion of obedience to law. The second implication of Tyler's findings speaks to the rate at which the experience of procedural injustice might be expected to erode compliance with law. Because, as shown in Figure 4-6, compliance is affected only weakly by legitimacy, which is itself only moderately affected by procedural justice judgments,

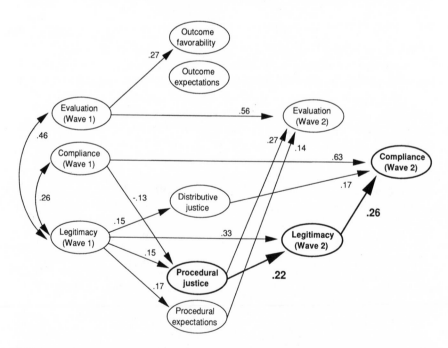

FIGURE 4-6. Causal paths linking procedural justice, legitimacy, and compliance with laws.

the procedural justice to compliance causal chain is not strong. The erosion of obedience to law just posited is supported by the data, but it is likely to be a gradual erosion. This is because there are other variables besides legitimacy that affect obedience to laws, and many of these variables would not be affected by procedural justice judgments. For example, obedience to the law is likely to be affected by perceptions of the probability of punishment as well as by attitudes and norms about the morality of lawbreaking, in addition to any effect of perceived legitimacy and support for the legal system.

Acceptance of Decisions

Tyler's work addresses the link between procedural justice and general compliance with laws. One might also ask whether there is a link between the perceived fairness of a dispute resolution procedure and the likelihood that the specific decision resulting from the procedure will be accepted and obeyed. Compliance with specific decisions is a perennial problem in law. Even when decisions are supposed to be binding, as is the case in adjudication and arbitration procedures, the enforcement of a decision can be very difficult in the face of active or even passive resistance. When the procedure in question is nonbinding, voluntary compliance is essential, making the issue of procedural justice effects on compliance even more important in such contexts.

Two field studies provide indirect evidence that procedural justice can enhance acceptance of decisions. McEwen and Maiman (1984) studied compliance with mediated and adjudicated judgments in small claims courts. They found that litigants were more likely to comply with judgments that they perceived to be fair. McEwen and Maiman did not assess procedural fairness—their fairness question dealt only with the fairness of the outcome—so we cannot be certain that differences in procedural fairness raised the level of compliance with the decisions. Because the link between procedural and distributive fairness is so well established, however, it is certainly reasonable to expect that procedural justice played a role in determining whether the decisions were obeyed.

Adler et al. (1983) report a similar finding in the context of a study of a nonbinding court-annexed arbitration program. They found that litigants' satisfaction was an important determinant of whether or not the arbitration award was accepted. Because, as we noted above, this study also showed a strong connection between procedural justice and litigant satisfaction, it provides additional evidence for the proposition that fair procedures lead to greater acceptance of decisions.

As we noted in Chapter 2, one of the most intriguing aspects of procedural justice is its apparent potential to enhance acceptance of decisions and thus to heal the social wounds produced by conflict. With respect to this idea, we note that some recent research on procedural justice in organizational settings suggests that fair procedures can act to reduce generally the level of conflict and dispute. Alexander and Ruderman (1987) have shown that higher levels of procedural justice judgments are associated with fewer reports of conflict and greater reported harmony in a large sample survey of federal employees.

Overview: Procedural Justice, Support, and Compliance

The research literature reviewed paints a striking picture of the consequences of the experience of procedural justice or injustice. Procedural justice matters a great deal in our attitudes and behavior. It may be difficult to get an overall sense of how profoundly attitudes and behavior are affected by the procedural justice experience. In this section we will review the major findings from a more personal perspective.

Imagine that you have just emerged from an encounter with the law; let us suppose that you have been to traffic court to defend yourself against a ticket that you believed was undeserved. You lost your case and have been ordered to pay a substantial fine and to go to traffic school for several evening sessions.

Having set this basic scenario, let us imagine and compare two variations upon it. In one variation, the procedures used in hearing and deciding your case seemed to you to be fundamentally fair; in the other variation, the procedures seemed to you to be fundamentally unfair. Suppose that in the fair procedure variation of our scenario you were given plenty of opportunity to express your views, beliefs, and arguments about the case. The judge was willing to hear about any individual circumstances that you believed to be relevant. In the unfair procedure variation of our scenario, we will imagine that you were not allowed to express many arguments that you believed to be important. The judge told you that your statements and evidence could only address what he believed to be the determining issue in the case. Your efforts to tell your side of the story were blocked in what seemed to you to be an arbitrary and unfair way.

Consider first the experience of a fair procedure. We would expect that you would be likely to emerge from the experience with somewhat more positive attitudes about the judge and the traffic court system in general. Because the procedure seemed to you to be fair, you would be more likely to accept the judge's decision and to view it as fair, and you would view the entire experience as more satisfactory. You might experience some increase in your overall support for the legal system, but this would be a less immediate result of the experience, and it might be "watered down" by your preexisting attitudes about the system or by other experiences that you had had in the past. You might well be more inclined to comply with the decision and attend the mandated traffic school classes, because the sense of procedural justice had led you to view the decision as fair. You also might be more inclined in the future to obey traffic laws, as well as laws in general, because your evaluation of the system of traffic laws and courts had been increased by the experience of a just procedure. Of course, the procedural justice experience would not be the only factor that would influence either your compliance with the court's decision or your future obedience of traffic laws. Both of these behaviors would also be affected by other factors, such as your assessment of the likelihood that you would escape punishment if you disobeyed either the order or the traffic laws, your own overall attitudes concerning the morality of lawbreaking, and your beliefs about the attitudes of peers and other important referent persons with respect to your actions.

In contrast, consider the consequences of a hearing procedure that seemed to you to be fundamentally unfair. The research suggests that your assessment of the hearing procedure as unfair would increase your discontent with the negative outcome. Your evaluation of the judge and the traffic court system would be quite negative. You would probably be very dissatisfied with the whole experience, and you might well be angry with the judge and the system. This single negative experience would certainly not undermine your support for the legal system, but it might well lessen it, making it more vulnerable to future reduction if you again encountered unfair procedures. This lessening of support for traffic laws and authorities might lead you to be less conscientious about obeying traffic laws; indeed, you might become more clever in breaking traffic laws if you were to become convinced that the system used unfair procedures. Your assessment that the procedures are unfair might make you less inclined to obey the judge's order that you attend traffic school, but your compliance with the decision would also depend on your assessment of the consequences of disobedience.

PROCEDURAL PREFERENCES

We reported in Chapter 2 that the Thibaut and Walker research on disputant preferences yielded two primary findings: that disputants prefer adversary procedures and that procedural fairness judgments are the major determinants of preferences for procedures. The clear implication of that research, and the thrust of the theoretical work that accompanied it, is that procedural preferences are greatly affected by procedural fairness judgments and that procedural fairness judgments are quite sensitive to variation in process control. We defer until the next chapter a review of recent research on the etiology of procedural fairness judgments in law; our concern here is with the role of fairness and other factors in determining disputant preferences for various dispute resolution procedures. As we will see, the overall implication of the research is that procedural fairness judgments do indeed play a major role in determining procedural preferences.

The material discussed in the preceding section is most relevant to a "top-down" perspective on the value of procedural justice, concerned as it is with the role of procedural justice in promoting support for and compliance with legal institutions. The material in this section looks at procedural justice research from a different perspective: from the bottom up. The central question we address here is what procedures are preferred by those who might find themselves subject to law and dispute resolution procedures. The importance of procedural preferences is expressed nicely by Sarat (1975, p.430), who notes that "[i]t would be strange, indeed, to call a legal system democratic if its procedures and operations were generally at odds with the values, preferences, or desires of the citizens over a long period of time." Procedural justice research has generated a substantial body of research on disputants' preferences for procedures, and we can now be more specific than ever about what disputants want from legal and dispute resolution procedures.

Kurtz and Houlden (1981) tested the generality of preferences for adversary adjudication procedures using a scenario method very similar to that used in the Lind et al. (1978) study described in Chapter 2. Noting that many early procedural justice studies had used student subjects, Kurtz and Houlden studied procedural preferences and perceptions of procedures in a quite different population: prisoners in a military stockade. The prisoners' overall preference ratings showed much the same pattern as had been observed by Thibaut et al. and Lind et al.: the pure adversary procedure was preferred to all others, and procedural evaluations declined as the procedures placed more control over the hearing in the hands of the judge and less in the hands of the disputants.

Kurtz and Houlden computed intra-subject correlations to index the extent to which ratings on various dimensions tracked the preference ratings for the various procedures. These correlations showed that ratings of the extent to which the subjects were favored by the procedure and the ratings of perceived procedural fairness were the two variables that were most closely related to preferences. The correlation between favorableness and procedural preference was somewhat higher than the correlation between fairness and preference, but the meaning of this difference is unclear because the strongest correlate of favorableness was perceived fairness. It may be the case, as Kurtz and Houlden suggest, that procedural preferences are largely determined by individual interests, and that their prisoners were more candid than were the student subjects used in previous research about the role of self-interest in determining their preferences. However, it may also be the case that what subjects mean by a favorable procedure is not necessarily one that promotes their own outcomes but rather one that is fair.[7] No doubt both of these views have some validity.

Houlden et al. (1978) examined the preferences of disputants and third parties for four dispute resolution procedures. The procedures represented all possible combinations of high or low process and decision control.[8] The high process control procedures gave the disputants more or less complete freedom in the presentation of their evidence; low process control procedures vested nearly absolute control over the presentation of evidence in the third party. The high decision control procedure allowed the disputants to reject the third party's decision and attempt to negotiate a resolution of the dispute. The low decision control procedure required the disputants to accept as binding any decision the third party made. The disputants in the Houlden et al. study were undergraduate students, the third parties were law students or military judges. The experiment used a role-playing method in which the disputant subjects were told that they would be asked to play the role of a disputant in a standard dispute and the law students believed they would have to play the role of third party in the dispute. The role-playing was made more relevant to the law student subjects by telling them that a monetary payment for one of the disputants was contingent on the outcome of the simulated dispute. The undergraduate student subjects were led to believe that the preferences they expressed would affect which procedure would be used when they themselves took part in a later phase of the experiment. The ratings were made prior to the enactment of the dispute resolution procedure.

[7]As noted in Chapter 2, testing relationships such as these using within-subject simple correlations, rather than a multiple regression approach, ignores the relationships among the factors thought to influence preferences. The difficulty in interpreting the Kurtz and Houlden results arises from this problem. In fairness to Kurtz and Houlden, we must note that the Lind et al. (1978) study also used the within-subject correlation technique.

[8]Some researchers speak of high versus low process control or decision control, adopting implicitly the perspective of the disputant; others speak of disputant process and decision control versus third-party process or decision control. We will adopt the former convention, unless emphasis on a specific transfer of control from the disputant to the third party is intended. As demonstrated in several experiments by Sheppard, described below, it is possible and apparently quite acceptable for the third party to control certain aspects of the dispute resolution hearing so long as disputants are allowed control over the parts of the hearing that are most important to them.

Houlden *et al.* found that disputants preferred high process control procedures to low process control procedures, especially if the procedure also included low decision control. Third-party preferences were less sensitive to variation in process control than were disputant preferences but more sensitive to variation in decision control. The results for ratings of procedural fairness were quite similar, but not identical, to those seen on the subjects' preference ratings. By and large, the results are congruent with the idea that variation in procedural fairness, produced by the manipulations in process and decision control, were a major factor in determining disputant preferences for a hearing procedure.

The strong relation between perceptions of process control and procedural fairness and disputant preferences for legal procedures is seen also in the study by Houlden (1980) on plea-bargaining procedures. Houlden asked inmates at a county detention center and college undergraduates for their preferences for a number of different plea-bargaining procedures and for their perceptions of the procedures on a number of dimensions. Within-subject correlations between the perceptual dimensions and preferences were computed, and it was found that the dimensions most strongly related to preferences for both inmates and undergraduates were the defendant's opportunity to present evidence and the fairness of the procedure.

There are a number of procedural details that are included in typical manipulations of process control—freedom to define the issues under dispute, freedom to express arguments, freedom to present evidence, the right to cross-examine or seek clarification, and so on. Sheppard (1984, 1985) has noted that, because of its multiple facets, process control can be subdivided. He hypothesized that people may view some facets of process control as appropriately vested in the third party, provided that some critical facets of process control remain in the hands of the disputants. In two scenario experiments, Sheppard solicited preferences for four procedures: an inquisitorial procedure that involved a single court-controlled investigator; a second inquisitorial procedure that involved two court-controlled investigators; a pure adversary procedure; and a hybrid procedure, which allowed the disputants free expression of their evidence and arguments, but also allowed the judge to ask questions and seek clarification. The first experiment used undergraduate students as subjects; the second used passengers awaiting flights at an airport.

Table 4-4 shows the preference results and fairness ratings of the four procedures. Sheppard found in both studies that significantly more subjects chose the adversary procedure than either of the inquisitorial procedures, but he also found that the great majority of subjects chose the hybrid procedure over any of the other three. Ratings of procedural

TABLE 4-4. Preferences and Fairness Ratings of Four Dispute
Adjudication Procedures

| | Procedure | | | |
| | Autocratic | | | |
Subjects/Measure	Single investigator	Double investigator	Adversary	Hybrid
Undergraduates:				
% Preferring procedure	4	10	18	68
Procedural fairness	3.05	4.21	6.18	7.16
Airport passengers:				
% preferring procedure	7	8	26	59
Procedural fairness	5.00	5.20	6.10	7.30

Note. Procedural fairness ratings were made on a nine-point scale; higher values indicate greater perceived fairness. Values derived from Tables 1 and 2, Sheppard (1985).

fairness tracked these preference effects very closely, suggesting that the hybrid procedure was preferred because it was seen as more fair than the other procedures. These two studies showed that even rather subtle variations in procedural features can have massive impact on procedural preferences by virtue of their effects on procedural fairness judgments, and that some limitations on process control appear to be quite acceptable, indeed desirable, to citizens.

Much of the research produced by the Thibaut and Walker group emphasized the role of procedural fairness judgments in determining procedural preferences. As more research has accumulated on disputant preferences, it has become clear that although procedural fairness is an important determinant of procedural preferences, it is certainly not the only factor influencing preferences. Recent research has suggested that disputants consider several other factors in deciding which procedures they prefer. Sometimes these other factors can be of sufficient importance to countervail against fairness concerns and lead disputants to prefer procedures that they see as less fair than others. A major task now facing procedural justice researchers is the investigation of the influence of situational factors on the relative importance of fairness and nonfairness concerns in procedural preferences.

Lissak and Sheppard (1983) interviewed sixty respondents concerning the criteria that they would use to evaluate or select a dispute resolution procedure. Each respondent was asked to describe a real dispute and then to generate criteria for a procedure to resolve that dispute. In order of the frequency with which they were mentioned, the ten most frequently mentioned criteria were: airing the problem, speed of resolution, fairness, personal control, animosity reduction, cost, minimizing disruption of everyday affairs, and reducing the possibility of future conflict. In a subsequent set of interviews, Lissak and Sheppard obtained ratings of the importance of these and other criteria. None of the criteria was seen as being more important than fairness, but several were as important as fairness.

Leung (1985) and Leung and Lind (1986) report two studies showing that process-control preference effects can be negated by countervailing effects based on other criteria. Both of these studies used a scenario method quite similar to that used in the Lind *et al.* (1978) cross-national preference study, reported in Chapter 2, to examine the procedural preferences of American and Hong Kong Chinese. We will discuss these studies in greater detail in Chapter 6, where we consider at some length cultural similarities and differences in procedural preferences and procedural justice judgments. For the moment it is sufficient to note that both of these studies showed culture-based variation in preferences. The Leung and Lind study found that the Chinese subjects were indifferent between adversary and inquisitorial adjudication procedures, apparently because they believed that adversary procedures promote conflict and this counterbalanced the process control advantage of adversary procedures. The American subjects showed the familiar preference for adversary procedures. In a later study, Leung found that Chinese subjects preferred mediation to adversary adjudication whereas Americans were indifferent between these two procedures. His study showed that differences in procedural preferences could be accounted for by cultural variation in beliefs concerning the characteristics of procedures (for example, whether the procedure is thought to promote fairness or reduce animosity, and so on) rather than by cultural variation in the extent to which various characteristics are seen as desirable (for instance, whether the respondent wants a fair procedure or a procedure that reduces animosity).

One additional set of studies has pointed to an additional qualification of what was once thought to be a pervasive preference for adversary procedures. Heuer and Penrod (1986) have shown that preferences for dispute resolution procedures depend in part on the nature of the relationship between the disputants and the opportunities for negotiated trade-offs. In particular, when trade-offs are thought to be possible, disputants appear to prefer procedures that afford them some decision control. In all instances, however, there remains a preference for procedures giving the disputants considerable process control. Further, the Heuer and Penrod studies showed, as have all of the studies reviewed in this section, that the perceived fairness of procedures is one of the most important determinants of procedural preference.

The studies reviewed above suggest that we must consider factors other than procedural fairness in our attempts to understand disputant preferences for various dispute resolution procedures, but they also confirm the importance of procedural fairness in affecting preferences. In every study, procedural fairness judgments have been found to be among the most important determinants of procedural preferences. The effect of procedural fairness on procedural preferences is remarkably stable. People as diverse as American military prisoners, French students, and Chinese workers make procedural fairness one of their primary considerations in deciding what dispute resolution procedures they want. Our current knowledge about procedural preferences has revealed that preferences for specific procedures are more variable than the early Thibaut and Walker research suggested, but more recent research has also provided impressive confirmation of the importance the Thibaut and Walker gave to procedural fairness in their theoretical and empirical work.

The final studies to be considered here look not at reactions to adversary or inquisitorial hearing procedures, but instead at various jury procedures. There is a good deal of psychological research on the objective effects of various procedures governing the legal institution of the jury: there are, for example, numerous studies of procedures specifying the size of juries, the decision rules that juries must follow, and the manner in which juries are to be instructed. A less extensive but no less important literature deals with the objective effects of nonjury procedures, such as those that govern witness identification sessions (lineups and photo-identifications). Unfortunately, both of these bodies of research have been largely ignored by researchers concerned with the underlying topic of this volume—the causes and consequences of the experience of procedural justice—and we have therefore had little to say about these important topics.[9]

MacCoun and Tyler (in press) had undergraduate subjects read a scenario involving a hit-and-run auto accident and evaluate one of four jury procedures for trying the case. The jury procedures varied along two dimensions that have been the subject of recent legal debate and considerable objective-criteria research: the size of the jury (six versus

[9]There are several excellent recent collections that summarize social psychological research on these topics. See, e.g., Kassin and Wrightsman (1985), Kerr and Bray (1982), and Hans and Vidmar (1986). The studies we describe next are the first to look at subjective reactions to two procedural variables that have figured largely in the jury decision-making literature. We hope that more studies on the subjective fairness effects of jury and identification procedures will follow and that we will see an end to the present discontinuity between the procedures examined by procedural justice researchers and those examined by other psychologists interested in legal issues.

twelve persons) and the decision rule that governs when the jury is said to have reached a verdict (unanimity versus majority vote required for a verdict). The subjects indicated their preferences for the procedure by rating its desirability, and they rated the procedure on a number of other dimensions, including its fairness.

Figure 4-7 shows a path diagram that reflects the study's findings with respect to the sources of the desirability ratings. The desirability ratings were found to be the direct result of three considerations: procedural fairness, thorough evaluation of evidence, and cost, with procedural fairness being the most powerful consideration. The fairness, thorough evaluation, and cost factors were in turn influenced by either direct effects of jury size and decision rule (for example, larger juries are

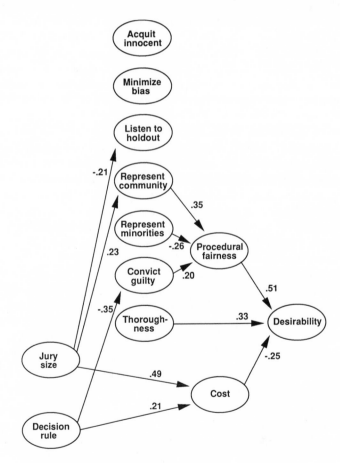

FIGURE 4-7. Model of jury procedure preferences.

likely to be more expensive) or indirect effects due to the perceived impact of the procedures on factors that in turn were seen as affecting the immediate causes of desirability (for example, larger juries are more likely to be representative of the community, which makes them more fair). As can be seen from the path diagram, sometimes one path could act to raise the desirability of one procedure while another path acted to lower the desirability of the same procedure; the ultimate desirability rating depended on which path was stronger for the respondent in question. Thus the twelve-person, unanimous procedure was viewed as the most desirable in terms of its fairness, and this same procedure was viewed as least desirable in terms of its cost.

In their second study, MacCoun and Tyler conducted telephone interviews with a relatively small sample of residents of Evanston, Illinois. The respondents were asked to rate each of the four jury procedures examined in the previous study as well as a bench trial (judge only, no jury) procedure. Again, large juries were seen as fairer but more expensive than small juries. The respondents were asked to rate the desirability of each jury procedure for a murder trial and for a shoplifting trial. MacCoun and Tyler found that the twelve-person, unanimous-decision jury was preferred by a substantial majority (68%) of the respondents in the case of a murder trial. When the case involved shoplifting, the twelve-person, unanimous-decision jury procedure was no longer chosen as most desirable by most respondents—only 22% chose it. Instead, the largest group (43%) chose the six-person, majority-decision procedure. The critical factor driving procedural justice judgments, cost judgments, accuracy judgments, and desirability ratings was the size of the jury, not the decision rule.

When MacCoun and Tyler compared respondents' attitudes about trial by a twelve-person jury and trial by judge, they found that the former was seen as more fair and more accurate than the latter, but also as more expensive. The respondents were asked to rate the desirability of jury and bench trial procedures under four assumptions: that the trial involved a murder charge, that the trial involved a shoplifting charge, that the respondent was the victim of the crime being tried, and that the respondent was accused of the crime being tried. By and large, the jury trial procedure was seen as more desirable for murder trials (93%). When the charge involved shoplifting, however, a majority (53%) of respondents choose the bench trial procedure. Even in this situation however, a substantial minority (44%) chose the jury trial procedure.

The MacCoun and Tyler studies show the important role of procedural justice judgments in determining preferences. This in turn points to an omission in psychological research on juries. If we think about why one might want to have lay juries, two rationales are apparent. One rationale focuses on the jury as a problem-solving group convened to attempt to reach a decision that is as accurate as possible given the facts in the case. The other rationale sees the jury as a political institution that is designed to increase the legitimacy of the justice system by allowing community participation and representation in legal decision-making. We psychologists have devoted enormous efforts to examining the efficacy of the jury with respect to its problem-solving ability, but we have largely ignored the efficacy of the jury with respect to its legitimizing function. The consequence of this emphasis is that we now know a great deal about how the jury functions as a group, but we know very little about how the jury functions as an institution. Before we can pretend to have a complete picture of the psychology of the jury, we must conduct more studies that examine consequences of jury variables for subjective, as well as objective, justice.

* * * * * * * * *

We have seen in the research reviewed in this chapter that disputants' concern with procedural issues in general, and their procedural justice judgments in particular, affect many important legal attitudes and behaviors. Indeed, the picture that seems to be emerging is of people much more concerned with the process of their interaction with the law and much less concerned with the outcome of that interaction than one might have supposed. The next logical question concerns what it is about legal procedures that drives perceptions of procedural justice. In the next chapter we consider the current state of knowledge about the sources of procedural justice judgments. We also discuss how our overall knowledge of the psychology of procedural justice judgments relates to our knowledge of the objective consequences of procedures and to issues of cost and of the social and political functions of law.

Chapter 5

Procedural Justice in Law II

Sources and Implications of Procedural Justice Judgments

SOURCES OF PROCEDURAL FAIRNESS JUDGMENTS

The material presented in the preceding chapter shows that procedural fairness judgments are important in determining reactions to encounters with legal and dispute resolution procedures and that procedural justice is one of the most important considerations affecting disputant preferences for different procedures. Sufficient justification for intensive study of the factors affecting procedural fairness can be found in its effects on any one of several variables: satisfaction, support, compliance, or procedural preference. All of these attitudes and behaviors have long been recognized to be worthy of study, and we now know that if we are to understand them we must understand the psychology of procedural justice. We believe, however, that additional justification for the study of the sources of procedural justice judgments can be found in the *variety* of attitudes and behaviors affected by procedural justice judgments. In other words, it is important that we understand the etiology of procedural justice judgments not only because they affect any specific attitude or behavior, but also because they affect so many different attitudes and behaviors. The variety of consequences of procedural justice points, we believe, to the importance that people accord to it. The experience of procedural justice (or procedural injustice) is a profound feature of social life, and one that is worthy of study in its own right.

In the following sections we examine the factors that have been found to influence procedural fairness judgments: control over the process and the outcome of the dispute resolution, opportunity for expression and consideration of arguments, the favorability of the outcome of the dispute resolution, and the procedure's correspondence to other procedural fairness standards. As was the case with the discussion of consequences of procedural justice, our presentation of research on the causes of procedural justice judgments will involve a considerable number of studies and a variety of findings. It might be helpful to keep in mind a personal scenario that can be used to judge and integrate the many different findings and their implications. We propose that our readers imagine that they have become involved in a landlord–tenant dispute. Because most of us have been tenants at one point or another in our lives, it might be easiest to imagine that you have just ended an apartment lease and that your landlord has retained all of the sizable damage deposit you had put down when you began the lease. Several efforts on your part to persuade the landlord to return the deposit have degenerated into arguments about what damage had resulted in the course of your occupancy, how clean the apartment had been when you left, and about your and the landlord's actions in maintaining the apartment. You have decided to pursue the dispute by filing a case in the local small claims court. The central issue of the following sections, as applied to this example, is how the procedures, events, and outcomes you experience will affect your judgments of procedural fairness.

CONTROL OVER PROCESS AND DECISION

One of the central themes of the Thibaut and Walker research is that procedures that provide high process control for disputants tend to enhance procedural fairness. More recent research has confirmed this general finding. Lind *et al.* (1980) replicated the original Walker *et al.* (1974) study with a larger set of measures designed to assess more precisely the effects of adversary and inquisitorial procedures on disputants' perceptions of adjudication. Lind *et al.* measured procedural fairness judgments, distributive fairness judgments, and a variety of other perceptions about the procedures. The independent variables manipulated in the study were the adjudication procedure (either a high process control adversary procedure or a low process control inquisitorial procedure), the outcome of the adjudication (either win or lose), and the timing of measures of perceptions of various specific features of the adjudication procedure (either before or after the verdict was announced). Table 5-1 shows the means for indices of the perceived fairness of the procedure and trial outcome. As can be seen from the table, the procedure manipulation had substantial effects on both types of fairness judgments. The experiment also permitted a comparison to be made between the perceptions of procedural features held by subjects who did not know how their case would be decided and those of subjects who knew whether they had won or lost the case. Lind *et al.* found that knowledge of the outcome did not change the relative perceptions engendered by the two procedures. Of particular interest is the fact that

TABLE 5-1. Procedural and Distributive Fairness
Judgments of Disputants in Adversary and
Inquisitorial Hearings

Outcome of hearing	Hearing procedure	
	Adversary	Inquisitorial
Procedural fairness index		
Disputant's team found innocent	.10	−.32
Disputant's team found guilty	.36	−.21
Distributive fairness index		
Disputant's team found innocent	2.53	1.93
Disputant's team found guilty	−2.11	−2.61

Note. Values are marginal means for standardized factor scores. Higher values indicate greater perceived fairness. From Lind *et al.* (1980, p. 649).

the experiment showed that even when subjects received an unfavorable verdict they showed no inclination to believe that the adversary
procedure was to blame.

In terms of the small-claims court example we posed earlier, the
process control effect would lead to greater perceived fairness if the
judge at the hearing allowed both parties to the dispute to control
the evidence and arguments presented. If the judge restricted your process control by requiring, for example, that you not mention your landlord's tardiness in making repairs, you would feel that the procedure
was less than fair. Note that the effects of process control restrictions on
procedural fairness judgments might run contrary to their effects on
objective fairness. It is certainly arguable that the issue of timeliness of
repairs is in fact irrelevant to the question of whether a damage deposit
should be returned, as long as the repairs ultimately were made and
were unrelated to the claimed damage, and it might be unfair in some
objective sense to have the issue raised at the hearing. Nevertheless,
rules that disallow the presentation of issues that seem to a disputant to
be important have the effect of restricting process control. The application of such rules to your case is likely to lead to feelings of procedural
unfairness, with all of the attendant lowering of satisfaction, support,
and compliance documented in the preceding chapter.

The psychological processes underlying the process control effect
have become the subject of some debate in recent years. The argument
centers around the issue, raised in Chapter 1, of whether outcomes and
outcome-related variables can account for the effect. Some explanations
of the process control effect, most notably those of Thibaut and Walker
(1978) and Brett (1986), are based on assertions linking process control to

the outcome of a procedure. An opposing view has been advanced by Tyler, Rasinski, and Spodick (1985) who assert that the process control effect is based on reactions to the procedure *per se*, independent of its relation to the outcome.

Thibaut and Walker contend that disputant process control promotes procedural justice because it promotes distributive justice in the outcome produced by the procedure. Presumably they would expect the process control effect to disappear if it were clear to the disputants that process control did not lead, at least in most cases, to the outcomes specified by the equity rule. Brett explains the process control effect by positing that disputants prefer to exercise personal control over outcomes. She argues that process control is viewed by disputants as the only way they can control their outcomes from an adjudication, because in adjudication disputants are not permitted more direct control over the decision. Brett hypothesizes that if disputants were allowed decision control, as is done in mediation procedures, they would have no need to use process control to exercise control over their outcomes. This leads Brett to predict that process control will not enhance procedural justice under conditions of high disputant decision control.[1]

We might label both of these positions "outcome-oriented." Neither suggests that process control is desired only to achieve positive outcomes, but both argue that it is something about outcomes, whether their fairness or control over them, that underlies the process control effect. A quite different etiology of the effect is suggested by Tyler, Rasinski, and Spodick, who attribute the enhancement of procedural fairness directly to the expression of values permitted under high process control. This value-expression explanation accounts for the process control effect by arguing that the mere experience of an opportunity for expression will be seen as fair—there is no reference to the outcome of the procedure. Because this explanation of the effect depends only on characteristics of the procedure and not on any view of the procedure as instrumental in securing or controlling outcomes, we label it "procedure-oriented."[2]

[1]Brett's explanation of the process control effect is only a small part of a larger body of work on mediation processes. We refer our readers to Brett (1986) and Brett and Goldberg (1983) for a more complete presentation of her work.

[2]Social exchange theorists might argue that the positive feelings prompted by the expression of values are themselves outcomes, and that this explanation of the effect is not fundamentally different from those that posit positive reactions on the basis of distributive justice or outcome control. We are aware of this argument, but we do not see it as relevant to the basic issue under consideration: whether procedural justice judgments are driven by something about procedures *per se* or something about procedures as means to outcomes. We will discuss this point in greater detail and consider its implications more fully in Chapter 10.

To date, there is no definitive resolution of the issues raised by the debate, but some recent studies provide evidence that the connection between outcomes and procedural justice is more tenuous than an extreme outcome-oriented position would suggest. If one supposed that immediate outcomes were the most potent determinants of procedural justice, one would predict that people would see as fair those procedures that favored their own interests. However, several studies (e.g., LaTour, 1978; Lind *et al.*, 1980) have shown a poor correspondence between ratings of the perceived favorableness of procedures to the disputant and procedural fairness ratings of the same procedures. The outcome-oriented position, in its simplest form, would predict that receiving a negative outcome from a high process control procedure should make it obvious to a disputant that process control has been ineffective in securing favorable outcomes, and any procedural fairness advantage of process control should disappear. In fact, virtually all of the studies of procedural fairness in dispute resolution have shown process control enhancement of procedural fairness judgments in conditions where subjects received negative outcomes.

Another piece of evidence against some of the outcome-oriented explanations of procedural justice judgments is to be found in the Lind *et al.* (1980) study, which showed little reevaluation of procedures in response to information on the verdict of an adjudication. The study gave some subjects unfavorable and inequitable outcomes and other subjects favorable and equitable outcomes. If outcomes were the major determinants of reactions to the adjudication procedure, the former condition should provoke judgments that the high process control procedures were as unfair as the low process control procedures. In fact, as we have already noted, the outcome did not affect basic perceptions of the procedures nor did it alter perceptions of the relative fairness of the two procedures.

These studies show some results that are inconsistent with extreme outcome-oriented explanations of the process control effect, but many of the results can be accounted for by less extreme positions such as those advanced by Brett and Thibaut and Walker. However, there are also several recent studies with findings that are contrary to the more moderate outcome-oriented explanations, especially that proposed by Brett. In one of these studies, Lind, Lissak, and Conlon (1983) tested the relative effects of process and decision control on reactions to conflict resolution procedures. Decision control was operationalized in this study as the opportunity to reject the decision put forth by the third-party. Decision control is a more direct means of controlling outcomes than is process control, and if Brett's explanation of the process control effect is correct, decision control should have greater effects on perceptions of procedural fairness than does process control. Indeed, one might expect from outcome-oriented explanations that process control would be of little importance, and therefore have little effect, when disputants have decision control.

Lind and his colleagues used the same experimental paradigm employed in the Walker *et al.* (1974), LaTour (1978), and Lind *et al.* (1980) studies, but they manipulated independently the process control and decision control that the hearing procedures afforded disputants. The process control manipulation involved the use of adversary or nonadversary procedures similar to those used in the Walker *et al.* (1974) study. High disputant decision control was created by including in the procedure the provision that the judge's decision could be rejected by either disputant (in favor of the option of attempting to negotiate a settlement); low decision control was created by specifying that the judge's decision was final and binding on both parties. In addition, the study included a manipulation of the outcome of the hearing—subjects were told either that they had been awarded two-thirds of the outcomes in controversy or that they had been awarded only one-third of the outcomes in controversy.

Table 5-2 shows the results of the process control and decision control manipulations on procedural fairness judgments. Even when they had considerable decision control, disputants showed higher procedural fairness judgments under high process control than under low process control. The decision control manipulation had little effect on procedural fairness judgments. These findings are contrary to those that one would expect if outcome instrumentality were the major force in the process control effect.

In a series of studies on the effects of process and decision control, Tyler, Rasinski, and Spodick (1985) used both survey and laboratory

TABLE 5-2. Procedural Fairness Reactions to Process and Decision Control

	Disputant decision control			
	High		Low	
	Disputant process control		Disputant process control	
Outcome	High	Low	High	Low
Favorable	6.54	5.97	7.12	6.04
Unfavorable	6.10	4.21	5.22	4.66

Note. Values are means of an index constructed by averaging two nine-point scales. Higher numbers indicate greater perceived fairness. From Lind, Lissak, & Conlon (1983).

data to test whether there were some unique process control effect on procedural justice judgments. Two sets of survey data, one consisting of defendant reactions to trial experiences and one consisting of student reactions to college courses, were analyzed to determine whether perceptions of process control had any effect on procedural fairness judgments over and above the effect of perceived control over decisions. In both surveys an independent effect of process control was found. (Both surveys also showed an independent effect of decision control over and above that of process control.) In their third study, the Tyler group manipulated the level of process control, the level of decision control, and the allocation setting described in scenarios. Both process control and decision control were found to have independent effects on ratings of procedural fairness. In another round of survey studies, Tyler (1987b) has replicated these findings.

There are some findings that are favorable to outcome-oriented explanations of the process control effect. Brett and Goldberg (1983) found that mediation procedures received higher procedural fairness ratings than did arbitration procedures.[3] At least one laboratory study of dispute resolution procedures (Houlden et al., 1978) has shown higher procedural fairness under high than under low decision control, as did the Tyler et al. study of allocation procedures mentioned in the preceding paragraph. Further, more favorable reactions to mediation than to adjudication have been observed in studies that have not directly measured procedural fairness, such as the McEwen and Maiman study (1984) mentioned in the section on compliance in Chapter 4.

Angela Ebreo (1985) conducted a study that shows that both the outcome-oriented and the procedure-oriented explanations of the process control effect have some validity. She manipulated process control through both the formal procedure and the enactment of the procedure in a laboratory adjudication. That is, subjects were allowed to contribute information either as a matter of right under the procedure or through the personal practices of the attorneys at the hearing. Her study showed that process control through formal procedure enhanced perceptions of freedom of expression but not perceptions of personal control over the hearing. In contrast, process control through enactment enhanced perceptions of personal control, but not perceptions of freedom of expression. Thus Ebreo's findings suggest that instrumental and noninstrumental process control can arise from quite different features of hearings. Notwithstanding their different origins, however, both feel-

---

[3]The difference in procedural justice may have been due to the higher level of decision control given disputants under mediation, or it may have been due to covarying differences in process control or some other feature of the procedures. Other research lends credence to the decision control explanation of the Brett and Goldberg results.

ings of personal control and perceptions of expression led to enhanced procedural justice judgments.

Returning to the small-claims court scenario, we can see what the various perspectives on process and decision control suggest about the experience of procedural justice or injustice. One prediction of the outcome-oriented position is that if the small-claims court rules allowed your case to be mediated, rather than adjudicated, you would find the procedure to be fairer, because mediation would give you more control over the outcome of the case.[4] An outcome-oriented perspective would predict that if your case were placed in mediation, your concern with process control would diminish, because you would have a more direct way of influencing the outcome of the case. In contrast, the procedure-oriented explanation of the process control effect would predict that whether your case were mediated or adjudicated, you would feel that the procedure was fairer if it allowed you considerable freedom of expression in presenting your arguments.

What can be concluded about the validity of these various explanations of the process control effect? The research conducted to date seems to suggest that process control effects on procedural fairness judgments are due to both outcome-related *and* expressive features of process control. This suggests two strategies for future work on this topic: we can refine and elaborate our conceptions of the various types of control that exist in dispute resolution procedures or we can search for the basic psychological mechanisms that underlie the process and decision control effects. We present next an example of work using the former strategy and we describe in a later section some studies that have used the latter strategy.

Sheppard (1983, 1984) has presented a conceptualization of control in dispute resolution that analyzes and elaborates control relations between disputants and the third party. Sheppard identifies four different stages of third-party dispute intervention at which control might be exercised, and he distinguishes four different types of control. His four stages of third-party intervention are: (1) definition of procedures and issues, (2) discussion of information and arguments, (3) alternative selection (that is, choice of a resolution for the dispute), and (4) reconciliation of the parties. Sheppard's four types of control are: (1) "process control," control over the choice of processes and procedures;[5] (2) "content control," control over the information and arguments considered by

---

[4]In fact, as noted in Chapter 2, Thibaut and Walker (1978) assume that in many legal disputes affording mutual decision control to the disputants would lead to no positive outcome because the parties would be unable to agree on an resolution.

[5]Note that Sheppard's use of the term *process control* differs from the use of the term by Thibaut and Walker and others. Sheppard's process control includes both what is some-

the parties; (3) "control by request," exercise of one of the other three types of control at the request of one of the parties; and (4) "motivational" control, the use of social power to force an action or enforce a decision.

The Sheppard taxonomy permits a more detailed description of the control relations in a given dispute resolution procedure, and it emphasizes that procedures can be designed that allocate various types of control in novel ways. This last point is especially important because it allows us to design procedures that give disputants enough of the types of control that promote procedural fairness, while at the same time avoiding some of the shortcomings, discussed later in this chapter, of unlimited adversariness. Recall that Sheppard (1985), in a study described in our discussion in Chapter 4 on disputant preferences, found that a procedure that called for sharing process control between the disputants and the third party was seen as more fair and was preferred to a procedure that vested all process control in the disputants. It is noteworthy, we believe, that this hybrid procedure allowed the disputants to retain sufficient control to be sure that they would have an adequate opportunity to tell their story.

EXPRESSION AND CONSIDERATION OF ARGUMENTS

As we noted in the previous section, there is considerable evidence that the process control effect involves something beyond instrumental control that can be used to assure the favorableness or equity of outcomes. The opportunity to express one's opinions and arguments—the chance to tell one's own side of the story—is a potent factor in the experience of procedural justice. A closely related finding is that, in order for procedural justice to be experienced in a dispute resolution, one must feel that the third party is giving due consideration to the views and information expressed by the disputants.

The Tyler, Rasinski, and Spodick (1985) studies, mentioned above, were undertaken to test competing predictions from instrumental and value-expressive views of the function of speech in political contexts. The value-expressive view is based on the notion that there are situations in which the opportunity to speak has value in and of itself, regardless of the capacity of the speech to secure other outcomes. The distinction between instrumental and value-expressive functions of

---

times called *processual control* (Bies & Moag, 1986), control over the enactment of procedures, and what is sometimes termed *procedural control*, control over the choice of procedures. The type of control that Thibaut and Walker called process control is termed *content control* in the Sheppard taxonomy.

speech was proposed by Katz (1960). Tyler, Rasinski, and Spodick tested these two functions of process control, using multiple regression to examine the effects of perceived process control over and above the effect of perceived outcome control and vice versa. They found, as mentioned earlier, that the relation between process control and procedural fairness could not be explained entirely by perceived influence over outcomes.

The Tyler, Rasinski, and Spodick studies showed that the etiology of procedural fairness includes factors other than control over outcomes, and it produced the results predicted by a value-expressive explanation of the process control effect. But additional evidence is needed to assure us that it is expression *per se*, and not some other non-outcome function of process control, that is the key to the effect. Several studies have shown results that point even more strongly to expression as a key factor in procedural justice.

Among these studies is a field study of procedural fairness judgments of court-annexed arbitration procedures, conducted by Adler *et al.* (1983), in which disputants were asked open-ended questions about what they viewed as fair or unfair in the arbitration hearings. A majority of the disputants who viewed the hearings as unfair complained that they had had too little opportunity to tell their story.

A study by Musante, Gilbert, and Thibaut (1983) provides additional evidence to support the proposition that procedural justice judgments are enhanced by an opportunity for the expression of views and opinions, whether or not the expression is instrumental in obtaining favorable outcomes. Musante *et al.* examined the effects of various types of participation on judgments of the fairness of procedures and outcomes. Subjects were assembled into six-person groups. Some groups were asked to discuss and decide on the rules governing a later adjudication that would affect the subjects' outcomes. Other groups were told to discuss their preference for the rules, but these groups were led to believe that their preferences would have no effect on the rules actually used and that in fact the rules to be used had already been selected. In half of these discussion-only groups the rules actually used matched the preferences expressed in the group discussion; in the other discussion-only groups the rules actually used did not match the group's preferences. Finally, some groups were not allowed either to discuss or to decide the rules to be used. The results of the study are shown in Table 5-3. Musante *et al.* found that instrumental participation (i.e., group discussion *and* decision control) led to the greatest enhancement of the judged procedural and distributive fairness of the subsequent adjudication but that *that group discussion alone, without any decision control,* led to some

TABLE 5-3. Procedural and Distributive Fairness Reactions
to Group Discussion and Control

	No control			Control
Fairness dimension	No discussion	Preference-mismatched discussion	Preference-matched discussion	Discussion and choice
Procedural fairness	−0.995	−0.559	0.282	1.275
Distributive fairness	−0.998	−0.207	0.431	0.779

Note. Higher values indicate greater perceived fairness. From Musante, Gilbert, & Thibaut (1983).

enhancement of both types of fairness relative to the condition with neither discussion nor decision control.

The Musante *et al.* findings are noteworthy on two grounds. First, on a practical level, they suggest that participation in the design of a procedure can enhance the perceived fairness of the procedure and its outcome. In this regard, the results of the study show that procedural variation in one social decision-making procedure can affect reactions to a subsequent related procedure. A practical implication of this finding is that procedures without process control might nonetheless be seen as fair if those subject to the procedure are allowed to participate in its design. For example, students who are not permitted to explain every feature of their examination answers might still feel that a grading procedure is fair if they are allowed to participate in the selection of the grading criteria. The second implication of the Musante *et al.* findings is of considerable theoretical importance to the issue under discussion in this section: It is remarkable that the study showed some enhancement of fairness in the conditions that encouraged discussion but explicitly ruled out any influence of this discussion on the decision. Discussion and the expression of preference, even in the absence of a response to the preference, leads to more positive procedural and distributive fairness judgments.

These findings support the value-expressive position advanced by Tyler, Rasinski, and Spodick (1985) that some process control effects may be due to value expression rather than any instrumentality in achieving outcomes. In the case of the Musante *et al.* discussion-only condition, an enhancement of fairness was observed in conditions that are purely expressive. In these conditions there was no suggestion of control or information influence over the outcome under discussion. Two additional studies suggest that it is important that the decision maker be seen as giving due consideration to the views expressed, even if he or she is not ultimately influenced by these views.[6]

Tyler (1987a) used cross-sectional survey data to test four possible limitations on the process control enhancement of procedural justice judgments. He tested whether the process control effect disappears: (1) when the decision maker is seen as biased; (2) when the decision maker is seen as not acting in "good faith"; (3) when the decision maker is seen as not giving the disputant's views due consideration; and (4) when the outcomes involved are substantial. Each limitation was tested by selecting individuals who did not believe they had any direct control over the decision and who also believed that the limitation in question was operative in their case. Within each set of individuals thus selected, the procedural fairness judgments of those who had experienced high process control were compared to the procedural fairness judgments of those who had experienced low process control. Tyler's results showed that only the third limitation, the lack of due consideration, removed the process control effect. Process control enhanced procedural justice even when the decision maker was seen as biased, when he or she was seen as acting in bad faith, and when the outcomes were important, but the effect disappeared when the decision maker was seen as not giving consideration to the respondent's views and arguments.

A recent laboratory study also showed that consideration of arguments is an important factor in procedural justice. Conlon, Lind, and Lissak (1987) studied the effects of various types of outcomes in the context of an adjudication. The study sought to test whether compromise outcomes induce feelings of injustice. Conlon *et al.* hypothesized that compromise outcomes might be interpreted as showing inadequate consideration of a disputants' views because a compromise can be suggested without considering the difficult issues of right and wrong that underlie many disputes. This in turn might lead to judgments that the procedure and outcome are less fair when a compromise decision is issued by a third party than when an all-or-nothing outcome is issued.

The experimental paradigm used was an adaptation of that used in the Walker *et al.* (1974) study, but only the adversary procedure was used. Recall that in this paradigm subjects compete for a monetary prize and are led into a dispute that can result in forfeiture of the prize. Some

---

[6]The results of the Musante *et al.* study might be seen as contradicting the statement that views must be given consideration for value expression to enhance procedural justice judgments. In the discussion-only conditions of that study it was clear to the subjects that the person deciding the rules would not see or hear their views. However, Musante *et al.* did imply that the experimenter was interested in the views expressed in the discussion-only group, and this may have constituted consideration by a sufficiently important figure in the experimental context to activate the effect.

subjects were told that they had been found innocent on all counts charged and would receive the full prize, others were told that they had been found innocent on most of the counts and would receive two-thirds of the prize, others were told that they had been found guilty on most of the counts and would receive only one-third of the prize, and others were told that they had been found guilty on all counts and would receive none of the prize. The major dependent variables were indices of perceived procedural and distributive fairness and ratings of the extent to which the judge considered the arguments favoring the subject's side of the case. Figure 5-1 shows the results. The outcome effects on both types of fairness judgments and on the consideration ratings are clearly nonlinear. As the outcomes moved from a total loss to a total win, fairness judgments first decreased and then increased. Ratings of the extent to which the judge considered all aspects of the case show a nonlinear outcome effect quite similar to that seen on fairness indices.

Judgments of whether one has received consideration are not based solely on the courtroom experience itself. Using panel data, Tyler (1987a) showed that views about whether one's arguments are considered by legal authorities are also affected by pre-experience attitudes. Among those who lost their cases, people with positive prior views of the courts were more likely to believe that their arguments had received consideration.

Limitations on the opportunity to express one's views and to have

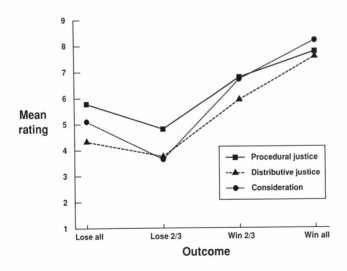

FIGURE 5-1. Fairness and consideration of the case.

those views considered can take a variety of forms. O'Barr and Conley (1985) document how the rules of evidence often run contrary to both the form and content of disputants' natural narrations about their disputes. They point out that the information and arguments advanced in less formal legal contexts, such as small-claims courts, are quite different than those that would be allowed at formal trials, and they note the rather ironic point that the freer narrations allowed in small-claims courts may be more satisfying to litigants but less likely to achieve favorable decisions, because the unrestrained narrations may not be adequate to constitute legal proof.

The perception that one has had an opportunity to express oneself and to have one's views considered by someone in power plays a critical role in fairness judgments. In our imaginary small-claims court experience, you would view the procedure as fair if you were allowed to tell your story and if the judge appeared to give consideration to your position. Rather remarkably, the experience of procedural fairness does not seem to turn on such issues as the impartiality of the judge—even if you view the judge as biased, you will see the procedure as fair if you think that he or she gave you a chance to tell your story and gave consideration to your perspective. The other side of the coin is that your judgment of the fairness of the procedure would probably be diminished if you were limited in the style and content of your expression or if you saw some evidence that your perspective was not being given adequate consideration. As we noted in the preceding section, if too strict rules of evidence prevented you from presenting information that you view as relevant to the dispute, you will experience procedural injustice. Similarly, if you see some indication that the judge has not considered your views, you will experience procedural injustice. The compromise outcome effect described above is a particularly striking example of the importance of expression and consideration. If you receive a partial repayment of your damage deposit but you believe that the judge is just attempting to mollify both parties rather than confronting the issue of who is right and who is wrong, you may well see the procedure as less fair than if you had received nothing at all.

The importance of beliefs about how thoroughly the judge considered the case touches on a point that often arises in debates about how court-annexed arbitration procedures should operate. Some procedures call for the arbitrator to provide an explanation or written opinion to justify his or her decision; other procedures call only for an announcement of the award itself. The research just described suggests that, to the extent that a written or oral explanation of the award provides evidence that the arbitrator has considered both sides' arguments, it will enhance procedural justice.

OTHER PROCEDURAL FAIRNESS STANDARDS

In a survey of Chicago residents, Tyler (in press) examined the role of a number of factors in determining whether people who had encounters with the courts or police felt that they had experienced fair procedures. The survey asked about a variety of procedural attributes that might affect the experience of procedural justice. Many of the attributes examined in the study were suggested by a theory of procedural justice in allocation situations proposed by Gerald Leventhal (1980; see Chapter 6 for a fuller discussion of Leventhal's theory). Leventhal proposed that people evaluate the fairness of procedures using such criteria as whether there was representation of the views of all interested parties,[7] the consistency of actions and rules across parties and in comparison to other disputes, the impartiality of the decision maker, the accuracy of the information used, the correctability of decisions, and the ethicality of those involved in the decision-making process.

Tyler asked his respondents about the level of process and decision control they felt they had in their encounter with the legal system ("representation"). He also asked respondents about the consistency of their experience relative to their previous experiences with the law, relative to their prior expectation, relative to what they thought usually happened to other people, and relative to what they knew of the specific experiences of friends, family, or neighbors. The respondents were asked about the impartiality of the legal authorities they had encountered, in questions about whether the authority was biased against the subject, whether the authority had tried hard to be fair, and whether the authority had done anything dishonest. Respondent attitudes about the quality or accuracy of decision making were assessed with questions about whether the authorities in question had gathered all of the information they needed to make a good decision and about whether the authorities had tried to bring all information into the open so that the problem could be solved. The procedural criterion of correctability was examined in a question about whether the respondent knew of an agency to whom they could complain about unfair treatment. The ethicality of decision making was examined in questions asking about the politeness of the authorities and about whether the authorities had shown concern for the respondent's rights.

[7]Note that Leventhal's "representation" criterion is *not* limited to legal representation, although that is one manifestation of the criterion. The critical feature underlying Leventhal's use of the term is allowing input to the decision-making process, whether through process control or any of several forms of decision control. We argue in Chapter 6 that several of Leventhal's criteria include multiple precursors of procedural justice; the representation criterion is a case in point.

TABLE 5-4. Determinants of Procedural
Justice in Dispute Resolution

Procedural attribute	Beta
Representation	.38**
Consistency	.12*
Impartiality of decision maker	
Bias	.06
Dishonesty	.15**
Effort to be fair	.07
Quality of decisions made	.16*
Correctability	.04
Ethicality	.21**

Note. Values are standardized regression weights in
an equation including all procedural attributes. From
Tyler (in press).
$*p < .05$
$**p < .01$

The study produced a number of findings. First, the correlation between responses to all of the questions mentioned above ranged from moderately positive to zero; no substantial negative correlations were found. This suggests that encounters that were seen as high in one procedural attribute tended to be seen as high in others. If some of the attributes had been negatively correlated, it might mean that respondents saw some of the procedural qualities as mutually exclusive, a finding that would pose a dilemma for anyone trying to design novel procedures that would be viewed as fair. In that situation those designing a new procedure would be forced to make a decision about which attribute of procedural fairness should be maximized. As we will see later in this chapter, there are dilemmas posed by the incongruence between objective and subjective desiderata of procedures. It is encouraging, however, that there does not seem to be any incongruence on the subjective level.[8]

This study also examined which of the criteria were most closely linked to the perception of procedural fairness. For example, how closely were perceptions of consistent treatment linked to individuals' judgment that their treatment was fair? Table 5-4 shows the result of a regression analyses testing the relationship between the various pro-

[8]There is another explanation for the generally positive correlations among procedural features. If some other variable, such as the outcome of the dispute, had a substantial effect on each feature of the procedure, moderate negative correlations might be concealed. Given the moderate outcome effects seen in this study, we doubt that this accounts for the positive correlations.

cedural attributes and respondents' judgments of the fairness of the procedures they encountered. The analysis shown in table considers only those respondents who encountered the courts or police in the course of a dispute; these results do not include respondents who encountered authorities outside a dispute context. It is clear from the table that some criteria are more powerful determinants of procedural justice than others. Representation, ethicality, and honesty showed especially strong independent relations to procedural justice. The study supports the Thibaut and Walker focus on issues of control in dispute resolution procedures: Representation, which includes process and decision control, was the feature most strongly related to procedural justice judgments. But the study also adds two new variables, ethicality and consistency, that appear to be an important part of the meaning of procedural justice in dispute resolution situations.

The importance that disputants accorded to ethicality is especially noteworthy. In Chapter 1 we noted that procedural justice appears to be linked to issues of social process beyond those related to decision making *per se*. The present study is one instance of data confirming a broad definition of procedural justice. Ethicality, as it was measured in this study, refers to such process issues as politeness and concern for rights (that is, respectful treatment by authorities). When authorities are seen as giving disputants their due with respect to these entitlements, procedural justice is higher; when authorities are seen as withholding due politeness and concern for rights, procedural justice suffers.

Because the respondents in the survey were exposed to legal procedures in a wide variety of circumstances and because the respondents themselves differed considerably along a number of dimensions, it was possible for Tyler to test whether differences among people and situations affect the meaning of procedural justice. Tyler could test, for example, whether people of different races or different political beliefs differed in the weight they gave each procedural criterion in forming procedural justice judgments. Similarly, he could test whether various aspects of the situation, such as whether it involved a dispute or some other type of legal matter or whether or not the citizen had sought contact with the legal system, changed the relation of each procedural criterion with procedural justice judgments.

The results of the Tyler analyses show that the personal characteristics of the respondents had little to do with which criteria most affected perceptions of procedural justice within a given situation. In other words, there were no subcultural differences in the definition of fair treatment within a given situation. Since the study was based on a highly diverse random sample of residents of the city of Chicago, the lack of person-based differences is especially striking. It suggests that legal procedures can be designed that will provide everyone with the feeling of fair treatment.

Although respondent characteristics were not related to judgments about the meaning of fairness, there were situationally based differences in the meaning of procedural justice. In different circumstances people used different criteria to assess the fairness of the process they experienced. For example, when the experience involved a dispute, representation of views (that is, process and decision control) exerted a more powerful influence on procedural justice and efforts to be fair exerted less influence than was the case when the encounter did not involve a dispute. When the encounter was voluntary, respondents' beliefs about the quality of decision making were relatively more important and their beliefs about representation of their views were relatively less important in determining their procedural justice judgments. These findings suggest that there may not be any single procedure that people will regard as the best way to resolve all types of problems. Different procedures maximize different aspects of fair process. Since people do not regard the same criteria as key issues in all situations, they are likely to prefer somewhat different procedures in different settings. These qualifications notwithstanding, there are probably some procedures that are always or nearly always seen as fair and others that are always or nearly always seen as unfair. We base this statement on the findings described earlier on the positive correlations among procedural criteria and the fact that situation-based differences in procedural criteria seldom made any criterion undesirable.

We can summarize the results of Tyler's study by referring again to our hypothetical small-claims court example. If you were one of the disputants in the landlord–tenant dispute we posited, it is likely that your decision about whether you had experienced procedural justice would be affected by several features of the experience. As we noted earlier, your procedural justice judgments would be affected by the amount of process and decision control you were afforded. But your procedural justice judgments would also be affected by other factors, such as the ethicality of the judge—the extent to which you felt you had been treated with politeness and concern for your rights. Tyler's results suggest that your procedural justice judgments would be based on the same basic criteria regardless of your race, income, or political philosophy.

OUTCOME EFFECTS ON PROCEDURAL FAIRNESS

Many of the studies described above and in Chapter 2 included manipulations of the outcome of the procedure; subjects were led to believe that they had received either a positive or a negative outcome from the dispute resolution process. Although there have been some studies that show no outcome effect on procedural fairness (e.g., Lind *et al.*, 1980), the most common finding is that procedural fairness judgments are higher following a favorable outcome than following an unfavorable outcome. (It is not clear whether it is the absolute level of outcome, the level relative to expectations, or the distributive fairness of the outcome that is the critical factor in determining how the outcome of the procedure affects procedural justice judgments—the outcome manipulations in experiments usually confound at least two of these dimensions by comparing a low-level, inequitable outcome with a high-level equitable outcome, and there is seldom any attempt to control expectations.) As noted earlier, outcome effects appear to operate independently of other determinants of procedural fairness, raising or lowering the patterns of perceived fairness caused by other factors.

We noted above in our discussion of expression and consideration effects on procedural justice judgments that the type of outcome that results from a procedure is sometimes used to infer whether the third party is giving due consideration to the issues. As shown by the Conlon *et al.* (1987) study (see Figure 5-1 above), there are instances in which small increases in the absolute level of outcome can lead to some decrease in perceived procedural fairness because of inferences that the outcome is the result of less consideration of case issues. It is important to remember, as we consider the procedural justice effects of outcome, that outcomes can function as information, as well as simply costs or benefits.

There are some instances in which outcome effects are complicated by interactions with other factors. Lind and Lissak (1985) used the Walker *et al.* (1974) paradigm to examine the effects of flaws in the enactment of an otherwise fair procedure. They exposed subjects to an enactment of an adversary procedure adjudication that either did or did not include evidence of what might be viewed as an improper interpersonal relationship. In conditions with an unflawed procedure the hearing was conducted without any information about the personal relationships of the judge and lawyers conducting the hearing. In conditions with a flawed procedure the subjects saw an apparently friendly social interaction between the judge and the lawyer representing the subject's opponent. The impropriety manipulation was crossed with a manipulation of the outcome of the hearing—the subject was told that he or she had either won or lost the case. Table 5-5 shows the effects of these manipulations on procedural fairness judgments. When the procedure was enacted without any suggestion of impropriety, no outcome effect was observed. However, when the ostensible impropriety was present, procedural fairness judgments were decreased by an unfavorable verdict and enhanced by a favorable judgment. Lind and Lissak speculated that

TABLE 5-5. Procedural Fairness Reactions
to Impropriety in the Enactment of Procedures

| | Impropriety | |
Outcome	Absent	Present
Disputant's team found innocent	6.28	6.85
Disputant's team found guilty	5.89	5.26

Note. Values are means of an index constructed by averaging five rating scales. Higher values indicate greater perceived fairness. From Lind & Lissak (1985, Table 1, p. 24).

the presence of a flaw in the procedure instigated a more elaborate attributional analysis of the procedure (cf. Wong & Weiner, 1981). This more extensive cognitive analysis led to greater use of the outcome in evaluating the procedure than would otherwise be the case. As in the Conlon *et al.* study described in the previous paragraph, the implication is that outcomes are sometimes used as information about the procedure. The additional finding in the Lind and Lissak study is that flaws in enactment of a procedure lead disputants to make greater use of outcome information.

Let us return to our hypothetical small-claims example. We would not be surprised to find that you would view the procedure to be fairer following a favorable decision than following an unfavorable decision. The verdict would act to raise or lower the procedural fairness judgment engendered by other features of the procedure. The elation or disappointment prompted by the verdict would not erase the effects of such factors as opportunity for expression of your side of the case. If you saw some evidence of a serious flaw in the enactment of the small-claims procedure, if, for example, it was evident to you that the judge was a neighbor of your landlord, the verdict would be of greater consequence for your judgment of the fairness of the procedure. But even this enhancement of the effect of the outcome probably would not rule out the effects mentioned in previous sections. Neighbor of your opponent or not, a procedure that permitted you a relatively free opportunity to express your views and a judge who gave evidence of giving your views due consideration would promote the experience of procedural justice.

OTHER DESIDERATA OF LEGAL PROCEDURES

If we are to interpret the policy implications of research and theory on the experience of procedural justice, we must know how the experience of procedural justice and its consequences relate to other aspects of justice. For example, as we seek to apply the much replicated finding that high disputant process control enhances felt fairness, we should consider the effects of process control on the accuracy of legal decisions, on the cost of litigation, and on other features that make a given procedure more or less attractive from a policy standpoint. Unfortunately, there is relatively little research on the effects of procedural justice variables on other desiderata of justice. An exception is the question of information accuracy, which Thibaut and Walker raised in their study on the topic and which has been addressed in subsequent studies.

ACCURACY OF EVIDENCE AND DECISIONS

Thibaut and Walker argued in their 1975 book that the adversary procedure is generally superior to the inquisitorial procedure on both objective and subjective grounds. Their endorsement of the adversary procedure on objective grounds was based in part on its capacity to limit biases from prior expectancy and order of presentation (Thibaut *et al.*, 1972; Walker *et al.*, 1972) and in part on their interpretation of an experiment on evidence discovery and presentation (Lind, 1975; Lind *et al.*, 1973). Subsequently, in their 1978 theory, Thibaut and Walker limited their endorsement of the adversary procedure to distribution of outcome disputes, although they asserted that this included most legal disputes. Implicit in the 1978 theory is the idea that, because no single procedure maximizes all desiderata of justice, one must consider how trade-offs can be made in the design or selection of procedures so that the most important consequences of a procedure are obtained. Thibaut and Walker argued that because fairness is more important than accuracy in disputes about the distribution of outcomes, it is reasonable to accept the lower accuracy of adversary procedures in order to obtain the greater procedural fairness of such procedures. But how much is accuracy compromised by adversary procedures? Recent research on the effects of adversary and inquisitorial procedures on information accuracy show that the fairness–accuracy dilemma may be more severe than was suggested by the original Thibaut and Walker research.

To begin our discussion of this issue, let us again consider the Lind *et al.* (1973) discovery and presentation experiment, which was described in Chapter 2. That study showed that adversary procedures led to presentations of evidence that did not accurately reflect the true distribution of facts when that distribution was unequally balanced between the two sides of the case. Only when the true distribution of facts favored neither side over the other did the adversary procedure show no bias in information processing. In contrast, the inquisitorial procedure always resulted in presentations that accurately reflected the true distribution of facts.

Thibaut and Walker (1975) and Lind (1975; Lind *et al.*, 1973) interpreted the conditional bias that characterized the adversary procedure as a positive feature; others have disagreed. We noted in Chapter 2 that the original Thibaut and Walker interpretation was based on two arguments: first, that the conditional bias would avoid premature cessation of investigation in circumstances of "sampling error," or spuriously biased early evidence; and second, that there is something appealing about a bias that favors the disadvantaged party in a case. There are some potent counterarguments to these interpretations, however. Contrary to the thrust of the first argument, there is no real evidence in the original experiment that inquisitorial procedures suffer from premature cessation of investigation. And with respect to the second argument, it should be noted that the type of "disadvantage" that is favored by adversary procedures is not social or economic disadvantage, but rather a paucity of evidence supporting the case of the party in question. To use an extreme example, the disadvantage is the type found in the unjustified accusations of the perpetrators of witch–hunts, rather than the sort of disadvantage that characterizes the poor and downtrodden of society. A less extreme example may be equally persuasive on this point: extrapolation from the conditional bias findings suggests that the use of adversary procedures promotes the continuation of frivolous lawsuits. Do we really want our legal procedures to favor those who are, in fact, unjustified in their claims? Perhaps we do—remember that Thibaut and Walker found that potential disputants behind a "veil of ignorance" based their fairness and procedural preference judgments in substantial part on just that feature of procedures—but one must wonder whether there is not some better way to structure legal procedures.

Vidmar and his colleagues (Sheppard & Vidmar, 1980; Vidmar & Laird, 1983) have conducted additional studies of the effects of adversary and inquisitorial procedures on the accuracy of evidence, and their findings have been generally unfavorable to the adversary procedure. These researchers were interested in whether the use of adversary procedures biases the testimony of witnesses. They noted that adversary procedures typically involve identification of each witness with one side of the case or the other and extensive interviewing of the witnesses by partisan attorneys.[9] In contrast, in inquisitorial procedures witnesses are

---

[9]In most real-world adversary forums there is some provision for witnesses to be called by the court; for instance, the U.S. Federal Rules of Evidence (Rule 614) allow the court to call witnesses. However, the exercise of this provision is rare.

called "for the court," rather than "for the plaintiff" or "for the defendant." Under inquisitorial procedures, witnesses are interviewed primarily by an impartial investigator for the judge.

Sheppard and Vidmar (1980) examined whether being interviewed by an adversary attorney biases testimony in the direction favored by the attorney. The results of two experiments show that a witness' subsequent testimony is indeed biased more by a prior interview with an adversary attorney than by a prior interview with a nonadversary attorney. The magnitude of the bias depended on the attorney's personality, as indexed by a Machiavellianism scale.

Because the Vidmar and Laird (1983) experiment showed a more straightforward and even more disturbing bias in adversary procedures, we will describe that study in some detail. The purpose of the experiment was to determine whether simply identifying a witness as representing one side in an adversary hearing would induce bias in the witness' testimony. The effect tested in this experiment is rather more subtle than that discovered in the Sheppard and Vidmar experiments; it is not a bias induced by persuasion or manipulation during an interview with a partisan attorney, but rather bias that results from the mere labelling of a witness as being for one side or the other.

Vidmar and Laird had their subjects watch a slide presentation concerning a barroom fight modeled on the written stimulus materials used in several of the Thibaut and Walker experiments. After the subjects had viewed the presentation, they were given mock subpoenas (modeled on actual Canadian subpoenas), which called them to testify for the plaintiff, the defendant, or the court. At a subsequent hearing before a panel of three judges, played by upper-level undergraduates and graduate students, each witness–subject was sworn and was asked to describe in his or her own words what had happened in the incident portrayed in the slide presentation. The judges rated the extent to which the witness' testimony favored the plaintiff or the defendant. The testimony was tape-recorded and rated again by impartial raters for the extent to which it favored the plaintiff or the defendant.

Table 5-6 shows some of the results of the study. The first two rows of the table show the ratings given by judges and raters, respectively, to the witnesses' testimony under the three role-assignment conditions. The third row in the table shows the witnesses' own ratings of whether they believed that the evidence in the case favored the plaintiff or the defendant. As can be seen from the table, both the judges and the raters saw substantial differences among the three conditions in the evidence presented at the hearing; witnesses called by the parties were seen as giving evidence more favorable to the party that had called them, and

TABLE 5-6. Ratings of the Testimony of Witnesses
for the Plaintiff, Defendant, and Court

Measure	Witness called by		
	Plaintiff	Court	Defendant
Judge's ratings of witness' evidence	4.3	5.8	6.2
Rater's ratings of witness' evidence	4.9	5.2	6.1
Witness' rating of evidence in case	5.1	5.0	5.4

Note. Higher ratings on the 11-point scales indicated evidence more favorable to the defendant. Values are mean ratings reported by Vidmar & Laird (1983, p. 893).

witnesses called by the court were seen as giving neutral evidence. The witnesses themselves did *not* show any differences in their own views of the case that were attributable to the party that had called them.

This pattern of effects shows that the witnesses were not influenced in their own opinions by the fact of having been called by one party or another, but that they were nonetheless biasing their testimony to favor the party that had called them to testify. The extent and consequences of the biasing is worth noting: judges who heard witnesses called by the plaintiffs attributed 38% of the responsibility for the incident to the plaintiff, compared to attributions of 47% and 52% plaintiff responsibility by judges hearing court-summoned and defendant-summoned witnesses, respectively. Vidmar and Laird report analyses of the content and style of the testimony that were designed to discover why the bias occurred. They found that the bias was relatively subtle. Witnesses did not omit unfavorable information in describing what they had seen. Instead, the witnesses varied their phrasing of the information in a way that loaded their statements in favor of the side that had called them.[10]

What then can we conclude about the wisdom of using adversary procedures? On one hand, there are the early Thibaut and Walker results (described in Chapter 2) that show either bias-inhibiting or conditional bias effects of adversary procedures. Further, it is now clearer

[10]It should be noted that the studies just described may overstate the case with respect to the evidence-biasing propensity of adversary procedures. In the Sheppard and Vidmar experiments there was no opportunity for opposing counsel to interview the witnesses, something that might have reduced the bias. Nor did the Vidmar and Laird study attempt any statement on the bias that might be present in an entire case, with witnesses on both sides. The original Lind *et al.* study found that in some circumstances the biases inherent in the presentations of individual adversary attorneys were canceled out by equal and opposite biases in the presentations of their opponents, leaving a total presentation that was quite similar, in these circumstances, to that of inquisitorial attorneys.

than ever that adversary procedures enhance subjective fairness. On the other hand, Vidmar and his associates have demonstrated biases in adversary procedures that are very difficult to interpret in any manner favorable to adversary procedures. The research literature poses precisely the type of problem to which we referred when we began our discussion of objective criteria in Chapter 2. Across-the-board endorsement of either the adversary or the inquisitorial procedure run counter to some research results. In policy terms we are faced with a dilemma of whether to choose the procedure that is seen as fairer and that seems to reduce decision makers' prior expectancy biases or whether to choose a procedure that provides the decision maker with the most accurate picture of case events. To resolve this dilemma we must either place some priority ordering on the various objective criteria and use that priority ordering to discount some criteria relative to others, or we must search for prescriptions that allow us to mix procedures in a fashion that optimizes all criteria. The former course runs very close to policy-making and may be outside our domain as scientists. The latter course, which is that used also in the 1978 Thibaut and Walker theory, is more attractive to us.

We believe that as our knowledge of psychology of procedural justice increases, it will be possible to design novel procedures that perform optimally in the situations to which they are applied. The first step in the search for such procedures is seen in Sheppard's (1985) study, described in the preceding chapter, which shows that a hybrid procedure can be designed that moderates disputant control over information while still allowing sufficient disputant process control to provide the opportunity for expression that is critical to perceived fairness. Given our growing knowledge of the precise psychological processes involved in procedural justice judgments, we should be able to design a variety of hybrid procedures that engender high levels of perceived fairness. For example, in light of the research described above on the role of expression in enhancing procedural justice judgments, we might find ways to allow free expression without placing all aspects of evidence production in the hands of the disputants. Once such hybrid procedures have been designed, additional research will be needed to determine whether such new procedures avoid the information bias that appears to plague pure adversary procedures and whether the hybrid procedure retains the protection against prior-expectancy bias that adversary procedures provide. If we can design a hybrid procedure that does indeed provide the benefits of the adversary procedure without its shortcomings, it would constitute the first instance of procedural engineering guided by science rather than intuition—a notable accomplishment for an area of research less than two decades old.

ISSUES OF CURRENT DEBATE

With the exception of methodological arguments, criticisms of procedural justice research have been of two general types. First, some researchers have taken exception to the conclusions emerging from procedural justice studies and have conducted additional research to resolve the issue by generating new data (e.g., Sheppard & Vidmar, 1980; Vidmar & Laird, 1983). The preceding section shows how this approach can broaden our base of knowledge about procedural justice and related legal processes and how this in turn can lead to a more sophisticated view of the strengths and weaknesses of various procedures. The second approach has been to criticize not the facts discovered by procedural justice studies, but rather the assumptions underlying the interpretation of procedural justice results. These criticisms are important, not only because they suggest where one must be cautious in applying procedural justice findings and theory, but also because they point out new directions for research that might be useful in future debates about the implications of procedural justice findings. Among the topics that have been the focus of criticisms of the second type are the question of the cost of using procedures found to engender procedural fairness judgments, the question of whether procedures high in procedural fairness help or harm post-conflict relations between the disputants, and the question of the policy implications of choosing procedures on the basis of perceived fairness, disputant satisfaction, or disputant preference.

Before we turn to a presentation and discussion of the debate on each of these topics, we would like to note that, at least with respect to the questions of cost and post-conflict relations, the focus of the controversy is the Thibaut and Walker (1975) endorsement of adversary over inquisitorial procedures. As we noted at some length above, procedural justice research has moved beyond investigations of the perceived fairness of adversary and inquisitorial procedures to more sophisticated procedural distinctions and fundamental psychological comparisons. This makes any debate that emphasizes the adversary–inquisitorial distinction rather dated; in many instances the criticism is directed toward a state of knowledge on procedural justice that has now been superseded. It is often the case, as we will point out below, that contemporary procedural justice research already offers solutions to the problems posed by the debate.

Cost

In their 1975 book, Thibaut and Walker themselves raise the issue of financial and other costs of adversary procedures (p. 119). The use of adversary procedures in American law has often been criticized as a major source of the enormous financial burden of litigation. For example, former Chief Justice Warren Burger criticized the use of adversary adjudication by noting, "Even when an acceptable result is finally achieved in a civil case, that result is often drained of much of its value because of the time lapse, the expense, and the emotional stress inescapable in the litigation process" (1982, p. 274). The cost consequences of various procedures have been discussed frequently by legal scholars and policymakers, but little research has been done on the question.

The question of cost can be subdivided into two separate issues. First, there is the question of whether the private financing of much adjudicatory activity, which is implicit in the use of adversary procedures but not in the use of inquisitorial procedures, leads to better legal services for the rich and thus to unfair advantage. There is no definitive research on this topic, but even the possibility of unequal justice with adversary procedures raises serious questions about the social dynamics of adversary justice. The traditional line of argument against this criticism of adversary procedures holds that the problem is counteracted by traditional provisions for legal financing. From the point of view of a plaintiff in a civil action, the use of contingent fees means that even a poverty-stricken plaintiff can acquire good legal services if he or she has a legitimate claim; the lawyer will be motivated to take the case on the basis of the likely award rather than on the basis of the plaintiff's current wealth. At least this is how the contingent fee system works in theory. In practice, it may well be that there are a substantial number of poor plaintiffs with claims that are legitimate and that involve sums that are quite important from the plaintiffs' point of view but that are not large enough to attract legal assistance. Whether or not the contingent fee system works as it is supposed to, however, poor defendants might suffer from inequality of financial resources; defendants have nothing to win and thus little other than their own resources to offer in return for legal representation.

The problem of unequal resources is especially serious when one considers the position of an unassisted defendant in a criminal case, and it is here that a second counterargument to the resource criticism of adversary procedures is seen most clearly. Ever since *Gideon v. Wainwright*, American criminal defendants have been provided with legal assistance when they could not afford to hire their own lawyers. The expansion of government-supported legal aid services in the 1970s gave support in civil cases for this second line of defense against economic inequalities, but recent years have seen this support erode substantially. Thibaut and Walker (1975) endorse the free provision of legal services as the answer to the unequal resources problem; they note that "the advantages of the well-manned adversary system furnish new and compelling argument for insuring that adequate resources be made available to all litigants" (p. 119).

The second major cost issue relevant to the procedural variations studied by procedural justice researchers is the overall cost of litigation. There is a widespread assumption that adversary litigation is more costly than inquisitorial litigation. To the best of our knowledge, there have been no studies that establish a cost advantage for inquisitorial procedures. Usually the implicit argument seems to be this: Litigation is extremely expensive in the United States and the United States has an adversary system of justice; therefore adversary justice must be extremely expensive. Absent comparative studies about the overall cost of litigation in adversary and nonadversary justice systems, the validity of this assumption cannot be assessed. However, the possibility that adversary procedures increase the cost of dispute resolution and the widespread credence given this possibility make overall cost a factor in any debate about the relative merits of adversary and inquisitorial justice.

There are additional points that should be considered with respect to the overall cost issue. One set of considerations has been raised by Lea and Walker (1979) in a theoretical analysis of the types of costs that arise in dispute resolution. Lea and Walker note that there are two types of process-linked costs: transaction costs and imposition costs. In litigation, transaction costs are the costs of seeking information, holding a hearing or bargaining session, and paying representatives and third parties—in general, the cost of running the procedural apparatus. Imposition costs include the costs associated with inaccurate third-party decisions; that is, the costs that arise because a third party usually does not know with complete accuracy the preference structure of the disputants. Lea and Walker argue that, although vesting process control in the decision maker may reduce transaction costs, the savings may be offset by increases in imposition costs resulting from inadequate knowledge of the dispute on the part of the decision maker. In essence, their argument is that adversary procedures have higher transaction costs than inquisitorial procedures, but because adversary procedures place the responsibility for information production in the hands of those who best understand the dispute, the ultimate decision will be the best for all involved and will result in an overall cost savings. Of course, a great deal more research will be needed before anyone can calculate the extent to which imposition costs offset transaction costs.

All of this points to the critical nature of the cost question in decisions about procedures. Procedural justice research supplies one additional point that should be considered in debates on the cost of adversary and inquisitorial procedures. It is arguable that much of the cost of adversary litigation results not from the basic provisions of the adversary model but from the substantial legal complexity that has come to be identified with adversary hearings. Given our current understanding of the psychology of procedural justice, there is no reason to think that such high levels of procedural complexity are necessary to glean the perceived procedural justice benefit of adversary procedures. We know of no study that has examined the effect of procedural complexity on procedural justice judgments, but a recent series of studies by Perry (1986) shows no substantial procedural justice effects for related variables, such as use of a judge versus use of an arbitrator or use of strict legal decision criteria versus informal rules of distributive justice. Recall also that the adversary and inquisitorial procedures that Thibaut, Walker, and their colleagues used in the laboratory to test subjective reactions to adjudication were quite simple in their structure and enactment. Since enhanced procedural fairness judgments are known to result even under conditions of relatively brief and informal adversary hearings, there is reason to think that one could reduce the cost of adversary procedures by making them less lengthy and less complex. Given that the procedural justice advantage of adversary procedures may be due at least in part to such factors as freedom of expression and argument consideration, it should be possible to design procedures that cut down on some of the more costly features of the pure adversary procedure and that nonetheless are seen as fair and satisfying. One might go so far as to suggest that redesigned procedures that relax somewhat the rules of evidence and thus minimize the opportunity for opposing counsel to limit the expression of views and arguments by the disputants might result in both greater fairness and, because of their simplicity, less cost.

Post-Conflict Relations

As we noted in Chapter 2, one of the primary motivations of the Thibaut and Walker research was the belief that fair procedures promote social harmony. The implications of the Thibaut and Walker project are contrary, however, to conventional wisdom in the social sciences about the effects of adversary procedures on post-conflict relations between disputants. Hayden and Anderson (1979) cite a number of anthropologists (e.g., Gluckman, 1969; Nader, 1969) in support of their claim that adversary procedures harm post-conflict relations.

In fact, if the question is whether adversary procedures, defined in terms of process control, harm post-conflict relations, there is little or no research on the issue. Most of the comparisons cited in support of the contention that adversary procedures are harmful in this regard have confounded three variables: decision control, process control, and the use of all-or-nothing versus compromise decisions. There is evidence (e.g., Sarat, 1976) that mediation is less harmful to post-conflict relations than adjudication, and, because the adjudication in question is adversary, it is often argued that adversary procedures are therefore harmful. In fact, the mediation procedures in question generally allow the disputants more process control than do the adjudication procedures, and therefore what these studies really show is that procedures high in disputant decision control, high in disputant process control, and using compromise decisions are more conducive to post-conflict relations than procedures low in disputant decision control, low in disputant process control, and using all-or-nothing decisions. But we do not know which of the differences is responsible for the effect.

What is needed, we believe, is research on this important issue that makes use of distinctions and concepts from modern procedural justice work. First, we must know whether procedural justice judgments in and of themselves do lead to more harmonious relations between former disputants. We must know also whether there are countervailing effects for factors that normally enhance procedural justice judgments. For example, we need studies that look at the post-conflict effects, in the context of various situations and relationship types, of procedures that allow disputants considerable opportunity for the free expression of evidence and arguments. One could argue plausibly either that the opportunity for free expression would promote positive post-conflict relations, by assuring that the resolution was seen as covering all issues in conflict, or that it would harm post-conflict relations, by raising the likelihood of angry exchanges and by promoting blaming. We hope to see this question receive the same sort of careful laboratory and field research that has resolved other issues in procedural justice.

Social Reform and Procedural Preferences

There are additional considerations that raise questions about using disputants' procedural preferences or other disputant perceptions as a major criterion in policy decisions. The arguments involved have been advanced by legal scholars such as Fiss (1984) and Resnik (1982, 1984). In essence, these arguments note that traditional ways of resolving legal dispute—through open trials with elaborate pretrial, trial, and posttrial procedures—have come to serve certain important social functions. For example, current procedures generate legal precedents that both guide future behavior and contribute to the development of law. If dispute resolution procedures are adopted or altered solely with the objective of matching disputant preferences or maximizing disputant satisfaction, we run the risk of having procedures that are ill designed for the social function of law. Further, we run the risk that procedures will be adopted that, having been designed to fit the preferences of some group of disputants whose interests are contrary to those of the population at large, will for this very reason produce results that are contrary to the interest of society.

An example might make the issue clearer. One would hardly have wanted the *Brown v. Board of Education* case to have been submitted to a mediation procedure that produced a private compromise decision without precedential value, however much the school board and the black student might have preferred such a procedure. Society had some interest in the *Brown* case, and the choice of procedure should take into account such societal interests. In terms sometimes used in debates on this topic, the dispute does not belong to the disputant exclusively, and it is therefore a mistake to weigh disputant preferences too heavily in deciding how the dispute should be resolved.

This line of argument suggests that we can go too far in basing procedural innovations on disputant preferences, but neither would one want to ignore such preferences altogether. What solution might we propose for this problem? We suggest two lines of attack. First, efforts should be made by legal scholars and theoreticians to determine which types of disputes are most likely to involve a substantial societal interest. In essence, we must know which disputes belong to the disputants and should be resolved with the procedures the disputants prefer and which disputes belong also to society and should be resolved with procedures that take societal interests into account.

Our second suggestion is that we begin to broaden the scope of our studies of the sources of procedural justice judgments to include the fairness judgments of nondisputants. Early studies of procedural justice judgments (e.g., LaTour, 1978; Walker *et al.*, 1974) often examined the judgments of both disputants and disinterested observers, but in recent years few studies have looked at the fairness judgments of nondisputants. Arguments that point out societal interests in the form and outcome of dispute resolution procedures serve to remind us that we must know more about what is seen as fair by those who are in the role of a citizen outside the immediate conflict. Most needed are studies that examine the effect of role variation in general on procedural justice judgments. Research of this sort will allow us to understand better the overall psychology of procedural justice, and it will provide information about how disputant perceptions might differ from those of citizens concerned with justice but not involved in the specific dispute in question. Some initial steps in the direction of understanding role-based differences have been made by Houlden *et al.* (1978) and Sheppard, Saunders, and Minton (1986), who have studied differences between disputants and third parties in their fairness-based reactions to various dispute procedures.

POLICY AND PROCEDURAL JUSTICE: THE CASE OF COURT-ANNEXED ARBITRATION

It might be instructive at this point to consider, in terms of a real-world example, the practical implications of procedural justice research. As we will see in later chapters, procedural justice research suggests novel policies and procedures for political and organizational decision making. Before we proceed to a discussion of applications in those areas, however, we owe the reader a demonstration of the policy relevance of procedural justice. The law is a particularly apt area for such a demonstration. In no other area of potential application has the psychology of procedural justice been so thoroughly studied as in law, and in no other setting are the trade-offs implied by attempting to maximize perceived fairness so well understood. Thus we can discuss the policy relevance of procedural justice to the law with greater sophistication about both its strengths and its limitations than would be possible in other contexts.

The policy issues we consider here concern a relatively new procedure for the pretrial resolution of civil lawsuits, "court-annexed arbitration." In general terms, the procedure requires that cases undergo a mandatory, but nonbinding, arbitration hearing prior to trial. The arbitrator is typically an experienced member of the bar. The hearing is somewhat less formal than a trial, but it is clearly an adversary hearing. The object of the hearing is to try the case, not to find a compromise position. In the course of the hearing both sides present their evidence under relaxed rules of evidence. The arbitrator then renders a decision. In most jurisdictions using the procedure, the arbitrator's decision becomes the judgment of the court if neither side rejects it. However, if either side rejects the award, a regular trial is available (sometimes termed a "trial de novo") and the case proceeds along the normal pretrial process. Of course, it is hoped that the award will be accepted in many of the cases exposed to the procedure. Interestingly, the policy debate concerning the use of court-annexed arbitration already involves arguments about the likely consequences of the procedure for disputants' procedural justice judgments. Some critics of the procedure have contended that litigants will believe that the procedure gives them "second-class justice" by shunting their dispute to a less formal procedure instead of giving them a real trial with a real judge or jury.

How might procedural justice research speak to the advisability and design of court-annexed arbitration procedures? First, in the case of court-annexed arbitration, as in other legal and dispute resolution settings, the research shows that procedural justice judgments matter. It is clear that procedural justice is likely to play a major role in acceptance of the arbitration program, in disputants' satisfaction with the litigation experience, and in their satisfaction with the outcome of the arbitration process. It is likely that procedural justice judgments will affect acceptance of arbitration awards, although we would expect that the behavior of accepting the award, like other compliance behaviors, is multiply determined and might show more modest procedural justice effects than do acceptance of the procedure and satisfaction.

The literature on procedural preferences, which we reviewed in Chapter 4, leads us to expect that procedural justice judgments will play a major role in disputants' willingness to use the arbitration procedure. This implication of the research is of greater importance than one might think. Policymakers often seem to assume that people are motivate solely by self-interest, that their preferences for procedures will be based entirely on whether they believe that a given legal procedure will result in greater likelihood of winning. One of the messages of procedural justice research is that perceived fairness is often a stronger factor in procedural preferences than is self-interest. If the court-annexed arbitration procedure is seen as fundamentally fair, it is likely to be acceptable to disputants whether or not it is seen as favorable to their interests.

Turning to the literature on the sources of procedural justice, we can begin to answer questions about the perceived fairness of arbitration relative to trial and about how arbitration procedures might be designed to maximize procedural fairness. First, consider the question of whether arbitration hearings will be perceived to be "second-class justice." The research reviewed above shows that process control, impartiality, ethicality, and the perceived quality of decisions are major determinants of procedural justice judgments. Only the last of these factors seems likely to be higher in trials than in arbitration hearings. The magnitude of this difference might be small, if the arbitrator were perceived to be nearly as good at making legal decisions as a judge or jury, or it might be large, if the arbitrator were perceived to be much less competent than a judge or jury. On the other hand, the relaxation of rules of evidence, if it allowed freer expression of arguments and views, might give arbitration a procedural justice advantage. We suspect that both effects will be small in most court-annexed arbitration programs and that the net result will be very little difference in the perceived procedural justice of the two forums.[11]

We can use this same knowledge to design arbitration procedures in

[11]We base this prediction on our belief that most of the differences between trial and arbitration are more salient to lawyers than lay people. For example, one of the major implications of the relaxed rules of evidence is that records can be introduced without in-person substantiating testimony. Thus, medical reports can be introduced as evidence without personal testimony by a physician. We suspect that few lay people would even notice the difference and that those who did would not see it as particularly relevant to the fundamental fairness of the hearing.

a way that enhances procedural justice judgments. The research shows convincingly that the opportunity to express views and arguments enhances procedural justice, and care can be taken to give disputants adequate opportunity to be heard at the hearing. This would lead one away from court-annexed arbitration procedures that involve very short hearings with decisions made largely on the basis of pre-hearing briefs. Research on other precursors of the experience of procedural justice suggests that care should be taken to assure the litigants of the impartiality and ethicality of the arbitrator. For example, procedures for assuring that arbitrators have no conflict of interest in hearing the case should be rigorous and well publicized, and having arbitrators take public oaths of impartiality would probably enhance perceived fairness. The use of procedures that involve the parties in the selection of arbitrators would probably also enhance disputants' perceptions of impartiality and, in turn, their procedural justice judgments. Ethicality has been found to be an important precursor of procedural justice judgments, and this procedural feature could be enhanced by instructing arbitrators to show particular concern for disputants' rights and to treat disputants with special politeness. As we noted earlier, quality of decisions is another feature affecting procedural justice judgments. To maximize the perceived fairness of the arbitration procedure, one would want to exercise care in the selection of the pool of arbitrators to keep high standards of training and experience, and one would want to make disputants aware of the qualifications of the arbitrators.

The procedural justice literature also suggests that two features of court-annexed arbitration procedures that might otherwise be thought to be likely sources of litigant discontent in fact do not have much impact on procedural justice judgments. One aspect of the "second-class justice" criticism is that inconsistency in the way different groups of cases are treated will lead to perceived unfairness. As we saw above, however, inconsistency of this sort does not appear to be a major factor in procedural justice judgments.[12] The second procedural feature arises from the practice in some court-annexed arbitration programs of assessing fees for demanding trial de novo or penalties when a party demands trial de novo and fails to do better than the arbitration award. Because trial de novo functions as a correction device for arbitration awards that seem to at least one disputant to be wrong, one might think that barriers to trial de novo would be seen as unfair. In fact, the research shows that the procedural feature of correctability is not a major factor in procedural

---

[12]As noted in later chapters, inconsistency of treatment *within* a relationship, as would occur if one party to a dispute was treated differently from the other, does produce feelings of procedural injustice.

justice judgments. At least from the perspective of disputants, disincentives to trial de novo are not likely to be seen as unfair.

But these recommendations should be tempered by consideration of the material presented earlier on objective justice studies and on debates about the cost of procedures and the legal value of disputes.[13] In the case of court-annexed arbitration cost considerations probably run in the same direction as do procedural justice judgments; arbitration may come out slightly ahead of trial. Considerations of objective justice and societal interest in case outcomes may well pull our assessment of the procedures in the opposite direction. Because arbitration hearings are as adversary as trials and because arbitration lacks some of the evidentiary restrictions that constrain adversariness in trials, it is likely that the information presented at the hearing will be at least as biased as that presented at trial. If this is the case, it might mean that arbitration, though as acceptable as trial on subjective grounds, would be less acceptable than trial on objective grounds. On the other hand, one would want this potential disadvantage of arbitration to be demonstrated (just as one would want the potential subjective advantage to be demonstrated) before deciding one way or the other. Similarly, because arbitration judgments do not carry the weight of trial decisions, one would have to decide whether any subjective justice advantage of arbitration was outweighed by the incapacity of the procedure to contribute to the development of law. Again, what is needed is a weighing of the magnitude and importance of each benefit and deficit, subjective and objective, of the procedure. We do not argue that research on subjective procedural justice replaces this weighing; we argue only that subjective justice must be one factor in the policy-making process.

Further, we suggest that procedural justice research can give the policymaker better choices. If, for example, it is decided that arbitration is desirable on cost and procedural justice grounds, but there remain concerns about objective justice, our knowledge of procedural justice can be used to design arbitration hearing procedures that increase the arbitrator's freedom to acquire information but leave substantial freedom of expression in the hands of the disputants. And if adversariness must be restricted, even more attention should be given to other precursors of procedural justice, using methods such as those we suggest above to increase perceived ethicality, impartiality, and quality of decision.

---

[13]Because the debate about the relationship consequences of disputes has neither research or convincing logic on either side of the question, it is difficult to see how one could apply it to policy considerations. Of course, once research is available, this might be a consideration that would either support or countervail against the recommendations made here.

Chapter 6

The Generality of Procedural Justice

The studies discussed in the preceding chapter show that procedural justice phenomena are ubiquitous in law and dispute resolution. Given this finding, it seems reasonable to ask whether phenomena such as the process control effect or the procedural justice enhancement of support for legal institutions are instances of a general human response to social decision-making procedures. Might not people react in much the same way to the myriad procedures that exist in business organizations and political institutions, or, for that matter, in personal relationships, as they do to legal procedures? Or are the procedural justice effects documented above unique to law and dispute resolution? In this chapter and those that follow we consider the substantial body of evidence favoring the first of these alternatives, that procedural justice phenomena appear in much the same form in a wide variety of social settings.

We begin our discussion of the basic psychology of procedural justice with a brief presentation of some theoretical work by Gerald Leventhal that contributed greatly to the recognition that procedural justice is a concept that can be applied to procedures in nonlegal contexts. Leventhal argued that procedural justice is an important determinant of perceived fairness in the context of almost any allocation decision. At the time Leventhal advanced his theory, researchers and theorists concerned with distributive justice had come to realize that justice in allocation is a fundamental feature of most human social behavior (see generally Berkowitz & Walster, 1976). By arguing that procedural justice was part of the experience of justice in allocation, Leventhal's theory provided a link to a wide variety of social settings.[1] Although there are still

[1]It is certainly arguable that there is no fundamental difference between dispute resolution and allocation and that we are on shaky theoretical grounds when we assert that Leventhal's work on allocation procedures is especially valuable because it prompted the field to look for procedural justice phenomena outside the realm of dispute resolution. One could argue that, in any dispute involving outcomes, dispute resolution is essentially

some gaps in our understanding of the extent to which procedural justice phenomena occur in different settings, it is becoming increasingly evident that Leventhal's assertions about the generality of procedural justice concerns were correct. Indeed, it is beginning to appear that procedural justice is an even more pervasive and influential concern than Leventhal thought.

LEVENTHAL'S THEORY OF PROCEDURAL JUSTICE

Leventhal's theory is presented in two analyses (Leventhal, 1980; Leventhal, Karuza, & Fry, 1980) of the current state of research and theory in the entire area of justice judgments. In both works, Leventhal considered both distributive and procedural justice factors as determinants of an overall sense of fairness in allocation situations. The analysis of distributive justice factors led Leventhal to suggest that distributive justice judgments are based on the correspondence of received outcomes to deserved outcomes, and that perceptions of deserved outcomes depend on a weighted combination of the outcomes thought to be deserved according to each of several allocation rules. The distributive justice rules used to determine deserved outcomes include a contributions rule (which is very similar to the equity rule proposed by Adams and others), a needs rule (which specifies that outcomes should meet the needs of the recipient), an equality rule, and several other minor rules that might govern a particular outcome distribution, such as a rule of "justified self-interest," an ownership rule, and a rule specifying that one must adhere to commitments. Leventhal suggested that the individual's goals for the interaction situation determine the weights assigned various distributive justice rules in deciding what outcomes are deserved. For example, if social harmony is an important goal of the interaction and the individual believes that equal distributions promote harmony, the equality rule will be weighted heavily in determining what outcomes are deserved.

---

an allocation process and that allocation in any relationship characterized by less than pure correspondence of outcomes involves dispute resolution. The distinction is clearer when one considers Greenberg's (1987a) argument that allocations are proactive distribution decisions and dispute resolution is a reactive attempt to redress an unfair distribution. In any event, without the encouragement provided by Leventhal's analysis of nonlegal procedures, the leap from studies of adversary versus inquisitorial justice to studies of such things as city council procedures or performance evaluation procedures would have been more difficult.

A Theory of Procedural Justice Judgments

According to Leventhal, a similar cognitive process determines whether procedures are thought to be fair. The procedure in question is compared to a fairness standard that is based on a number of procedural justice rules. Leventhal identifies six general procedural justice rules. As can be seen from the descriptions below, each rule can have a wide variety of manifestations in any given procedural situation. It should be noted at the outset that, unlike the distributive justice rules mentioned above, most of which had been found empirically to affect allocation preferences and fairness judgments, Leventhal's procedural justice rules are largely the result of his intuition and speculation about what makes a procedure fair. Leventhal drew on some of the early Thibaut and Walker research in developing his hypotheses about procedural justice, but he did most of his theoretical work prior to the real explosion of research on procedural justice. As we shall see in later chapters, some of his ideas have been borne out by later research and some have not. However, because Leventhal's six procedural justice rules have stimulated a good deal of research, there is value in considering all of them in some detail:

1. *Consistency.* For a procedure to be fair, it must be applied consistently across persons and across time. Consistency across persons generally takes the form of equal treatment for all affected by the procedure. In practical terms, this aspect of the consistency rule requires that all parties believe that they have the same rights under the procedure and are treated similarly. Consistency across time requires that the procedure follow the same rules and be enacted the same way each time it is used. This aspect of the consistency rule requires that procedural change be made carefully and with full notification of all who might be affected by the procedure.
2. *Bias suppression.* Although many types of bias might arise in allocation procedures, Leventhal mentions specifically only two sources of bias in his description of this justice rule. First, procedures are unfair if the decision maker has a vested interest in any specific decision. Second, procedures are unfair if the decision is made on doctrinaire grounds, in other words, if the decision maker is so influenced by his or her prior beliefs that all points of view do not receive adequate and equal consideration. The examples that Leventhal gives for both aspects of the bias-suppression rule have to do with assuring that the decision maker(s) are unbiased, rather than with suppressing biases that might arise within the procedure itself. (Some procedural biases are covered by some of Leventhal's other justice rules.)

3. *Accuracy of information.* According to Leventhal, procedures are perceived to be unfair if they appear to be basing decisions on inaccurate information. To the extent that the procedure includes provisions that assure that decisions will be based on accurate information and on well-informed or expert opinion, procedural fairness will be enhanced. Thus, if an allocation procedure requires keeping full and accurate records of contributions, the fairness of the procedure will be higher.
4. *Correctability.* Leventhal suggests that the fairness of a procedure is enhanced to the extent that it contains some provision for correcting bad decisions. He mentions specifically grievance and appeals procedures. Leventhal notes that all of the other procedural justice rules are involved in the fulfillment of this rule; the appeals procedure must itself meet the standards set by the other rules.
5. *Representativeness.* Of all of Leventhal's rules, the representativeness rule seems the broadest. It includes the process control and decision control variables that figured so prominently in the work of Thibaut and Walker, and it also includes subgroup representation in the decision-making group. Leventhal (1980) says the representativeness rule "dictates that all phases of allocation process must reflect the basic concerns, values, and outlook of important subgroups in the population of individuals affected by the allocation process" (p. 44).[2]
6. *Ethicality.* According to Leventhal, procedural justice depends on the extent to which an allocation procedure conforms to personal standards of ethics and morality. Leventhal mentions several examples of how a procedure might run afoul of the ethicality rule, including the use of deception, bribery, invasion of privacy, and spying. Leventhal suggests that this procedural justice rule may be rather weak because it is "based on the assumption that judgments of fairness and justice are related to a larger intrapsychic system of moral and ethical values and standards," and his intuition is that "linkages between the components of this moral-–ethical system are probably quite weak" (p. 46).[3]

In Leventhal's analysis the weighting of procedural rules, like the weighting of distributive rules, depends on a goal-based analysis of the likely effects of each rule—justice rules will be influential to the extent they are seen as promoting the basic goals of the perceiver. In addition,

[2]In our subsequent reference to this rule, we will use the term *representation.*
[3]In fact, subsequent research, including the Tyler (1986a) study described in Chapter 4, has shown that ethicality is one of the stronger determinants of procedural justice judgments.

Leventhal suggests that procedural rules are given higher weights when they are thought to promote the attainment of either favorable outcomes for the perceiver or fair outcomes for all involved.

Leventhal notes that procedures typically contain a number of structural components, each of which might be judged according to the six procedural justice rules. He considers seven components: (1) selecting agents to gather information and make the decision, (2) setting ground rules and establishing criteria for receiving an allocation, (3) gathering information, (4) defining the decision structure (for example, setting up group decision rules), (5) processing appeals from the decision, (6) safeguarding the procedure by monitoring and sanctioning the behavior of those who participate in the procedure, and (7) providing mechanisms for changing the procedure when it is not working properly. Although Leventhal argues that each justice rule can be applied to each procedural component, he admits that some of the rules are especially important for certain components. For example, accuracy of information is a particularly important feature of the information-gathering component.

Having analyzed both the structure of procedures and the justice rules that are used to evaluate procedural fairness, Leventhal turns to two additional questions: How are distributive and procedural justice judgments combined to reach a general assessment of the fairness of a situation, and what activates the entire justice judgment process? In answering the first question, Leventhal asserts that distributive fairness is generally more salient than procedural justice, and he suggests that distributive justice judgments are likely to be more important in determining overall fairness judgments. He bases his assertion on several suppositions: that people often do not understand how procedures work, that procedures often fade into the perceptual background because they are routine and therefore invariant properties of the social system, and that people in a well-functioning social system simply have little concern with procedures. Leventhal mentions two factors that lead to greater attention to procedural matters and, presumably, greater influence of procedural fairness on general fairness judgments. First, when organizations are being created, more attention is paid to procedures and procedural fairness is more salient. Second, when people are dissatisfied with the distribution of outcomes, procedures are examined more closely in order to find justifications for change. When substantial pressure for procedural change surfaces in the organization, both those dissatisfied with current distribution and those satisfied with the current distribution will be stimulated by the debate to become concerned with procedural justice.

With respect to when the entire justice judgment process is activated, Leventhal mentions four determinants of the importance of fairness. First, a person's social role might increase or decrease his concern with fairness. For example, judges and mediators are expected to be concerned with fairness as they enact their roles. Second, a person's interest in fairness may be decreased as he or she becomes preoccupied with other social goals. Concerns such as efficiency, productivity, or social control might lead people to endorse procedures or distributions that are unfair. Third, when there are obvious and salient violations of distributive or procedural justice rules, people are likely to pay more attention to fairness. According to Leventhal, when the violation of procedural rules results in public scandal or when the individual in question receives an unfair allocation, the justice judgment process is instigated. Finally, Leventhal suggests that fairness is of greater concern in pluralistic social systems than in monolithic social systems. Leventhal argues that fairness is more salient when there is dissension among the members of an organization or society about procedures or distributions.

COMMENTS AND CRITIQUE

In addition to stimulating the study of procedural justice in nonlegal settings, Leventhal's theory pointed out that procedural justice is affected by factors other than process control and decision control. His six justice rules have been the basis of a number of procedural justice studies, including the Tyler (1987b) study mentioned in Chapter 5, several of the studies described in the next section of this chapter, and several studies of organizational procedures which we will describe in Chapter 8. The research suggests that some of Leventhal's justice rules, especially consistency, ethicality, and accuracy of information, are quite potent factors in determining whether procedures are seen as fair.

However, as researchers have tried to operationalize Leventhal's procedural justice rules, it has become increasingly apparent that the rules sometimes involve more than one procedural justice criterion. This is certainly true of the representation rule, which includes variation in decision control, instrumental process control, and expressive process control. As we saw in the preceding chapters, each of these three factors appears to have an independent effect on procedural justice and the psychological processes underlying each seem to quite distinct. Similarly, researchers have sometimes broken down Leventhal's consistency rule into subdivisions that distinguish consistency across persons and consistency across time and have found, as will be seen in one of the studies described below, that these two types of consistency differ substantially in their importance. In general, Leventhal's procedural justice rules seem to be too broad to be more than a first cut.

The most serious inaccuracy of Leventhal's theory is his belief that procedures were of less importance than outcomes in determining overall fairness judgments. As we saw in Chapter 4, procedural fairness plays at least as large a role as distributive fairness in determining overall justice judgments in legal settings, and it plays a much larger role than distributive fairness in determining reactions to legal authorities and institutions. In chapters 7 and 8 we will describe a number of studies that show much the same pattern of effects in political and organizational settings. There is now little doubt that procedural justice is at least as potent a determinant of satisfaction and overall fairness judgments as is distributive justice.

Leventhal also overestimated the role of outcome favorability and distributive fairness as factors affecting procedural justice judgments. Procedural justice judgments are often affected by the favorability and apparent fairness of the allocation outcome, but it is now clear that these factors are not as important as Leventhal suggested. As did Thibaut and Walker, Leventhal underestimated the importance of procedure *qua* procedure and overestimated the extent to which procedures would be seen and judged simply as mechanisms to generate outcomes.

CONTEXT, CULTURE, AND THE GENERALITY OF PROCEDURAL JUSTICE CONCEPTS

Leventhal's theory provides one justification for thinking that procedural justice processes generalize beyond legal and dispute resolution contexts, but there is also need for empirical confirmation of the generality of procedural justice findings. Confirmation might, and in fact has, taken several different forms. First, there are a few studies that have made direct comparisons of procedural justice effects across a variety of settings. Second, there are studies that have examined how procedural justice phenomena are affected by what might be viewed as the ultimate contextual variation: culture. And finally, there are studies that have simply looked for familiar procedural justice effects in novel settings. Each of these approaches has its accompanying methodological strengths and weaknesses. For example, the studies involving direct comparisons among different social contexts or different cultures have generally used scenario methods, and the findings of these studies might be questioned on the grounds that they tell us how people *think* they react to procedural justice, rather than how they *actually* react. On the other hand, although the studies that have tested procedural justice phenomena in novel settings have generally studied reactions to real experiences with procedures, they have been conducted in only one context at a time, making it difficult to judge the relative strength of procedural justice effects across contexts. Fortunately, the results from all the studies have been generally congruent with the idea that procedural justice judgments are important in a wide variety of contexts and that many of the same factors determine whether a procedure is seen as fair, regardless of the context. We describe in the remainder of this chapter several studies that made direct comparisons of procedural justice effects in different contexts and in different cultures. In the following two chapters we will present studies that have found procedural justice effects in novel contexts.

STUDIES OF CONTEXT AND PROCEDURAL JUSTICE

The first attempts to assess the generality of procedural justice phenomena were conducted by Fry and Leventhal (1979) and Fry and Cheney (1981). Both studies examined college students' ratings of the fairness of six procedures in various hypothetical social settings. The procedures examined in both studies consisted of one procedure in which all of Leventhal's structural components were fair and five procedures in which one of the structural components was unfair. In both studies, violation of different justice rules was used to render different components unfair. For example, in the Fry and Cheney study, violation of the consistency rule was used to render unfair the procedural component dealing with setting ground rules, and violation of the representation rule was used to render unfair the provisions for changing the procedure. This methodological approach confounds the justice rule that was violated and the structural component involved in the violation, and this limits the interpretability of the findings. For this reason, these studies can speak only to the fairness of specific combinations of rules and components. They can tell us, for example, how serious a threat to procedural fairness is the violation of the consistency rule in the context of setting ground rules because this combination was studied, but the studies cannot tell us much about the fundamental importance of either the ground-rules component or the consistency rule because neither factor was considered independently of the other.

The Fry and Leventhal study varied the sex of the subject, the nature of relations in the hypothetical social setting (harmonious, disharmonious, or unspecified), and the context of the allocation (business versus family). Each subject judged the relative fairness of one procedure in which all components were fair and the following five unfair procedures: (1) a procedure with unrepresentative selection of decision makers, (2) a procedure with inconsistency in setting ground rules, (3) a procedure with biased information gathering, (4) a procedure with a biased appeal procedure, and (5) a procedure with inaccurate safeguards. The central question of interest to us here was the extent to which procedural fairness ratings of the six procedures would vary as a function of gender of subject, social harmony, and social context.

The results of the Fry and Leventhal study showed that each of their manipulations affected procedural justice ratings for the six procedures, but the changes were relatively minor compared to the effects of different procedures. Figure 6-1 shows reactions to each procedure in a business and a family context. As can be seen in the figure, the pattern of fairness ratings was quite similar for the two contexts, although there were some differences that point to occasional context-specific judgments of what constitutes procedural fairness. For example, the context manipulation had little effect on any of the procedures except that involving a biased appeal procedure, where the procedure was viewed as less fair in a business setting than in a family setting. The other procedures appeared to inspire similar fairness judgments across both contexts. Thus inconsistency in setting ground rules was seen as a very serious violation of procedural justice and unrepresentative selection of decision makers was seen as a relatively less serious violation of procedural justice, regardless of whether the procedure was used in a family or a business setting. Similar effects were observed for the other independent variables. Occasional effects for social harmony or gender of subject did not mask the overall procedure effects. Notwithstanding the occasional differences, the general implication of the Fry and Le-

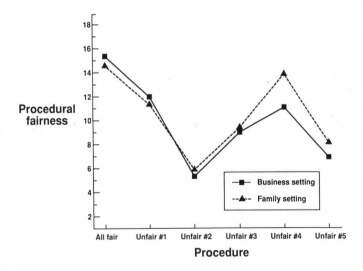

FIGURE 6-1. Fairness of six allocation procedures.

venthal study is that procedural justice processes are not radically different across contexts.

Fry and Cheney (1981) used the same method to study the effects of the closeness of the relationship and of various distributive justice rules on procedural fairness judgments. They found that the fairness of various procedures was unaffected by whether the allocation was among friends or among acquaintances and by whether the distribution was to be made according to merit, equality, or needs. The ratings given to specific procedures were similar to those found in the Fry and Leventhal study.[4] In particular, inconsistency in setting ground rules was seen as a very serious violation of procedural justice.

A more extensive study of the effect of context on the importance of procedural justice concerns is reported by Barrett-Howard and Tyler (1986). They presented undergraduate students with brief scenarios describing allocation situations. The subjects were asked to imagine that they were in the situation and were asked to rate the importance of making the allocation with fair procedures. The allocation situations varied following a $2 \times 2 \times 2 \times 2$ factorial design. The situations were designed to represent the 16 possible combinations of situations high or low on four basic dimensions of interpersonal relationships: socio-emotional versus task orientation; informal versus formal relationship; cooperative versus competitive interaction; and equal versus unequal power between the parties and the decision maker.

In each situation a scenario was constructed describing an allocation problem appropriate to that particular type of interpersonal setting. For example, in the socio-emotional, informal, cooperative relationship with equal power respondents read this scenario:

> Sue, Lisa, and Ellen have been best friends since grade school. Over the years their friendship has grown stronger. During their college years they roomed together, went to parties together, and studied for tests together. Now that they are finished with school, they no longer live together, but they do visit each other often and keep in close contact. Sue recently won a weekend trip for two to San Francisco. She wants to invite one of her best friends, but can't decide whether to ask Lisa or Ellen, both of whom would like to go.

Let us consider first the results with respect to ratings of the importance of procedural justice, distributive justice, and nonjustice factors as criteria to be used in selecting an allocation procedure. Figure 6-2 shows the overall pattern of the importance ratings given each of these three types of criteria across the 16 situations, in order to illustrate the general level of situation-based variability in the importance ratings. Several

---

[4]The Fry and Cheney study used some of the same procedures as did the Fry and Leventhal study.

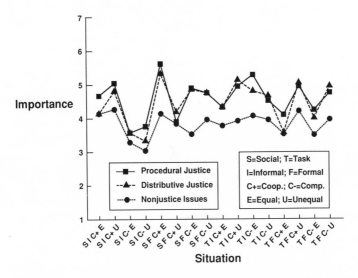

FIGURE 6-2. Importance of fairness and nonfairness considerations.

findings are of particular interest. First, the importance accorded procedural justice and the importance accorded distributive justice showed quite similar patterns across the 16 situations. As can be seen from the figure, the curves for procedural and distributive justice tend to rise and fall together. This indicates that situational differences resulted in heightened or lessened importance for fairness concerns in general, rather than affecting the importance of one type of fairness at the expense of the other. A second major finding was that, in general, fairness concerns were seen as more important than other concerns—the curves for both types of fairness are generally higher than the curve for nonfairness factors. A third finding was that there was some variability in the importance of fairness. Barrett-Howard and Tyler found that fairness concerns were rated as especially important in situations that involved formal social relationships or informal task relationships, perhaps because such relationships are seen as susceptible to conflict and fair procedures and outcomes are seen as protecting against conflict. Fairness was also perceived to be more important in task-oriented relationships involving unequal power, again perhaps because of the potential for fair procedures and outcomes to smooth relationships that might otherwise suffer from chronic conflict (cf. Thibaut & Faucheux, 1965).

A second set of findings of the Barrett-Howard and Tyler study are also of interest to our discussion here. Subjects in their study were asked to rate the importance of each of the Leventhal justice rules in determin-

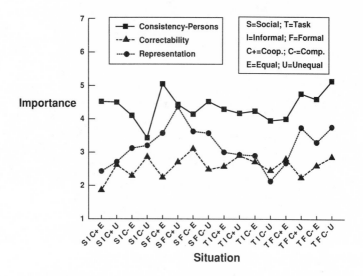

FIGURE 6-3. Importance of three procedural justice rules.

ing whether an allocation procedure was fair in the situation in question. (Barrett-Howard and Tyler had separate rating scales for each of the two types of consistency mentioned by Leventhal, consistency across people and consistency across time.) In general, this part of the study showed that there are situation-based differences in the importance accorded various justice rules but that these differences are not so massive as to suggest that the meaning of procedural justice changes entirely from one situation to another. Figure 6-3 illustrates this finding by showing the importance accorded three of the justice rules—consistency across persons, representation, and correctability—across the 16 situations.[5] As can be seen from the figure, the importance curves for each rule do occasionally show substantial variation from one situation to another, but it is also clear that there are some universal effects as well. Across all the situations consistency across persons was seen as more important than correctability.

What can we say about the generality of procedural justice phenomena on the basis of these three studies? First, the studies support the notion that procedural justice is a concept applicable far beyond the legal context in which most of the early work was done. There is no evidence

[5]The three justice rules included in the figure were chosen because they include one rule that was high in overall importance (consistency across persons), one rule that was moderate in overall importance (representation), and one rule that was low in overall importance (correctability).

in any of the studies that subjects had any difficulty dealing with the concept of procedural justice. In the two studies by Fry and his colleagues, subjects distinguished among various procedures in terms of procedural fairness, regardless of the context in which the procedure was said to be used. In the Barrett-Howard and Tyler study, mean ratings of the importance of procedural fairness seldom dropped below the mid-point of the rating scale and were never lower than "3" on the seven-point scale. Further, there appears to be substantial generality for some of the specific factors that determine the fairness of procedures. For example, in all three studies, and across all of the various contexts studied, consistency across persons appeared to be a very strong determinant of procedural justice and correctability appeared to be a rather weak determinant.

Notwithstanding these cross-situational constancies, the studies just described do suggest that there is some situation-linked variation in the causes and consequences of procedural justice judgments. The studies by Fry and his colleagues did show that the potency of some justice rules increases and decreases depending on the social context, and the Barrett-Howard and Tyler study showed situational variation in both the perceived importance of procedural justice and the importance of various justice rules in determining whether a procedure is fair. It is clear that procedural justice processes are affected by the context within which the procedure is used. At the present time what can be concluded is this: Wherever research has examined procedural justice it has been found that people care about the fairness procedures. People may give different weight to various concerns as they decide in different situations what constitutes procedural justice, but they appear always to make procedural justice judgments and these judgments are always important to them. Further, there appear to be some factors that always have substantial impact on judgments of procedural justice.

STUDIES OF CULTURE AND PROCEDURAL JUSTICE

Another way to determine whether it is reasonable to expect procedural justice phenomena to generalize to novel contexts is to look at cross-cultural studies of procedural justice effects. To the extent that we see similarities of response across different cultures, we can have greater confidence in the robustness of an effect, and we would expect the effect to generalize to different subgroups within a culture. If, however, differences appear between cultures, we would wonder whether intracultural variation in the background of those exposed to a procedure might not also limit procedural justice phenomena. In this section we will describe several studies that seem to us to be particularly revealing about which procedural justice effects are robust in this respect and which are not.

Using West German undergraduates as subjects, Barrett-Howard and Lamm (1986) conducted a partial replication of the Barrett-Howard and Tyler study, which used American undergraduates. There were a few differences between the two studies—the German study examined only equal power relationships and it examined a larger set of justice rules—but the studies were sufficiently similar that any substantial differences in their results can be attributed to the cultural difference. Barrett-Howard and Lamm found,as did the earlier study, that procedural fairness concerns by and large were seen as more important than non-fairness concerns in choosing allocation procedures. Indeed, comparison of the results of the two studies suggests that the Germans accorded relatively more importance to procedural justice and showed less situation-based variation in the procedural justice importance ratings than did the Americans.

Similarly, when Barrett-Howard and Lamm examined judgments of the importance of various justice rules for deciding whether or not a procedure is fair, they found, as had the American study, that there was some variability across situations in the importance of each rule. However, these ratings also showed that some rules, such as consistency across persons and ethicality, were deemed more important in all situations than were other rules, such as consistency across time. Again, these findings are similar to those of the American study. Direct comparisons of the importance ratings for specific justice rules by the Germans and the Americans show that the curves are sometimes remarkably similar. Figure 6-4a shows an example of the similar ratings that were seen on one justice rule, consistency across persons, and 6-4b shows an example of dissimilar ratings, in this case for the correctability rule. It is noteworthy that even when the Germans differed from the Americans in the overall level of importance they accorded a particular rule the pattern of importance across the eight social situations was quite similar in the two national samples. For example, as can be seen from Figure 6-4b, the Germans accorded much more importance to correctability than did the Americans, but the general shape of the two curves was quite similar. Taken as a whole, the Barrett-Howard and Lamm findings imply that, although there are some cultural differences in the weight accorded various factors that determine whether a procedure is seen as fair, much of the psychology of procedural fairness, including its importance in influencing reactions to allocation procedures, generalizes beyond American culture.

A similar message emerges from some recent cross-cultural work on procedural fairness in dispute resolution. In the first of these studies,

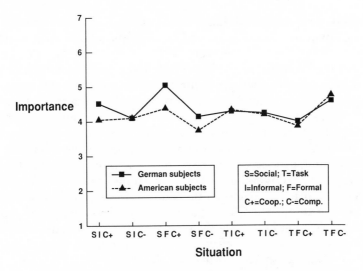

FIGURE 6-4a. Importance of consistency across persons rule.

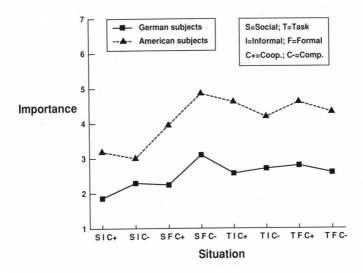

FIGURE 6-4b. Importance of correctability rule.

conducted by Leung and Lind (1986), two dispute resolution procedures, adversary adjudication and inquisitorial adjudication, were described to Hong Kong Chinese and Midwestern American undergraduates, and the subjects were asked to rate their preference for using the procedure to resolve the hypothetical dispute and their perceptions of each procedure on a number of dimensions, including procedural fairness. Leung and Lind hypothesized that the Chinese subjects would be less likely to prefer the high process control adversary procedure because their culture discourages the overt competitiveness that often accompanies high process control in dispute resolution. The results of the study support this hypothesis. The study found greater preference for adversary than for inquisitorial procedures among the American subjects, but not among the Chinese subjects. The Chinese sample showed no preference for either procedure over the other. Additional analyses of the correlations between preference ratings and perceptions of the procedures produced some information about the causes of procedural preferences in the two cultures. Both the American and the Chinese samples showed significant positive correlations between measures of process control and procedural preferences, indicating that in both cultures disputant process control was seen as a positive feature of adjudication procedures. Leung and Lind reconciled this finding with the absence of any significant preference for the adversary procedure among the Chinese subjects by hypothesizing that the Chinese subjects saw the adversary procedure as having some other characteristic that was undesirable and that counteracted the favorable evaluation that would otherwise have been provoked by high process control.

Leung (1985, Study 1) tested this explanation of the results of the Leung and Lind study. He again used a scenario study methodology that asked subjects to imagine that they were involved in a dispute with either a friend or a stranger. Four procedures—bargaining, mediation, inquisitorial adjudication, and adversary adjudication—were described and the subjects were asked to rate their preference for and perceptions of each procedure. The study was conducted in the United States and Hong Kong using both student and nonstudent subjects.

Leung found that the Chinese subjects preferred mediation most highly, adversary adjudication somewhat less, and the other two procedures substantially less. He found that the American subjects were ambivalent between mediation and adversary adjudication but preferred both to the other two procedures. The preference differences are themselves interesting, since they confirm and extend the Leung and Lind finding that procedural preferences are in fact variable across cultures. Even more interesting, however, were the results of regression analyses that examined the relation between preferences and several perceptual dimensions. Leung regressed the procedural preferences on perceptions of the fairness of the procedure, the extent to which the procedure allowed disputants control over evidence presentation, the capacity of the procedure to reduce animosity between the disputants, and the extent to which the procedure favored the subject. Analyses comparing the regression equation across the different samples revealed that the regression equation *did not vary with any of the sample characteristics* (i.e., whether the subject was Chinese versus American or student versus nonstudent). Across all subjects the regression of procedural perceptions on procedural preferences produced the following standardized coefficients:

Preference = .05 × Process Control + .13 × Animosity Reduction +
.27 × Favorability + .34 × Procedural Fairness

These findings show that, regardless of their culture, all the subjects gave substantial weight to procedural fairness, favorability, and animosity reduction in deciding how much they would prefer or not prefer to use a dispute resolution procedure.[6] This in turn suggests that the cultural differences seen in procedural preferences did not result from cultural differences in the weight accorded various desiderata of dispute resolution procedures. Rather, differences in procedural preferences appeared to result from cultural differences in the extent to which various procedures are believed to exhibit each desired characteristic. For example, Leung found that the Chinese subjects were more likely than the American subjects to believe that adversary adjudication fails to reduce animosity. Given the positive weight that all subjects placed on animosity reduction, this difference in beliefs about the consequences of adversary adjudication explains the cultural differences seen in preferences for adversary procedures.

As did the Barrett-Howard and Lamm study, the Leung study suggests that procedural fairness maintains its importance across different cultures. The Leung study shows that the underlying values that drive procedural justice judgments are much the same across cultures. Leung's findings can be summarized with a statement that is borne out by all of the theory and research described in this chapter: Some procedural justice *effects* are clearly variable, but basic procedural justice *processes* are remarkably invariant across the contexts and cultures studied thus far.

[6]The low weight given to process control can be explained by the likely mediation of any process control effect by the procedural fairness variable. That is, process control probably acts on preferences through its effects on procedural fairness, with relatively little direct effect.

Chapter 7

Procedural Justice in the Political Arena

The distinction between the political arena and the legal arena differs widely across societies and across history. For example, during the colonial period in the United States almost all of the functions we will be describing as political were performed by the legal system (Friedman, 1985). If, for example, a decision had to be made concerning whether a road should be built, that decision was made by the same body of leaders and at the same meeting as a decision about punishment for the town drunk. In other societies the decisions that we think of as legal are handled by "political" officials and no distinction between law and politics is made.

However, under the current American system of government a distinction is made between politics and law and separate branches of the government deal with these two issues. The key distinction between the two lies in the concerns that preoccupy the authorities in each group. The function of legal institutions is to interpret the laws and rules made by legislators and to apply those laws and rules to specific decisions in order to resolve disputes and decide allegations of rule breaking. In contrast, the political system makes the rules that guide the disposition of public resources, shape public policies, determine appropriate penalties for rule violations, and regulate economic transactions and private lives. In other words, the executive and legislative branches of government set the rules by which government operates, laying out the rights and obligations of citizens. These rules must, of course, be consistent with the Constitution and other documents that describe the basic structure of government and the principles it seeks to achieve. The political system also creates the institutions that allow it to enact and implement public policies.

Because the political system, like the legal system, is a collection of

147

institutions and rules, it is another arena within which procedural justice-based evaluations might occur. As is the case with judicial actions,
citizens might judge their satisfaction with budget allocations or social or
economic policy decisions by considering the processes through which
the decisions are made. Procedural justice concerns may also affect citizen evaluations of political leaders and institutions of government.

The political arena is an important site for testing the generality of
procedural justice effects because the range of actions undertaken by
political authorities is so broad. Political authorities decide where roads
will be built, where and how economic development will be allowed,
and how citizens will be regulated when they deal with each other. The
government also decides issues of public morality; determining for example whether homosexuality and premarital sex will be illegal, and
more generally determining the degree to which government will play a
role in controlling the private lives of citizens. Government decisions
can send citizens to their deaths in battle, change the environmental and
industrial safety standards that influence their risk of injury or death,
and outlaw or ignore such potentially dangerous public practices as
carrying guns or drunk driving. The direct impact of the political system
on citizens' lives is broader and more pervasive than is the case in the
legal arena. Hence, finding procedural justice effects in the political
arena would add considerable strength to arguments that such effects
are important.

Although the study of American politics tends to focus upon citizen
reactions to existing political systems, politics can also involve the process of creating the basic structure of government itself and deciding on
the principles that the government will promote and use. Such a process
occurred in American history during and just after the revolutionary war
period and still occurs in other societies. Although the structure and
principles of American government have been largely unchanged for the
past several hundred years, it is important to recognize that politics can
also involve development of the basic procedures and structures of government, in addition to the operation of political processes within existing structures. However, this chapter will accept the reality of American
politics and focus on decisions and policies made within the context of a
preexisting government structure.

One interesting consequence of the fixed nature of American politics is that there has been little attention paid to the underlying procedural preferences of citizens, that is, to the procedures that Americans
would prefer if they were creating a new government. It is typically
argued that our government rests on a "consensus" of support for its
basic procedures (McClosky, 1964; Prothro & Grigg, 1960). Studies of
this consensus suggest that it exists on an abstract level, in support for
procedural rules such as "one person, one vote" and "free speech for all

no matter what their views might be." In concrete instances, however, there can be substantial disagreement about whether to apply these principles. Extensive research on free speech, for example, shows that citizens are more likely to support the principle of free speech for all as an abstract concept than they are to support allowing homosexuals, Nazis or communists to demonstrate on specific occasions (McClosky & Brill, 1983; Stouffer, 1955; Sullivan, Pierson, & Marcus, 1982). These inconsistencies suggest that a systematic exploration of views about procedural fairness in the political arena might be very interesting.

CONSEQUENCES OF JUDGMENTS ABOUT THE FAIRNESS OF GOVERNMENT

From the perspective of a citizen in our society there are a number of potential targets of concern in thinking about politics. First, citizens evaluate the policies developed and implemented by their government. Government policies intrude upon the everyday life of citizens by affecting whether they can form unions, whether they receive welfare, whether they will be helped or hurt by government loans for education or affirmative action programs, and whether they will be able to buy a home. In each case citizens may feel that the government has adopted policies that are wise or foolish and that may help or hurt them, their family or friends, and other citizens like themselves.

Public reactions to policies are also important because they are likely to influence reactions to political authorities. In addition to reacting to government policies, citizens evaluate the leaders who make those policies. In American politics, a focus of much public attention is the President, who has a major role, of course, in deciding and implementing government policy. Studies have suggested that the President is blamed or praised for public policies to a much greater extent than is reasonable given his or her actual power to create personally desired policies. Legislators and members of the Supreme Court are also the focus of much public attention.

Distinct from the evaluation of authorities are public views about the system of government itself. Unlike citizens in many other countries, most Americans have not had the experience of seeing the basic structure of their government change in a major way. Nonetheless, they might have opinions about how well their existing government structures and institutions work. Political scientists distinguish between support or opposition to particular incumbent authorities (labeled "specific" system support) and support or opposition to the system of government itself (labeled "diffuse" system support: Easton, 1965). Positive evaluations of the institutions of government have been posited to provide a "cushion of support" that allows authorities to undertake actions that may not be in the short-term self-interest of citizens (Rasinski, Tyler, & Fridkin, 1985).

If citizens oppose incumbent authorities they may work within the system to remove them and replace them with other authorities (Kinder & Sears, 1985; Rasinski & Tyler, in press). If they oppose the system itself they are unlikely to try to work within the system to change incumbent authorities. Instead, they will work to change the system itself. On occasion, such efforts might also involve working within the system, as when communists run for political office promising to use their power to abolish the office they seek to obtain. More frequently it involves working outside the system to disrupt and destroy it. In the United States there have been few examples of major efforts to change the political system since the Civil War, but many groups have engaged in acts of violence, such as riots, that are less steadily sustained and less well organized expressions of opposition to the existing political structure (Muller, 1979).

Opposition to the political system itself, however expressed, is likely to be much more difficult for the political system to deal with than is opposition to particular political authorities. Hence, discontent with the political system itself represents the true threat to political stability. If citizens support the system but dislike incumbents, then their energies will be directed within preexisting channels that do not threaten to disrupt society. Thus, Democrats continue to support the political process even after a Republican has been elected President. Instead of rioting, attacking the police, bombing buildings, or otherwise attempting to destroy the political system, the American political opposition works within the system to remove the incumbent.

Concern over public support for government has been especially strong in recent years, since it is widely believed by political analysts that public support for the political system has been declining. Regardless of whether the focus of study is presidential endorsement, public evaluations of legislators or Supreme Court justices, or evaluations of government institutions, the survey evidence suggests that public support for government has declined markedly during the post–World War II period (Lipset & Schneider, 1983; Miller, 1979; Wright, 1981). Some social commentators have suggested that this decline in support represents the most uniform and striking trend in public opinion polls in the last twenty years (Caddell, 1979; Shaver, 1980). Although recent evidence suggests that the decline in support for government may have stopped and may even be reversing (Miller, 1983), the potential danger of failing public confidence has emerged as a major concern in political psychology.

Public support has become an especially important issue to political psychologists because there have been many suggestions that the nature of American politics may be fundamentally changing. A number of political commentators have argued that the United States is entering an era of resource scarcity and economic decline during which conflicts over the allocation of collective resources will intensify (Blumberg, 1968; deCarufel, 1981; Deutsch, 1981; Greenberg, 1981; Lerner, 1981). Resource conflicts are expected to lead to particularly intense stresses on the American political system. This is the case because the American political system is based upon the assumption that the disadvantaged will be given access to collective resources through the creation of new wealth, rather than by taking wealth away from those who already have it (Ophuls, 1977). If no new wealth is being created, then the disadvantaged can improve their lot only by taking resources from advantaged groups. The advantaged groups, unaccustomed to such redistributive pressures, would be expected to resist efforts at redistribution, resulting in substantial pressures on the political system.[1]

THE BASIS OF PUBLIC REACTIONS TO GOVERNMENT POLICIES AND AUTHORITIES

The importance of public views about government policies, leaders, and institutions to the fate of political candidates and the viability of the political system itself has led political psychologists to be very interested in the basis of public support for government. Given this interest, political psychologists have sought theories or models of the citizen that might be useful in understanding public reactions to political decisions and leaders. The public choice model is currently the dominant model of the citizen used by political scientists and policy makers to explain public political reactions. It represents the application of economic choice models to the political arena. The public choice model has two components: a theory of utility and a theory of judgment or choice.

Public Choice Theories

The theory of utility underlying public choice models makes three assumptions about the nature of human values. The first assumption is that the citizen will attempt to maximize his or her gain from the political system, just as a person would do in a financial marketplace transaction such as buying a car. This is the major assumption of public choice theory and provides the distinctiveness that sets that theory apart from

---

[1]This view is quite similar to John Thibaut's insight, described in Chapter 2, that procedural justice might provide an ever more important source of satisfaction as society's resources become more and more limited.

other models of political behavior. A second assumption is that actors are primarily motivated by a desire for *material* rewards (Laver, 1981). Finally, it is assumed that citizens focus on immediate, short-term gains and losses. These latter two assumptions have been relaxed (or abandoned) in recent versions of public choice theories (see Tyler, 1986a, and Tyler, Rasinski, & Griffin, 1986), leaving the first assumption as the key characteristic of public choice models of the citizen's values.

The basic assumptions of public choice theory are similar to those of social exchange theories in social psychology (Kelley & Thibaut, 1978; Thibaut & Kelley, 1959). Social exchange theories also assume that people are motivated to maximize their own gain in interactions with others and behave in a manner designed to do so. One difference between social exchange and public choice theories is the proposition in the former that satisfaction with outcomes is the result of relative, rather than absolute, outcome levels.

The second component of the public choice approach is a theory of judgment. Since the work of von Neumann and Morgenstern (1947), the major theory of judgment and action underlying public choice theory and other economic models has been the familiar subjective expected utility model. According to the subjective expected utility model, actions are governed by calculations involving the multiplicative combination of probabilities and values (see Feather, 1964; Luce & Raiffa, 1957; Luce & Suppes, 1965; Savage, 1954). In public choice theory, this suggests that citizens decide what to do and how to feel about policies and leaders by combining their judgments of personal gain (values) with their expectations about which alterations would lead to personal gain or loss (probabilities).

Theories of public choice have been important in political psychology for two reasons. First, they have provided the image of the citizen that has dominated political science and policy studies. This image is of a self-interested individual whose actions are determined by a desire to maximize short-term personal material gain. Irrespective of whether citizens are deciding whether they should vote or riot, whom to vote for, or which store to burn down, their decisions are thought to be governed by their beliefs about which actions will benefit them. Similarly, citizen policy preferences and leadership evaluations are seen as driven by self-interest-based judgments.

The influence of public choice theories on political psychology can be seen in the traditional explanation of public support for policies and political leaders. This area of study has been dominated by the assumption that poor outcomes from the political system will lead to dissatisfaction with the system and its leaders. Two types of poor outcomes have been emphasized: the failure to solve problems or provide benefits, and policy incongruence. Thus, public dissatisfaction is thought to arise from the failure of government leaders to solve social and economic problems and provide desired government programs (Citrin, 1974; House & Mason, 1975; Miller, 1979; Wright, 1981). According to this view of public discontent, the public wants leaders who are competent and who can solve the social problems that are of personal relevance to the citizen. For example, citizens who are unemployed will be angry with government leaders whose economic policies have hurt their industry and will vote against those leaders.

Political discontent may also result from disagreements between citizens and leaders over which social or economic policies are appropriate. Here the self-interest assumption is represented in the belief that citizens have values about what social and economic policies are appropriate, and they want their leaders to follow those policies (see Wright, 1981). If, for example, a citizen opposes abortion he or she will want the political system to develop policies that make abortions difficult or impossible to obtain.

Theories of public choice have also had an important influence upon the problems that political psychologists view as important to study. In particular, attention has been directed toward those political behaviors that appear paradoxical or problematic when viewed from an economic perspective. The fact that many people vote, for example, appears unreasonable when viewed in the context of subjective expected utility theories. The likelihood that one vote will influence an election is very small, and the act of voting necessarily involves some personal inconvenience. As a result, no self-interested citizen should take the trouble to vote. In spite of this logical analysis, many citizens do vote, even in the face of difficulty, risk, and hardship.

Another important consequence of the focus on issues of outcome favorability has been the neglect of procedural issues. Recent political psychology has ignored the possible effects of the political decision-making *process*. This neglect is not universal—some political psychologists have been very interested in the role of process in establishing and maintaining government legitimacy (see Anton, 1967; Edelman, 1964; Engstrom & Giles, 1972; Murphy & Tanenhaus, 1969; Scheingold, 1974; Wahlke, 1971)—but reactions to the decision-making process have been seen as less important in political analysis as the field has become increasingly dominated by public choice theory.

Justice-Based Models

Although political psychologists, political scientists, and policy analysts have been heavily influenced by economic models of the citizen in recent years, this image of the citizen has not always predominated. As early as the seventeenth and eighteenth centuries political philosophers were arguing that citizens' political behavior is influenced by a natural desire to be considerate of others (Shaftesbury, 1710; Hutcheson, 1728). More recently, Wilson and Banfield (1964) cited evidence of non-self-interested voting behavior by citizens in support of a "public regardedness" motive in political behavior. Additional evidence in support of such a motive is found in historical studies (Moore, 1978), in studies of legal authority (Sarat, 1977), and in studies of citizen support for government policies (Cook, 1979; Rasinski, 1987).

As we have noted in previous chapters, psychological theories of justice have identified two types of justice judgments that might be important in citizen's judgments of fairness: judgments of distributive justice and judgments of procedural justice. Judgments of distributive justice compare the outcomes a person receives to some standard of fairness or deservedness. Judgments of distributive injustice form the basis of feelings of relative deprivation (Crosby, 1976, 1982) and inequity (Walster, Walster, & Berscheid, 1978). According to distributive justice theories, those who receive low levels of outcomes from the government will evaluate the government negatively only if they feel that they have not received what they deserved or that the overall distribution of outcomes across citizens is unfair.

Judgments of procedural justice are by now familiar. In the political arena they involve judgments about the fairness of the process by which policy decisions are made. Procedural justice judgments in the political arena are typically more abstract and general than those in the legal arena. In the work of Thibaut and Walker, for example, disputants judged the fairness of the procedures used to resolve a particular case. Specific judgments are sometimes studied in the political arena: Katz, Gutek, Kahn and Barton (1975) asked people to judge the fairness of their treatment when they went to a federal agency, such as the social security administration, to resolve a claim or grievance. However, most procedural justice studies in the political arena have tended to ask respondents to make evaluations of the general policy-making process. General procedural justice judgments are more abstract than are assessments of a particular experience and therefore the importance of procedural judgments will have to be proven anew at this new abstract level.

Judgments about procedural and distributive justice are like the public choice judgments already outlined in that they also involve assumptions about personal values. But the major assumption of justice-based models is that individuals are motivated by a desire to be treated fairly, either through receiving fair outcomes or through having decisions made in a fair way. This assumption is the key difference between justice-based and public choice perspectives.

The model of judgment that underlies most justice-based theories is the same subjective expected utility model that underlies economic approaches, but the model is broadened to include terms reflecting the value of fair outcomes and fair procedures (Leventhal, 1976, 1980). Our earlier discussion makes it clear that the dominant models in political psychology and policy studies in recent years have not viewed citizens as interested in either distributive or procedural fairness. If one accepted this view, there would be little point in looking for procedural concerns in the political process. Therefore, the first issue to be addressed is whether there is in fact evidence that justice-based concerns, and especially concerns about procedural fairness, matter in the political arena. This issue has been resolved in a series of recent studies directly examining the influence of fairness judgments on political evaluations and behavior.

Research examining the importance of justice-based concerns in political evaluation and behavior has relied heavily on the use of survey data. This reflects the greater use of survey methods in the field of political science, where the laboratory experiments favored by social psychologists have traditionally been viewed with suspicion. Survey methods allow two issues to be addressed. The first is whether judgments of the fairness of a decision-making procedure are naturally distinct from judgments of the personal gain or loss resulting from the procedure. Economic analysts have suggested that ethical judgments are epiphenomenal, arising as socially acceptable justifications for evaluations and behaviors actually governed by concerns of self-interest. If this were true, then concerns about justice could not be found to be empirically separated from judgments of personal gain and loss.

The second empirical issue addressed in political surveys is whether judgments of distributive and procedural justice exert independent influence on political evaluations and behavior. Citizens could potentially distinguish between fairness and personal gain but react largely in terms of personal gain. If this were the case, it would make fairness judgments considerably less interesting.

INFLUENCES ON POLICY EVALUATIONS

Tyler, Rasinski, and McGraw (1985) examined the influence of self-interest and fairness judgments on policy evaluations. A random sample of 300 residents of Chicago were interviewed over the telephone about their support for or opposition to the policies of the Reagan administration. Respondents were asked to indicate both the absolute number benefits they received from the federal government and the number of benefits they received relative to those they received at the beginning of the Reagan administration. Most respondents indicated that they currently received "a few" (33%) or "no" benefits (39%) from government, with 63% indicating that their current level of benefits was lower than it had been at the beginning of the Reagan administration. A large number of respondents (49%) also reported paying a higher percentage of their income in taxes than at the beginning of the Reagan administration. As might be expected, many respondents expressed dissatisfaction with the level of benefits they currently received (48%) and with the level of taxes they were required to pay (64%).

Respondents were also asked to judge the fairness of their level of benefits (distributive fairness). Forty-nine percent indicated receiving a fair level of benefits, whereas 44% said that the number of benefits they received was less than fair. In the case of taxes, 38% indicated paying a fair level of taxes, while 59% said that they had to pay too much in taxes. When asked about the fairness of the procedures used to allocate benefits, 39% indicated that they were fair. In the case of the procedures used to decide tax levels, 28% felt that they were fair.

In addition to evaluating government benefits and taxes, the respondents were asked to consider the government's economic and social policies. Thirty-five percent of respondents agreed with the Reagan administration's economic policies, 39% agreed with its social policies. Forty-seven percent indicated that they had been hurt by current economic policies and 8% indicated that they had been helped; 22% indicated that they had been hurt by current social policies and 6% indicated that they had been helped.

When asked about the distributive fairness of economic policies, 39% of citizens indicated that they were fair, 55% that they received unfairly low levels of benefits from those policies. Forty-three percent felt that the Reagan administration's social policies were fair to them, 52% that they were less favorable to them than was fair.

To assess the procedural fairness of the Reagan administration's policy-making process, respondents were asked to evaluate four aspects of policy-making: whether the President considered the views of all sides before making decisions, whether he took enough time to consider decisions carefully, whether he had enough information to make good decisions, and whether he was unbiased and impartial. Depending on the specific item in question, 25% to 30% of those interviewed said the President's policy-making procedures usually had such characteristics, 20% to 30% that they sometimes did, and 40% to 50% that they seldom did.

Respondents were also asked a number of background questions, including political party affiliation, liberalism, age, education, race, income, and sex. These background characteristics were included in the analysis to control for differences among the respondents involved in the study.

The goal of the study was to explore the basis of policy evaluations. Two issues were addressed: the basis of public satisfaction with the level of government benefits received and taxes paid and the basis of public agreement or disagreement with social and economic policies.

The correlations between judgments of personal gain and fairness are shown in Table 7-1. As can be seen, judgments of outcome favorability and fairness were substantially independent. In the case of

TABLE 7-1. The Relationship among Outcome Judgments

	Outcome level		Fairness	
	Absolute	Relative	Distributive	Procedural
	Benefits			
Outcome level				
Absolute	—			
Relative	.10*			
Fairness				
Distributive	.14**	.38***	—	
Procedural	.14**	.17**	.17***	—
	Taxes			
Outcome level				
Absolute	—			
Relative	.11*	—		
Fairness				
Distributive	.03	.30***	—	
Procedural	.10*	.11*	.30***	—

	Personal benefit	Fairness	
		Distributive	Procedural
	Economic policies		
Personal benefit	—		
Fairness			
Distributive	.52***	—	
Procedural	.25***	.40***	—
	Social policies		
Personal benefit	—		
Fairness			
Distributive	.36***	—	
Procedural	.29***	.43***	—

Note. Entries are Pearson correlations.
*p < .05.
**p < .01.
***p < .001.

TABLE 7-2. Influences upon Satisfaction with Benefits and Taxes

	Satisfaction with benefits		Satisfaction with taxes	
	Beta	R^2	Beta	R^2
Outcome level				
Absolute	.18***	.06***	.03	.00
Relative	.10	.06***	−.10	.06***
Total	—	.11***	—	.06***
Fairness				
Distributional	.18**	.10***	.32***	.22***
Procedural	.26***	.12***	.31***	.19***
Total	—	.19***	—	.31***
Demographics				
Party	.05		.15**	
Liberalism	−.13*		−.15**	
Age	−.08		−.04	
Education	.10		.03	
Race	.07		−.01	
Income	−.04		—	
Sex	.05		.02	
Total		.07***		.08***
Total		.24***		.34***
Usefulness analysis				
Outcome level beyond fairness and demographics		.03***		.01***
Fairness beyond outcome level and demographics		.08***		.22***
Demographics beyond outcome level and fairness		.01**		.02***

Note. Entries in the columns marked beta are the standardized regression coefficients. Entries in the column marked R^2 are the adjusted square of the multiple correlation coefficient.

*$p < .05$.
**$p < .01$.
***$p < .001$.

benefits and taxes, judgments of outcome favorability and fairness were only moderately correlated (mean $r = .17$, $p < .01$). For policy judgments, respondent agreement was more strongly related to fairness judgments (mean $r = .36$, $p < .001$). In both cases, judgments of distributive fairness and procedural fairness were only moderately related to each other (with benefits and taxes $r = .24$, $p < .001$; with policy judgments $r = .42$, $p < .001$). These results suggest that people differentiate between receiving favorable outcomes, receiving fair outcomes, and having decisions made by a fair process.

The second issue of concern was the role of each type of judgment in shaping citizen evaluations of policies and benefits and taxes. The various inputs were used as independent variables in regression equations examining their influences on evaluations of policies and benefits and taxes. The results for satisfaction with benefits and taxes are shown in Table 7-2; the results for policy agreement are in Table 7-3.

The major influence on satisfaction with benefits and taxes was perceived fairness. In the case of benefits, fairness judgments accounted for 8% of the variance not accounted for by other factors, while in the case of taxes fairness judgments accounted for 22% of unique variance. Outcome favorability, on the other hand, only accounted for an average of 2% of unique variance. Thus reactions to government benefits and taxes

TABLE 7-3. Influences upon Policy Agreements

	Agreement with economic policies		Agreement with social policies	
	Beta	R^2	Beta	R^2
Personal benefit	.20***	.18***	.29***	.21***
Fairness				
Distributive	.22**	.25***	.21***	.22***
Procedural	.32***	.33***	.21***	.22***
Total	—	.41***	—	.31***
Demographics				
Party	.14**		.15**	
Liberalism	.11*		.13*	
Age	.02		−.03	
Education	.09		.12*	
Race	.19***		−.01	
Income	−.07		−.02	
Sex	.07		.13	
Total		.32***		.21***
Total		.52***		.43***
Usefulness analysis				
Personal benefit beyond fairness and demographics		.03***		.08***
Fairness beyond personal benefit and demographics		.12***		.22***
Demographics beyond personal benefit and fairness		.08***		.05***

Note. Entries in the column marked beta are the standardized regression coefficients. Entries in the column marked R^2 are the adjusted square of the multiple correlation coefficient.   N = 300.
  *$p < .05$.
  **$p < .01$.
  ***$p < .001$.

were clearly linked to judgments of fairness. Further, both distributive and procedural fairness had an influence on respondents' evaluations of benefits and taxes.

In the case of policy agreement, fairness was also the major factor considered by respondents. Fairness judgments accounted for 12% of the unique variance in the case of economic policy, 22% in the case of social policy. Again both distributive and procedural fairness were important influences upon agreement.

The results of this study suggest that people make judgments about the fairness of government benefits, taxes, and social and economic policies that are distinct from their assessments of whether they benefit from the policies and actions. Fairness judgments are important in both satisfaction with government actions and agreement with government policies. In each case both distributive and procedural justice are important concerns.

INFLUENCES ON INCUMBENT AND SYSTEM EVALUATIONS

In addition to studying reactions to policies, the Tyler, Rasinski, and McGraw study examined the basis of public support for or opposition to President Reagan and to the general political system itself. Evaluations of the President were assessed with measures of performance competence and feelings about the President; system evaluations were assessed with measures of trust in government.

In examining the basis of evaluations of the President and the political system, respondents' evaluations of the favorability and fairness of benefits, taxes, and economic and social policies were combined to generate overall indicators of favorability and distributive and procedural fairness. These indicators were then used as independent variables in a regression equation that examined the basis of public support for the President and the political system.

The results of the regression analysis are shown in Table 7-4. They reveal that fairness judgments were important determinants of both Presidential and system evaluations. For both types of evaluation, respondents were primarily concerned with judgments of fairness, not with the extent to which benefits, taxes, or policies were favorable to them. In the case of Presidential evaluations, fairness explained 19% of the variance beyond that explained by favorability; in the case of system evaluations, fairness explained 28% of the variance not explained by favorability. Outcome favorability judgments, on the other hand, explained only about 1% of the variance not explained by fairness judgments. In other words, when people evaluate government leaders and institutions they appear to do so primarily in terms of fairness.

TABLE 7-4. Justice and the Endorsement of Political Authorities

	Evaluation of President Reagan		Trust in the national government	
	Beta	R^2	Beta	R^2
Outcome level				
Absolute	.09	.08***	.11	.08***
Relative	−.04	.00	−.04	.00
Total	—	.08***	—	.07***
Fairness				
Distributional	.11*	.18***	−.01	.03**
Procedural	.47***	.41***	.61***	.34***
Total	—	.45***	—	.34***
Demographics				
Party	.20***	—	−.10	—
Liberalism	.16***	—	−.03	—
Age	−.07	—	.00	—
Education	.00	—	−.02	—
Race	.06	—	.00	—
Sex	.13**	—	−.05	—
Total	—	.30***	—	.00
Total	—	.54***	—	.34***
Usefulness analysis				
Outcome level beyond fairness and demographics	—	.00	—	.01***
Outcome fairness beyond level and demographics	—	.19***	—	.28***
Demographics beyond level and fairness	—	.09***	—	.00

Note. Entries in the columns marked beta are standardized regression coefficients. Entries in the columns marked R^2 are the adjusted multiple correlation coefficient.
*$p < .05$.
**$p < .01$.
***$p < .001$.

Procedural fairness mattered in evaluations of both President Reagan and the political system. In both evaluations the major concern was the fairness of the process by which benefits were distributed, tax rates determined, and economic and social policy formulated. In evaluating the President, respondents considered both distributive and procedural fairness. In the case of system evaluations, only procedural fairness was important.

These results suggest that a focus on outcomes, such as that underlying public choice theory, is too limited a basis for understanding how citizens evaluate political leaders and the political system. In making such evaluations, citizens focus heavily on issues of fairness, especially procedural fairness. Similar results were found in another series of studies examining the relationship between procedural justice and leadership evaluations (Tyler & Caine, 1981).

It is interesting to compare these findings to those of procedural justice studies in the legal arena, which we examined in Chapter 4. In both the political and legal arenas procedural justice has been shown to have impressive effects on important attitudes, and in both areas these effects are strongest in system-level evaluations. A particularly noteworthy feature of the political arena findings is the fact that procedural justice effects are found when citizens are making general evaluations of government policies. (Previous legal arena studies had shown procedural justice effects only in reactions to specific experiences.) This shows the generality of procedural justice findings and demonstrates their robustness across variations in question style and level.

IMPLICATIONS

The major implication of the Tyler, Rasinski, and McGraw study is that the image of the citizen used in political analysis should include a fairness component. In particular, assessments of citizen judgments of the fairness of decision-making procedures must be made. Altering our image of the citizen to incorporate moral concerns such as questions of justice and fairness requires changes in the way we think about many political issues. For example, citizen dissatisfaction with government should be thought of as arising at least in part from views about the fairness of the policy-making process, rather than arising solely from the failure of government to solve problems or provide benefits. This is especially true of evaluations of the political system itself, evaluations that have been found to be linked to anti-system actions such as rioting (Muller, 1979) and to positive actions such as obeying the law (Tyler, 1987b).

Several more general questions are raised by these results. First, if much of citizens' dissatisfaction with government results from perceived injustice and, as public opinion polls suggest, if dissatisfaction is high, does this mean that the public believes the political process to be procedurally unjust? Are people personally experiencing injustice in their dealings with government officials or are they reacting to a general culture of mistrust, perhaps created by mass media accounts of government actions? It is also important to determine the extent to which judgments that government is unfair have some objective basis. Is public alienation a reflection of an actual decline in the quality of the political system's decision-making procedures? It may be that public support for government can be increased only through improvements in the quality of government decision-making.

Policy Implications

These findings suggest that political leaders should recognize that citizens are evaluating them in terms of judgments about their fairness. When formulating public policy, leaders should be concerned with using procedures that citizens will view as fair. In addition, policies should be presented to citizens as having been developed in a fair manner and as being in accord with citizens' views about distributive fairness. Although citizens may react to policies in part on the basis of personal gains and losses from those policies, their sense of distributive and procedural justice will act as a cushion of support, leading them to accord some support to policies and leaders if they view them as having acted fairly.

The view of the citizen we are articulating has positive implications for government leaders attempting to follow policies that solve social problems. Leaders may often feel unable to advance policies that involve sacrifice or loss on the part of some portion of the citizenry because they believe that their policies will be evaluated by each citizen only in terms of his or her own self-interest. In fact, the results of procedural justice research suggest that leaders are freer than they imagine to follow policies that lead to high-quality, if occasionally painful, solutions. This freedom comes from the receptivity of citizens to justifications based on procedural and distributive justice.

An example of the difficulties of a political strategy based on the assumption that citizens are responsive only to their self-interest is provided by recent efforts to cut the federal budget. Congressmen, relying on their view that cuts in programs favorable to their constituents would hurt them politically, have been reluctant to make spending cuts. As a result, budget reform has been difficult. What has been overlooked is the possibility that citizens, who are quite responsive to fairness issues, would accept an overall package of cuts if they believed it was arrived at fairly and if they thought it distributed costs fairly.

But this same procedural focus can on occasion have negative consequences for citizens. Because people focus on process and procedure rather than on outcomes, leaders may be better able to beguile citizens into accepting policies that benefit the leaders and harm the citizens than they could if people focused on outcomes (Tyler, Rasinski, & Spodick, 1985). Leaders might induce citizens to accept objectively poor outcomes or poor procedures by leading citizens to develop a "false consciousness" about what is actually in their best interest.

Both the positive and the negative potential consequences of procedural justice effects outlined above depend on leaders' correctly identifying what it is that leads people to see decision-making procedures as fair. At the present time, applications of procedural justice in the political arena must rely on intuitions about what constitutes procedural fairness; there has been little research on what citizens view as fair in political procedures.

It may also be the case that the priorities of leaders will differ from those of the general public, resulting in the implementation of policies that do not accord with citizen views about fairness. Those charged with designing welfare programs may, for example, be concerned with issues of efficiency and may limit opportunities for potential recipients to express themselves. Citizens may see efficiency issues as less important and may want the opportunity for an extended presentation of their cases. In such a situation leaders may understand public views about fairness but be unwilling to implement procedures that reflect those views.

How to Make Public Policy

The findings outlined above suggest that it is important that public policies be formed in such a way as to be favorably received by the public. One obvious implication of procedural justice research is that procedural aspects of the policy formation, implementation, and operation should be made clear to the public. In evaluating a policy citizens will focus on how it was made and how it will work. These aspects of policy-making should, therefore, be in the foreground.

A recent example of a policy that fails to emphasize process issues is the use of comparable worth standards as a solution to sex discrimination in pay. Comparable worth proposals highlight the distributive justice goal of equal pay for equal work, regardless of sex. But advocates of the policy have not presented the public with clear procedures that show how comparable worth will be implemented. Instead, the distributive justice goal the policy seeks to attain has been emphasized. The research described in this chapter would suggest that this outcome-oriented strategy would hinder public acceptance of the policy. In fact, the policy has not been widely accepted by the public, and a frequent question raised about it is how it will operate procedurally.

Of course, specification of procedures will help in the acceptance of a public policy only if the procedures accord with public sentiments about what is fair. One example of a policy the procedures of which might sometimes violate public conceptions of fairness is affirmative action. Studies of procedural justice have shown that people see consistency of treatment across persons as an important aspect of fair process (see Barrett-Howard & Tyler, 1986). Affirmative action, a policy that deliberately creates inconsistency of treatment by giving preferential treatment to some people over others, violates traditional conceptions of procedural justice. In these circumstances, more detailed specification of affirmative action procedures would not necessarily help the policy gain acceptance and might actually hurt it. It is certainly true that affirmative action policies have encountered widespread public hostility (Austin, Friedman, Martz, Hooe, & Ball, 1978). This hostility is congruent with the idea that citizens are unlikely to support a policy with the goal of distributive justice if they see the process by which that goal is achieved as contrary to their conceptions of procedural justice.

On the basis of the argument we have been making, we would hypothesize that hostility to comparable worth or affirmative action policies could be lessened if the policy included procedures that conformed more closely with public conceptions of fairness. There is evidence to support this hypothesis in some recent work by Rubert Nacoste (1985). Nacoste presented subjects with two affirmative action policies: "discrimination in reverse" and "preferential treatment." In the Nacoste study discrimination in reverse referred to a distribution-based policy that assigned opportunities entirely on the basis of ethnic or gender group membership (that is, a quota system). Preferential treatment was a policy that awarded greater opportunities to minority group members only when they were qualified for the position in question. The preferential treatment procedure is more consistent with the procedural justice standards held by the public. Nacoste found that the preferential treatment procedure was judged to be fairer and was more acceptable to the subjects in his study.

One way in which leaders can increase public support for policies is to provide a justification for those policies that links them to public conceptions of fair process and fair outcomes. Research has shown that justifications can, at least to some extent, excuse procedures that have resulted in poor outcomes (Bies, 1986; Bies & Shapiro, 1987), especially if the excuse itself appeals to a sense of procedural justice (Folger, Rosenfield, and Robinson, 1983). Thus the acceptance of social change could be maximized by presenting policies in ways that emphasize that both the policy change process and the new policies themselves conform to public conceptions of procedural justice. The general message of our analyses of policy-making in this section is that policy can and must be justified not only in terms of its distributive fairness but also in terms of its procedural fairness.

Procedural Justice and Political Behavior

Underlying the study of political evaluations is the belief that such evaluations actually influence what citizens do. One of the clearest instances of this assumption is the widely held view that citizens' evaluations of political leaders influence their voting behavior. If this is true, then an examination of voting choices should find that they are influenced by judgments of the relative fairness of the candidates in an election.

Rasinski and Tyler (in press) recently conducted two surveys to examine the influence of fairness judgments on vote choices in the 1984 presidential election. The first survey was conducted in August 1984, early in the campaign, the second during the final days of the campaign (October and November). Both surveys were of random samples of citizens; of Chicago in the first study, of Cook County, Illinois, in the second.

Both surveys focused on the area of social policies and pitted voters' judgments of their own self-interest and the self-interest of their group against their assessments of the fairness of the two presidential candidates. Partisanship was included as a control variable in the analyses. Since the dependent variable was a dichotomous choice, logistic regression analyses were used to analyze the factors affecting vote choice. The results are shown in Table 7-5. They indicate that judgments about the relative distributive and procedural fairness of the two candidates influenced vote choice. Of the two types of fairness judgment, procedural justice was the more important factor. As would be expected, party membership also had a substantial effect on vote choice.

These findings raise an interesting question for the study of the 1984 presidential election. The data suggest that fairness influenced vote choice more than self-interest. An examination of the fairness ratings, shown in Table 7-6, indicates that Walter Mondale was generally viewed as a fairer decision maker than Ronald Reagan, yet Reagan won the election, and by a large margin. This seems to contradict the suggestion that fairness influenced vote choice. However, the results of the study are not so contradictory as they seem. First, the studies were conducted in Chicago and Cook County, where Reagan did not win the election by the same wide margin he held in the country as a whole. In addition, the election involved many issues other than social and economic policy-making. As the incumbent President, Reagan came to the election campaign with advantages in terms of name recognition and access to the media. He also benefited from his personal charisma and his image as a successful leader in handling the economy. All of these factors worked in his favor in the election. The data from this survey suggest that Mondale was viewed as fairer in his policy-making procedures and that

TABLE 7-5. Logistic Regression of Vote Choice

	Vote For Reagan	
	Survey 1 August	Survey 2 November
Distributive fairness	Lambda	Lambda
Reagan	3.290(20.92)	.436(.370)
Mondale	−2.398(1.675)	−.454(.362)
Procedural fairness		
Reagan	5.561(2.780)*	2.024(.731)**
Mondale	−3.349(2.433)	−1.285(.605)*
Benefit		
Past	.661(1.392)	.324(.564)
Reagan	2.800(1.486)	1.432(.707)*
Mondale	−1.440(1.278)	−1.491(.543)**
Background characteristics		
Party Identification	.954(.366)*	.761(.201)***
Ideology	−.011(.392)	−.064(.245)
Race	2.472(1.334)	1.752(.730)*
Income	−.029(.322)	.025(.181)
Education	.160(.345)	−.120(.191)
Age	.039(.033)	−.033(.019)
Sex	.596(1.004)	.277(.570)
G² (df)	36.26 (153)	101.37 (.343)

Note. Entries are unstandardized logistic regression coefficients (Lambda) with standard errors in parentheses. The difference in magnitude of the fairness coefficients between the two surveys is due to the use of different scales of measurement.
*p < .05.
**p < .01.
***p < .001.
Source. Rasinski and Tyler (in press).

TABLE 7-6. Fairness and the Presidential Candidates

	Reagan	Mondale
Distributive justice		
He would distribute benefits in a way fair to all or most people	40%	52%
You would receive at least your fair share of benefits	55%	72%
General welfare of old people, children, sick and poor would increase if he were elected	64%	92%
Procedural justice		
Would usually consider the views of all sides before making decisions	38%	42%
Would give citizens a great deal or some opportunity to express their views before making decisions	48%	68%
Would be equally influenced by the views of all citizens in making decisions	22%	42%
In making appointments would choose people who would give equal weight to the views of all citizens	27%	54%

Source. Rasinski and Tyler (in press).

he gained from this relative fairness judgment. He did not gain enough, though, to overcome Reagan's many other advantages in the election.

It is also interesting to note that citizens did not agree about who was the fairer candidate. In a further study of public views about Reagan and Mondale (Rasinski, 1987) it was found that citizens who endorsed a conservative, equity-based ideology viewed Reagan as fairer, whereas those who endorsed a liberal, equality-based, ideology viewed Mondale as fairer. Both liberals and conservatives view fairness as important, but the two groups differed in how they defined fairness. In fact, Rasinski found that the political judgments of conservatives were more strongly influenced by issues of procedural justice, as they defined it, than were those of liberals. Liberals were influenced by procedural justice issues, but they relied more on judgments of distributive justice and less on judgments of procedural justice than did conservatives.

Although vote choice is a natural focus of attention, it is not the only important political behavior that might be related to procedural justice. Rasinski (1986) examined the role of fairness in two other types of political behavior: taking political action in response to some specific policy or benefit and being generally active in political campaigns. His study was based on a survey of 398 residents of Chicago. The design of the study was similar to that used in the Rasinski and Tyler studies except that the political behaviors studied were different.

The results of the study are shown in Table 7-7. Policy-related behavior refers to actions in response to some particular policy or benefit; general campaign activity to involvement in political activities. The results of the study suggest that, as with voting behavior, policy-related activity was linked to assessments of procedural fairness. In deciding whether to act in response to particular policies citizens are more concerned about the fairness of the process by which the policy was made than about either the actual consequences of the policy for them or its distributive fairness. Regardless of whether they benefited from the policy, citizens accepted policy decisions if they believed that the game was being played fairly. Those who did not view the game as being played fairly complained.

On the other hand, general political activity was based more heavily on long-term individual characteristics than on any reaction to contemporary policy issues. The results of this study accord with suggestions that general political activity is a "life-style" characteristic that does not relate closely to contemporary issues (Kinder & Sears, 1985). Some people are involved in politics, others are not. This difference is clearly linked, however, to background characteristics. Those characteristics that seem particularly important are income and education. On the other hand, vote choice and responses to particular policy issues—behaviors en-

TABLE 7-7. Logistic Regression Analysis of the Effect
of Outcome and Justice Concerns

	General activity			Policy-related activity		
	Lambda	SE	p	Lambda	SE	p
Economic outcomes						
Global self-report	−.13	.13	ns	−.24	.13	.0529
Tally	.13	.09	ns	.14	.09	ns
Relative to past	.17	.18	ns	−.11	.18	ns
Relative to others	.42	.27	ns	.12	.27	ns
Economic justice						
Procedural	.32	.17	.0589	.42	.17	.0103
Distributive	.46	.29	ns	.23	.28	ns
Background						
Party identification	.14	.10	ns	.20	.10	.0503
Ideology	.04	.15	ns	−.03	.15	ns
Race	−.30	.28	ns	.08	.27	ns
Income	.22	.09	.0096	.00	.08	ns
Education	.14	.08	.0699	.18	.08	.0172
Age	−.003	.008	ns	−.00	.01	ns
Sex	−.15	.25	ns	−.60	.25	.0170
G square	398.11		.0002	405.34		.0001
df	304			304		

Note. Entries are unstandardized regression coefficients (Lambda), corresponding standard errors (SE), and levels of significance (p).
Source. Rasinski (1986).

gaged in by larger proportions of the population—are very much related to fairness issues.

It would be interesting to know what leads citizens to take anti-system actions such as rioting. Muller and Jukam (1977) explored the antecedents of violent anti-system behavior among 2663 German workers. They found that process-based judgments about the political system were the key factor in anti-system actions. When workers lacked faith in the basic processes of government they were more likely to take a series of actions that were destructive of the political order. These findings are congruent with the general implication of procedural justice research in that process-based, procedural justice judgments have been found to be a major factor in system-level evaluations. Procedural justice may be the key force that binds members of a political group together. Even those disadvantaged by a particular decision will maintain their allegiance to a political system if they feel that the system's decision-making procedures are generally fair.

It is also interesting to ask whether those who are chronically disadvantaged within a group, such as members of the lower class, also focus primarily on issues of procedural justice. The research evidence (Tyler, Rasinski, & McGraw, 1985) suggests that people of all income levels place more emphasis on procedural justice than distributive justice in forming evaluations of government. However, there is some evidence that the disadvantaged place less emphasis on procedural justice than do those who are better off (Tyler & McGraw, 1986). Similarly, Rasinski (1987) found that conservatives focused more heavily on issues of procedural fairness in evaluating government than did liberals. These findings suggest that procedural concerns may be more important to those who are well-integrated into society.

WHAT IS PROCEDURAL JUSTICE IN POLITICS?

Up to this point the case we have been making has been directed primarily toward establishing that procedural justice is a factor of some importance in the political arena. We have not confronted a second question that is of concern once the importance of procedural justice has been established: what do people mean by procedural justice in political contexts? Unfortunately, there is very little research on which we can draw to answer this question, so our comments will be somewhat speculative.

VOICE

One clear finding from research in other arenas is that people like to have an opportunity to present their views before policy decisions are made. This desire for voice or process control has already been discussed in terms of research in the legal arena, and there is evidence that it is equally important in the political arena. Tyler, Rasinski, and Spodick (study 3; 1985) conducted a scenario study in which they varied the opportunity citizens had to present their views to a government council before budget decisions were made. They found that greater opportunities for voice heightened assessments of fairness and evaluations of the council.

Political voice represents the opportunity for citizens to express their views about government decisions before policies are formed. Such opportunities for free expression of views seem to be as highly prized and as strongly linked to the assessment of procedural justice in the political arena as in judicial settings. The value that citizens attach to voice suggests that political allegiance is enhanced by allowing open argument about government policy. Allowing citizens to express their opinions and disagreements leads to feelings that fair process has occurred in decision making, promoting diffuse support for the political system. These findings are congruent with suggestions by political psychologists that tolerance for political expression by minority groups can add stability to political systems (McClosky & Brill, 1983; Sullivan *et al.*, 1982).

Tyler, Rasinski, and Spodick (1985) also found that citizens value opportunities to speak whether or not this voice is linked to influence over the decisions made by the political body. As noted in Chapter 5, the key to the effectiveness of voice in enhancing perceived fairness appears to be the judgment that citizens' expressions are given due consideration (Tyler & McGraw, 1986).

The capacity of voice without decision control to raise procedural justice reinforces our earlier suggestion that there are dangers inherent in citizens' strong concern with procedural justice when evaluating political leaders or their decisions. Leaders may be able to create the impression that citizens have a say in the decision-making process without actually giving them any real control. The possibility that leaders might use voice to try to mislead citizens has been suggested in radical critiques of American politics (Edelman, 1964; Scheingold, 1974).

Tyler and McGraw (1986) have suggested that citizens' acceptance of voice without decision control could be the basis for solving a traditionally puzzling problem in political science; why the poor do not revolt. In American society, as in most societies, those without wealth outnumber those with wealth. In a democracy, the large group of poorer citizens could use their political power to vote for massive income redistribution, yet they do not do so. A number of political psychologists have attempted to explain this absence of political mobilization by reference to the confusion the poor feel about appropriate norms of distributive justice in American society (Hochschild, 1981; Lane, 1962). Tyler and McGraw suggest that the real answer is that, like all citizens, the poor focus on procedures instead of on outcomes.[2] In the United States the procedures for allocating goods involve, at least in theory, a free and open contest in which those with intelligence and ability can rise to the top through their own efforts. This procedure seems fair to people. A focus on distributive justice, that is, on the fairness of the outcomes of such a procedure, might reveal that most people actually make little progress beyond the social position in which they begin life. However, because citizens focus on the seemingly fair procedure rather than on its unfair outcomes, they accept the system, without much careful attention to whether the procedure actually leads to positive outcomes for them or other members of their group (Lane, 1986).

It is important not to overstate the case. Although citizens focus on

---

[2]As noted earlier, although the poor care less about procedural justice than do the rich, they still do care about procedural justice more than they care about distributive justice.

procedures in evaluating the social and political system, they also pay attention to issues of distributive justice. As a result, the procedural justice explanation cannot completely account for the political inactivity of the poor. The disadvantaged may also feel that political actions would be ineffective, or they may be so busy coping with disadvantage that they have no time to think about strategies for change.

A THEORY OF FAIR POLITICAL PROCESS

Our discussion has focused on one source of procedural fairness in political settings: voice. Lane (1986) has recently attempted to generate a more general set of criteria of procedural fairness in political settings. His list includes four such criteria. The first is the extent to which a process recognizes and reinforces the citizen's dignity. Lane argues that citizens value procedures that treat them in a manner that recognizes their rights and builds their self-respect as persons and citizens.

A second procedural criterion is the efficiency or ease of operation of a procedure. Citizens do not like to be subjected to decision-making procedures that are time-consuming and laborious. Instead, they value methods of decision-making that are simple, efficient, and quick.

Third, citizens would like political decisions to be made by leaders who share common values with them. This means that those making decisions should accept the basic set of moral and political beliefs that are held by the citizenry.

Fourth, the procedure should lead to fair decisions. According to Lane, citizens judge a process by whether it results in fair decisions. This criterion is already familiar to us from the legal literature. As we noted in Chapter 5, outcome fairness is often a factor in judgments about the fairness of procedures.

Lane's list of procedural criteria is the only one that has been developed to date in the political arena. Unfortunately, it has not yet been used in research and therefore the importance of his four criteria has not yet been tested. Establishing the meaning of procedural justice in the political arena is an important task for future research.

Chapter 8

Procedural Justice in Organizations

In previous chapters we have made reference to potential applications of procedural justice theory and research to organizational settings. Like courts and political institutions, organizations must make decisions concerning the evaluation of individuals and groups, the allocation of resources and outcomes, and the resolution of disputes. And like other social entities, organizations develop procedures that specify how information is to be gathered and used to make these decisions, who is authorized to make decisions, and how decisions are to be executed. We discuss in this chapter psychological reactions to organizational procedures. Research and theory to date show that, although some special considerations arise in procedural justice in organizations, by and large the same basic psychological processes occur here as in other procedural contexts.

PROCEDURES IN ORGANIZATIONS

It is likely that more people encounter formal decision-making procedures in the course of their work than in any other area of their lives. Procedures are a ubiquitous feature of organizations. Most of us have been exposed to organizational procedures for hiring new employees, for evaluating and rewarding performance, and for allocating organizational responsibilities and resources. Other common organizational procedures are those used to decide whether employees will be transferred among various offices and divisions of the organization, to decide whether an employee will be fired or laid off, to set goals for the future performance of individuals and organizational entities, and to manage conflict within the organization.[1] Procedural justice researchers have

[1]Because we have reviewed research on organizational dispute resolution procedures and practices in Chapters 4 and 5, we will focus here on organizational procedures other than those used to resolve disputes. This certainly does not mean that dispute resolution

conducted studies on most of these kinds of procedure, and have found that procedural justice judgments play a major role in affecting organizational attitudes and behavior.

From the point of view of procedural justice research, one of the very nice things about organizational procedures is that they vary more widely than do the procedures used to make political or legal decisions. Because organizations are to a large extent free to set up their procedures as they see fit, there is substantial variation in the procedures used by different organizations to address the same question. For example, one of the authors has experienced professional-level performance evaluation procedures in four different organizations: two university psychology departments, one government agency, and one private corporation. All used rather formal procedures for evaluating performance, giving feedback, and deciding salary increases, but each procedure was quite different from the others in terms of the complexity of the procedure, the organizational level at which the decision was made, the amount of voice mandated by the procedure, and the specificity of the criteria considered. In some instances the variation was hardly what one would expect from popular stereotypes about the organizations in question; the government agency used by far the simplest procedure and one of the universities used the most elaborate.

Additional variation in organizational procedures arises from the variety of decisions addressed by the procedures. It is not at all unusual to see procedures within the same organization varying substantially along dimensions relevant to procedural justice. The same organization, for example, might allow employees substantial input in performance evaluation decisions but little input in deciding how organizational resources should be allocated, even though the allocation decision might actually have greater impact on the employees' day-to-day work experience than the performance evaluation. Sometimes there is variation in the procedures used to make the same decision with respect to different groups in the organization; for example, clerical personnel might be subject to a performance evaluation procedure that does not permit voice while professional personnel might be accorded considerable voice in their performance evaluation procedure. The variability of organizational procedures can create natural variation that can be used to good purpose in field studies of procedural justice. Later in this chapter we will describe a field study by Lissak that used natural variation among

---

procedures are not an important part of organizational procedural justice. Work by such researchers as Blair Sheppard and Roy Lewicki demonstrates that dispute resolution is an essential part of management and that organizational settings are fruitful locales for the study of third-party procedures and their psychological consequences.

posting decision procedures in the Canadian Armed Forces to test the generality of the voice-to-fairness relation.

For those of us interested in the basic psychology of procedural justice, the variability of organizational procedures makes organizations an exciting context for study and analysis. The variety of organizational procedures suggests previously unexplored variables that might affect procedural justice judgments. For example, Leventhal's (1980) analysis of procedural characteristics that might influence procedural justice judgments, described in Chapter 6, was based in part on his own experience with a university procedure for allocating intramural research funds and his consideration of how the procedure might have been viewed by those who encountered it. As we look at variations in real or possible organizational procedures we can see new dimensions that should be included in theory and research on procedural justice.

There is another interesting aspect of the study of procedural justice in organizations that make this context exciting. In many studies of procedural justice in organizations, it has been possible to study procedural justice effects on performance, allowing us to examine another class of behaviors that might be affected by procedural justice experiences. Compared to the behavioral consequences that appear in other contexts, such as compliance in law or voting behavior in politics, performance is easier to observe directly. As we will see below, research that has examined the relationship between procedural justice and performance has shown that the experience of procedural justice does affect performance, sometimes in a straightforward fashion and sometimes not.

Before we begin a description of the "state of the art" of procedural justice in organizations, it might be helpful to consider some topics that have traditionally been of interest to organizational psychologists and that have some bearing on procedural justice. Especially relevant are the study of distributive fairness and the study of participatory decision-making procedures, which were of interest to organizational psychologists well before anyone attempted to apply procedural justice ideas to organizational procedures. Our understanding of procedural justice phenomena in organizations (and elsewhere) benefits from the results of these areas of research.

PROCEDURES AND FAIRNESS IN ORGANIZATIONAL PSYCHOLOGY

Equity and Motivation

We mentioned in Chapter 2 that theory and research on distributive justice helped set the stage for the study of procedural justice as a topic of interest in its own right in social psychology; much the same was the case in organizational psychology. Adams' (1963) equity theory has received a great deal of attention with regard to issues of motivation in organizations. Adams theorized that deviations from proportional reward would produce a negative motivational state, which he termed "inequity distress," and that one response to this distress would be to vary the level of one's contributions to the organization so as to reestablish equity. Thus, according to Adams' theory, if there were no other easier way to reestablish equity, workers who were unfairly overpaid would increase their level of effort, and those who were unfairly underpaid would reduce their level of effort. To the extent that performance is linked to effort, inequity could thus produce increases or decreases in performance.

A review of the considerable literature on distributive justice and motivation in organizational settings is beyond the scope of this book; the reader is referred to excellent reviews by Greenberg (1982; 1984; 1986a). By and large, research has borne out the positive relationship between distributive fairness and performance that is one of the key elements of equity theory. As is the case in other areas of justice research and theory, however, the literature on distributive justice in organizations has shown a need for greater sophistication about both the causes and the consequences of distributive fairness judgments. We now know that proportionality is only one rule for judging the fairness of outcomes (cf. Greenberg, 1986a). There are some circumstances in which distributions that allocate outcomes equally or that allocate outcomes according to needs are judged fair, to mention two of the most potent alternatives to proportionality rules for fair allocations. There is also considerable evidence that the performance effects of inequitable payment are more complex than Adams thought. Although some studies have shown the effects predicted by equity theory, other studies have shown either no effect or, occasionally, effects opposite to those predicted by the theory (Campbell & Pritchard, 1976).

PARTICIPATION AND SATISFACTION

Another shared interest of procedural justice researchers and organizational psychologists is a concern with the relationship between participation in decision making and satisfaction. We have seen in the preceding chapters that one of the most potent determinants of the procedural fairness of a social decision-making procedure is the extent to which those affected by the decision are allowed to participate in the decision-making process through the exercise of process control or voice. The research we have reviewed in the previous chapters on legal and political procedures has also shown that satisfaction is one of the principal consequences of procedural fairness. These two findings fit well with the longstanding interest of organizational psychologists in the connection between participation and satisfaction.

Folger and Greenberg have reviewed the literature on participation in organizational decision making and discussed the relevance of procedural justice to that literature (Folger & Greenberg, 1985; Greenberg & Folger, 1983), and we will not duplicate their effort here. It is worth noting that procedural justice research has the potential to explain some of the complexity seen in participation effects (cf. Locke & Schweiger, 1979) by offering a finer understanding of the psychology of different types of participation than previously has been available. For example, as our knowledge of the psychological consequences of voice procedures has increased, we have discovered that there are some circumstances in which fair procedures do not enhance satisfaction. We describe below some research that shows that voice-based procedural justice effects can be attenuated or reversed when the procedure is weak or when there is social criticism of the procedure. This finding may explain the occasional studies that have shown negative attitudinal effects for participatory procedures in organizations.

The real proof of the value of a procedural justice perspective in explaining and understanding organizational behavior lies not in its similarity to ideas that have long been accepted in organizational psychology, but rather in its capacity to generate new and interesting findings. We turn now to a discussion of the consequences of procedural fairness judgments for organizational attitudes and behaviors. After we have reviewed the studies that show that procedural fairness has important consequences for organizations, we will describe the factors that have been shown to lead to the experience of procedural justice or injustice.

CONSEQUENCES OF PROCEDURAL JUSTICE IN ORGANIZATIONS

ORGANIZATIONAL ATTITUDES

Alexander and Ruderman (1987) studied the relationships between justice judgments and organizational attitudes in a survey of more than 2,000 federal employees. Initial factor analyses of twenty fairness-related items produced three procedural justice factors (participation, performance appraisal fairness, and appeals procedure fairness) and three distributive justice factors (pay fairness, promotion–performance contingency, and sanctions for poor performance). Alexander and Ruderman studied six organizational variables that they thought might be affected by fairness concerns: job satisfaction, conflict and harmony in the workplace, trust in (upper-level) management, turnover intention, perceptions of tension and stress, and evaluations of supervisors. They examined the relationship between the various procedural and distributive justice factors and the six organizational variables using a multiple regression approach.

Table 8-1 shows the unique contribution of each type of justice judgment to the six variables. (The effects of each type of justice judgment were tested by entering the entire set of factors related to that type of justice judgment in the regression equation). Alexander and Ruderman found that five of the six variables showed substantial justice effects; only perceptions of tension and stress were unrelated to either procedural or distributive justice. Of the five variables affected by justice concerns, four were affected more by procedural justice than by distributive justice. Job satisfaction, evaluations of supervisors, reports of conflict or harmony, and trust in management all showed substantial unique effects of procedural justice and only minor effects for distributive justice. The remaining variable, turnover intention, showed a stronger effect for distributive justice than for procedural justice.

The Alexander and Ruderman study shows that important organizational attitudes are affected by procedural justice judgments. The effects of procedural justice ranged from modest to moderate; 10% to 21% of the variance in the organizational variables was attributable entirely to procedural justice. The appearance of the effects in a sample as large and diverse as that used in this study is impressive. Other studies have

TABLE 8-1. Procedural and Distributive Fairness as Predictors of Organizational Attitudes

Dependent variables	Procedural fairness R^2	Distributive fairness R^2	Total R^2
Job satisfaction	.105*	.019*	.189*
Evaluation of supervisor	.212*	.029*	.375*
Conflict–Harmony	.144*	.020*	.245*
Turnover intention	.009*	.134*	.142*
Trust in management	.114*	.046*	.261*
Tension–Stress	.001	.000	.001

Note. Entries in Procedural fairness and Distributive fairness columns are incremental R^2 when the three predictors in each fairness category are entered after the predictors in the other category.
*$p < .001$

produced findings congruent with those of the Alexander and Ruderman study. Lissak, Mendes, and Lind (1983) studied the relationship between procedural and distributive justice and job satisfaction among Canadian Armed Forces enlisted personnel. They found that procedural justice showed a larger unique contribution to job satisfaction than did distributive justice. Additional support for the effect of procedural justice on evaluations of supervisors is seen in the results of two recent laboratory experiments. Experimental conditions that produced high ratings of procedural justice (by affording subjects voice in performance evaluation or by providing a more accurate procedure for monitoring performance) also produced high ratings of the subjects' supervisor (Greenberg, 1987b; Kanfer, Sawyer, Earley, & Lind, 1987).

On the basis of these studies and the studies described in previous chapters on the consequences of procedural justice in law and politics, we expect procedural justice judgments to have substantial effects on a variety of important organizational attitudes. The general finding seen in all of these studies has been that procedural justice is a remarkably potent determinant of affective reactions to decision making and that procedural justice has especially strong effects on attitudes about institutions and authorities, as opposed to attitudes about the specific outcome in question. These findings lead us to suspect that, in addition to job satisfaction and evaluations of leaders in organizations, a number of other organizational attitudes are affected by procedural justice judgments. For reasons that we present in Chapter 10, we believe that attitudes toward the organization as a whole, including such things as organizational commitment, loyalty, and work group cohesiveness, are strongly affected by procedural justice judgments. Fair procedures, we hypothesize, are a critical aspect of the quality of work life and are well-nigh essential to good employer–employee relations. Organizations that ignore procedural justice concerns run the risk of engendering negative organizational attitudes, dissatisfaction with organizational outcomes and decisions, noncompliance with rules and procedures, and, in some instances, lower performance.

DISTRIBUTIVE FAIRNESS AND OUTCOME SATISFACTION

The relationship between procedural justice, distributive justice, and outcome satisfaction has received considerable attention from procedural justice researchers interested in organizational settings. One reason for this attention is the discovery quite early of an apparent contradiction of the usual finding of a positive relationship between fair procedures and judgments of distributive justice. Folger (1977), in the first procedural justice study to examine allocation procedures (as opposed to dispute resolution procedures) found what he later termed a "frustration effect": in one condition in his experiment an inequitable outcome from an ostensibly fairer procedure was judged *less* fair than the same outcome from an ostensibly less fair procedure. The frustration effect has not been observed frequently, but it deserves attention because it stands in such sharp contrast to the more usual effect of procedural justice—higher distributive fairness judgments under fair procedures.

Let us begin our consideration of the frustration effect with a description of Folger's (1977) initial study. In a laboratory experiment, sixth-grade boys were confronted with an allocation situation in which their payment for work on a task was decided by another boy, who was designated their manager and who supposedly allocated money to the subject and to himself from a constant sum. Thus the allocator and the subject were in what Thibaut and Kelley (1959) term a severely noncorrespondent relationship. The allocation was repeated over a number of trials. In the conditions of interest to the current discussion, the allocation to the subject was always inequitably low. In some conditions the subject's outcomes were constant across the series of allocations; in other conditions the subject's outcomes improved across the series of allocations; always, however, the total payment was inequitable. The allocation procedure in the experiment either did or did not include a limited opportunity for voice. Subjects in the voice condition were permitted to notify the allocator of the division of money that they deemed fair, but subjects in the mute condition were not permitted to communicate at all with the allocator. In the voice condition, the communication was prompted by an apparently off-the-cuff suggestion by the experimenter following the second of ten work trials that the subject send the allocator a copy of a card showing the subject's preferred percentage split.

Table 8-2 shows the levels of perceived procedural and distributive fairness observed in the Folger experiment. When the subjects' outcomes were inequitable and constant, normal procedural justice effects were seen—the voice condition resulted in greater perceived procedural fairness and greater perceived distributive fairness than did the mute condition. However, when the subjects' outcomes were inequitable and improving, the (rather small) procedural justice advantage of the voice condition was not reflected in the distributive fairness ratings. Instead a frustration effect was seen—perceived distributive fairness was substantially lower in the voice condition than in the mute condition. As can be seen from the table, the voice effect on procedural fairness is attenuated in the improving outcome condition, suggesting that the negative reaction to the outcome may have carried over to reduce the perceived fairness of the voice procedure itself.

TABLE 8-2. Procedural and Distributive
Fairness Judgments by Recipients
of Inequitable Allocations

Trend in allocations	Allocation procedure	
	Voice	Mute
Procedural fairness rating		
Allocations constant	4.7	3.4
Allocations improving	4.5	4.3
Distributive fairness rating		
Allocations constant	4.0	2.2
Allocations improving	2.6	4.3

Note. Higher values indicate greater perceived fairness. From Folger (1977).

Cohen (1985) has suggested that the frustration effect occurs when recipients of an allocation recognize that the allocator has a vested interest in the allocation, prompting the recipients to believe that the apparently fair, high participation process is being used to seduce them into accepting a self-serving allocation by the allocator. Cohen points out that the enhancement of distributive fairness by procedural fairness is found almost universally in studies of legal procedures, where the decision maker has no vested interest in a particular outcome, and that the frustration effect appeared in the first study to examine a hierarchical, business-like allocation setting, where the allocator received whatever he did not pay to the subject. In other words, Cohen suggests that when the allocator and the recipient are in a noncorrespondent relationship it is likely that the recipient will see voice procedures as an insincere attempt to give the allocation the trappings of fairness rather than a real attempt to solicit views. According to Cohen, when this happens, the recipient will not experience any enhancement of procedural fairness from the voice procedure, and he or she will be likely to view the allocation outcome as unfair and dissatisfying.

Folger *et al.* (1979) conducted two experiments that attempted to replicate the frustration effect seen in Folger's initial study. Subjects in the experiments were female high school and college students. Both experiments manipulated the procedure used to allocate pay for performing a task along the same lines as did the Folger experiment. The subjects, who always received an inequitable payment, either were or were not given an opportunity to send a card with allocation preferences to the allocator. In the first experiment, this voice versus mute procedure manipulation was crossed by a manipulation of the extent to which the allocator might be tempted to bias her allocation and by a manipulation of other recipients' comments about the allocation. Contrary to what Cohen might have predicted, Folger *et al.* found no effect for allocator bias. They did, however, find something rather like a frustration effect when another recipient had confirmed that the allocation was inequitable, as can be seen from Table 8-3. When the inequity was confirmed, voice had no effect at all on procedural fairness, distributive fairness, or satisfaction. In contrast, when there was no comment from the other recipient, normal procedural justice effects were seen: procedural fairness, distributive fairness, and satisfaction were all enhanced by voice.

In their second experiment, Folger *et al.* used a situation in which the allocator's interests were more strongly in conflict with the subjects. In this experiment, the other recipient either confirmed the subject's belief that the allocation was inequitable or she disconfirmed that belief. Table 8-3 also shows the results of this experiment. The apparent decreases in procedural fairness, distributive fairness, and satisfaction in the inequity-confirmed *voice* condition, relative to the inequity-confirmed *mute* condition, were not significant; under the voice procedure and the inequity-disconfirmed condition the increases in all three variables were significant. Thus, as in the first experiment, there was no

TABLE 8-3. Responses of Recipients
of Inequitable Allocations

Measure	Inequity confirmed		No co-worker comment	
	Voice	Mute	Voice	Mute
Experiment 1				
Procedural fairness	7.0	6.7	8.8	5.6
Distributive fairness	6.4	4.9	7.8	6.0
Satisfaction	7.7	8.1	9.5	7.6

Measure	Inequity confirmed		Inequity disconfirmed	
	Voice	Mute	Voice	Mute
Experiment 2				
Procedural fairness	4.9	5.5	8.7	6.2
Distributive fairness	2.7	3.7	6.0	5.5
Satisfaction	6.7	7.3	7.7	7.1

Note. Higher values indicate greater perceived fairness and satisfaction.
From Folger *et al.* (1979).

straightforward frustration effect, but when there was social support for the perception that the allocation was unfair, there was an attenuation of the normal enhancement of fairness and satisfaction by voice procedures.

What can be concluded about the frustration effect? First, in its purest form—lower distributive fairness or satisfaction under ostensibly fair procedures—it is a very rare phenomenon indeed. For each of the few studies that have shown a frustration effect, many studies in organizational, legal, and political settings have shown procedural justice enhancements of the distributive fairness of and satisfaction with negative outcomes. However, the fact that similar negative satisfaction effects have been observed in studies of the effects of worker participation in decision making shows that the frustration effect is a real phenomenon and points to the importance of understanding it. We believe that it is worth noting that the voice manipulations in all of the experiments reviewed above were relatively weak; in none of the studies, so far as we can tell, were the subjects given the opportunity for full expression of their views, opinions, and values. We suspect that the attenuation and occasional reversal of normal procedural justice effects occurs under a special set of circumstances. In particular, we suggest that frustration effects will occur when the characteristics that give the procedure a procedural fairness advantage are relatively weak. When a weak procedural advantage is opposed by negative outcomes whose impact is strengthened, either by repeated disappointment in the face of rising expectations (as in the Folger, 1977, experiment) or by social support for the perception that the outcome is unfair (as in the Folger *et al.*, 1979, experiments), a rare response is instigated—the fairness of the procedure is reevaluated with an eye to discovering possible corruption in the decision-making process. When reasons are found to suspect that the procedure is indeed corrupt, a new procedural justice judgment is formed reflecting both the corrupt nature of the procedure and any nefarious motives that might be inferred from the corruption (see Lind and Lissak, 1985, for evidence of such a process). If it appears that someone is manipulating the process in an attempt to mask personal gain behind a facade of procedural justice, a particularly negative reaction will occur that can create a true frustration effect.

Our explanation of the frustration effect is similar to that suggested by Cohen (1985), but we place a great deal more emphasis on the necessity that the procedure be weak in terms of the characteristics that make it ostensibly fair. The infrequency of genuine frustration effects or attenuation of the normal procedural justice effect leads us to believe that, even under conditions of severe conflict of interest between the allocator and the recipient, any relatively strong procedural justice difference will produce higher satisfaction and distributive fairness.[2] Our reading of the literature on procedural justice in organizations and other contexts leads us to the conclusion that people are remarkably willing to accept procedures at face value. Even ad hoc justifications for otherwise objectionable inconsistencies of treatment appear to be accepted and to ameliorate discontent, especially if the justification is couched in procedural terms (Folger, Rosenfield, & Robinson, 1983). This tendency to believe that procedures function as they are said to function accounts, we believe, for the rare occurrence of frustration effects and suggests that such effects will occur only when there is overwhelming social or factual support for the supposition that the procedure is corrupt.

As we have noted, the usual finding, in organizational settings as elsewhere, has been that fair procedures enhance the perceived fairness of the outcomes they produce. A particularly striking instance of this effect is to be found in a laboratory experiment on organizational procedures by Paese (1985). Paese varied the procedure used to evaluate subjects' performance on a series of tasks and the nature of the outcomes that the subjects received. The performance evaluation procedure was either high in procedural fairness (the subjects were allowed considerable input in deciding the criteria to be used) or low in procedural fairness (no input was allowed). The subjects always received three consecutive negative outcomes, and in some conditions the outcomes were so poor that it was evident after the second outcome that the subject would never receive a positive outcome from the procedure. Thus the experiment permitted a test of whether the procedural justice enhancement of distributive fairness would persist in the face of repeated negative outcomes, and especially whether the effect would occur in the face of no prospect for positive outcomes from the procedure.

Figure 8-1 shows the distributive fairness ratings of subjects in the conditions that allowed no prospect of positive outcomes. Remarkably, the procedural justice effect appeared *after* the second negative outcome, at the very time that it became apparent to the subjects that they could never receive a favorable outcome. Even after three negative outcomes, the fair, high-input procedure produced higher distributive fairness ratings than did the unfair, low-input procedure; the apparent diminution of the effect after the third outcome was probably due to a "floor effect" on the ratings of subjects in the unfair procedure condition.

The enhancement of distributive fairness by procedural fairness has been seen in other laboratory studies and in at least two field studies in organizational settings. In a laboratory experiment, Cornelius (1985) var-

---

[2]Note, for example, that the Folger et al. (1979) experiments never showed significant frustration effects, but they did sometimes show significant procedural justice effects, even when the allocator's interests were strongly opposed to those of the subject.

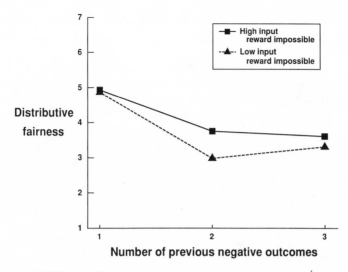

FIGURE 8-1. Effect of repeated failure on distributive fairness.

ied the consistency and accuracy of a performance evaluation procedure. He found that procedural justice judgments were affected by the
accuracy manipulation but not by the consistency manipulation. Subjects' judgments of the fairness of the outcome showed the same pattern
of effects as their procedural fairness judgments: there was an effect for
the accuracy manipulation, but no effect for the consistency manipulation. Kanfer, Sawyer, Earley, and Lind (1987) observed a similar effect in
a laboratory experiment examining performance evaluation procedures.
They found that procedures allowing subjects to express their opinions
about their performance enhanced judgments of both procedural fairness and distributive fairness. Greenberg (1987b) conducted a laboratory
experiment on fairness reactions to the use of diaries in performance
appraisals. He found that both procedural and distributive justice judgments were enhanced by the use of diaries. Additional evidence for the
enhancement of distributive fairness by procedural fairness is seen in
the Folger et al. (1983) study mentioned above. In that study the discontent that otherwise accompanied unfair relative deprivation was blunted
by an explanation couched in procedural terms. Even though the explanation was brief, the invocation of procedural issues was apparently
enough to ameliorate the discontent.

Lissak (1983) reports two field studies, one of which used a randomized experimental design, that show clear procedural justice effects
on perceptions of outcome fairness. Both studies examined the fairness
judgments of enlisted personnel in the Canadian armed forces. In the

experimental study, Lissak found that judgments of the fairness of performance evaluations were higher for respondents who were evaluated under a procedure that allowed them the opportunity to present information about their performance than for respondents who were given no such opportunity. As expected, the voice procedure was seen as much more fair than the non-voice procedure. In a second, nonexperimental, study, Lissak examined reactions to personnel transfer procedures that either did or did not allow individual input concerning preferred postings. He found that respondents who were permitted input believed that their transfers were more fair than did those not permitted input, even after actual postings were controlled statistically. The distributive justice judgments mirrored similar effects on measures of procedural justice.

Thus there is substantial evidence for the enhancement of the perceived fairness of outcomes and concomitant satisfaction when procedures engender perceptions of procedural justice. Before we leave this topic, however, we should note that in organizational settings, as in legal settings, there is some question about whether the enhancement occurs for evaluations of positive, as well as negative, outcomes. Greenberg (1987a) reports a laboratory study that showed a substantial procedural justice effect for negative outcomes, but no such effect for moderate or positive outcomes. In Greenberg's study, as in legal studies showing procedural justice effects only on judgments of negative outcomes (e.g., LaTour, 1978), there is some possibility that what is happening is a "ceiling effect" that arises because all of the positive outcome ratings cluster around the highest scale intervals. As it happens, in Greenberg's study, there was simply no room on the rating scale for subjects in the moderate and positive outcome conditions to show a procedural justice effect of the magnitude seen in the negative outcome condition.

On the other hand, it is certainly possible, and perhaps likely, that under some circumstances the procedural justice effect is obliterated by a generalized hedonic glee when outcomes are positive. Future research should search for circumstances that promote or inhibit outcome-based evaluations. In the meantime, perhaps more confidence should be placed in the likelihood of procedural justice effects when outcomes are negative than when they are positive. However, it is when outcomes are negative that organizations have the greatest need to render decisions more palatable, to blunt discontent, and to give losers reasons to stay committed to the organization. Thus, the enhancement of outcome fairness and satisfaction by procedural justice is most likely to occur in precisely the situation in which such an effect is most valuable to the organization.

COMPLIANCE WITH ORGANIZATIONAL RULES AND DECISIONS

There is mounting evidence, in organizational settings as in legal settings, that fair procedures lead to greater compliance with the rules and decisions with which they are associated. We mentioned in Chapter 4 a study by Friedland *et al.* (1973) that examined compliance with rules as a function of the fairness of surveillance procedures, the penalties for rule violation, and exploitation of those subject to the rules. The Friedland *et al.* experiment showed that unfair procedures lead to higher levels of disobedience and to more "efficient" and clever disobedience than did fair procedures. This study found also that the noncompliance effect of unfair procedures was magnified when the rules were used exploitatively by those in power. A similar effect was observed in another laboratory experiment by Thibaut, Friedland, and Walker (1974), which also studied compliance with rules under a variety of conditions. Thibaut *et al.* found that when a rule-maker was seen as acting unfairly—by promulgating a decision procedure that was patently self-serving—compliance was lower than when the rule-maker was seen as acting fairly. Further, when the rule-maker had induced those subject to the rule to participate in a procedure that ultimately led to the adoption of an unfair decision rule, the rate of compliance was particularly low. Thibaut, Friedland, and Walker concluded that when participation was thought to be a sham, especially strong behavioral reactions against the procedure were instigated.

A field study by Lissak (1983) suggests that unfair procedures may carry the seeds of their own destruction. Lissak studied the relation between perceptions of procedural fairness and self-reports of attempts to subvert or avoid the decision process mandated by the procedure. The study examined the reactions of enlisted personnel in the Canadian Armed Forces to the procedure used to determine their transfers and postings. Lissak found that respondents who perceived existing procedures to be unfair were more likely to admit to attempting improper influence. Of course, it is possible that the lower procedural justice judgments were rationalizations for the use of improper channels, but Lissak's findings at least suggest that future research should look at the relation between procedural justice and adherence to procedurally mandated processes. Lissak's findings are congruent with the results of the laboratory study by Kanfer *et al.* (1987), which found that subjects were more willing to change unfair procedures than fair procedures.

Additional evidence for the relation between procedural justice and the desire to change procedures is to be found in a recent study by Greenberg (1987a). Greenberg conducted a laboratory experiment in which subjects were paid for participation in the experiment according to either a fair (performance-contingent) or unfair (essentially random) procedure. Further, the subjects were told that the source of the payment procedure was either the particular individual in charge of their session or the organization that sponsored the research. Greenberg's experiment also included a manipulation of the subject's outcome. The experiment included a behavioral measure of desire to change the procedure—subjects could take a slip of paper with a telephone number from a notice on a bulletin board that bore the legend "STOP UNFAIR EXPERIMENTS" and that urged subjects to report unfair treatment to an ethical responsibility board. Greenberg found that all of the subjects who took the telephone numbers had experienced both the unfair procedure and a low outcome. Further, most of those who took the telephone number were in the condition in which the unfair procedure had been ascribed to an organizational decision.

PROCEDURAL JUSTICE AND PERFORMANCE

Organizational researchers have long recognized that the relationship between work performance and attitudinal variables is far from straightforward (see, e.g., Locke, 1976). Performance is multiply determined, and it is probably unreasonable to expect any attitudinal variable, including judgments of procedural justice, to have simple effects on performance. As we shall see below, there have been studies that show straightforward procedural justice enhancement of performance-related attitudes and performance *per se*, but there have also been studies that show much more complex relationships.

Earley and his colleagues report four studies that have shown procedural justice enhancement of performance, apparently by altering attitudes closely related to performance. In a laboratory experiment and a field experiment, Earley and Lind (1987) studied the effects of direct and expressive control over task assignments and over the procedures used to determine task assignments.[3] In both experiments, the effects of the manipulations on an attitudinal measure of task commitment and on a behavioral measure of performance mirrored the effects seen on sub-

---

[3]True variation in control could render ambiguous any effects seen on performance by allowing subjects to select working conditions or tasks that they knew would fit well with their particular skills or work habits. For this reason, most studies of performance and procedural justice that involve manipulations of control use deception to induce the perception of whatever form of control is of interest without actually giving the subjects true control. For example, Earley and Lind led subjects to believe they had control over the task assignment or the task assignment procedure, but the choices presented to the subjects were constructed so that nearly all the subjects made the same choice or endorsed the same option.

jects' judgments of procedural justice. In order to test whether procedural justice judgments actually caused the performance effects, Earley and Lind used LISREL (Jöreskog & Sörbom, 1981) structural equation models to analyze the data from both studies. They found evidence that procedural justice caused higher performance in the laboratory study, but not in the field study.

In another pair of studies, Earley (1984) showed that goal-setting procedures high in procedural justice lead to enhanced performance. Again, one of the experiments was conducted in the laboratory and one in the field and the same results were obtained in both settings. The particular procedural variable that Earley studied was the amount of voice that workers had in a goal-setting procedure. In the laboratory experiment, one of three goal-setting procedures was used. Some subjects were allowed to express their opinions about the goal and the task prior to receiving a goal from the experimenter, others were allowed to express their opinions after receiving the goal, and others were not given an opportunity to express their opinions. The field experiment replicated the pre-decision voice and no voice conditions. Table 8-4 shows the results of both studies for fairness judgments, ratings of acceptance of the set goals, and task performance. In both experiments, the opportunity for expression, either before or after the decision was made, increased perceived fairness, goal acceptance, and performance.

The relationship between procedural justice and performance has also been studied in the context of pay and performance evaluation procedures. Here the findings have been much less straightforward.

TABLE 8-4. Procedural Justice, Goal Acceptance, and Performance

Measure	Predecisional voice	Postdecisional voice	Mute
Laboratory experiment			
Procedural fairness	3.64	3.03	2.35
Goal acceptance	.23	.12	−.35
Task performance	6.63	5.85	4.67
Field experiment			
Procedural fairness	3.86	2.50	—
Goal acceptance	.10	−.79	—
Task performance	30.77	27.5	—

Note. Higher values indicate greater perceived fairness, goal acceptance, and task performance. In laboratory experiment values are unweighted marginal means averaging across supervisor input manipulation. From Earley (1984).

Cornelius (1985), in a laboratory study referred to above, studied performance under several payment schemes (piece-rate, hourly, or bonus payment schedules) and under performance evaluation procedures that varied in their consistency and accuracy. He found that high fairness procedures were more likely to be accompanied by improved performance than were low fairness procedures, but that this relationship was present only in some combinations of the two procedural characteristics and three payment conditions.

Kanfer *et al.* (1987) found a *negative* correlation between procedural justice judgments and task performance. Their experiment involved performance evaluation procedures that either did or did not give subjects an opportunity to explain their work product prior to an evaluation; as one would expect, the voice procedure led to greater perceived procedural justice than did the no-voice procedure. The negative correlation between performance and procedural justice may have occurred because subjects who had an opportunity to explain their work product felt that the product did not need to "speak for itself" and worked less diligently. In contrast, under the unfair, no-voice procedure, subjects may have felt that exceptional performance was the only way to assure themselves of a positive outcome. In any event, the negative correlation was only moderate ($-.22$) and it is probably best not to make too much of the apparent negative relationship between procedural fairness and performance.

In general, the evidence of performance enhancement by high fairness procedures has been most clear when the procedures in question are closely related to the task itself and least clear when the procedures in question concern the evaluation of performance and reward. If performance were our only concern, it would make more sense to concentrate on improving the fairness of procedures for task assignment or for the allocation of work resources, rather than improving the fairness of pay or promotion procedures. Given the relatively few studies looking at procedural justice and performance, a generalization of this sort may be premature, but we advance the idea nonetheless because we believe that a hypothesis of this sort might motivate further study.

Even if future studies do show that fair task procedures are more likely to enhance performance than are fair evaluation and reward procedures, however, we would hardly support limiting our concern to task-related procedures. The research reviewed in previous sections of this chapter quite often involved manipulations of the procedural fairness of evaluation and reward procedures, and it is in the context of such procedures that many of the nonperformance benefits of procedural justice have been seen. We believe that, notwithstanding the importance of performance in organizational settings, the great practical value of procedural justice lies in its capacity to enhance the quality of work life and in its value as a source of both satisfaction and positive evaluations of the organization. This last point is perhaps the most important. We will argue in Chapter 10 that procedural justice acts to make individuals more willing to subordinate their own short-term individual interests to the interests of a group or organization. If this proposition is correct, the benefits of procedural justice for organizations far exceed its effects on individual performance—fair procedure may be one of the crucial elements of organizational viability.

* * * * * * *

As is the case in legal and political settings then, procedural justice has positive consequences for organizations. The preceding material shows that procedural justice judgments affect a variety of very important beliefs and attitudes in organizations. In organizations, as in other settings, procedural justice appears to be a major concern, and the experience of procedural justice or injustice is a critical element in the organizational psychology of decision making. Thus, in organizations, as in other contexts, it is natural to look for the causes of procedural justice judgments. It is to this topic that we now turn.

ANTECEDENTS OF PROCEDURAL JUSTICE IN ORGANIZATIONS

CONTROL AND EXPRESSION

Given the findings of research in other contexts, it would be surprising indeed if procedural justice judgments in organizations were not enhanced by control over the decision-making process and by opportunities to voice opinions and values. In fact, the studies that have looked at control and voice variations in organizational procedures make it clear that the same social psychological processes are at work in organizations as in other contexts.

Three studies, one conducted in the laboratory by Kanfer *et al.* (1987) and two conducted in field settings by Lissak (1983), support the generalization of the voice or process control effect to organizational procedures. Kanfer *et al.* manipulated two features of procedures for evaluating and rewarding performance. The subjects, in the role of the person being evaluated, were either given or not given an opportunity to provide information as part of the decision-making process, and they were either given detailed information about the criteria to be used in the evaluation or given only superficial information about the criteria. The Kanfer *et al.* experiment also included a manipulation of the outcome of the evaluation: the subjects either received a favorable evaluation and a cash bonus or they received an unfavorable evaluation and no bonus. The results of the experiment showed substantially higher procedural justice judgments in the voice condition than in the no-voice condition, regardless of the outcome of the evaluation.

Lissak (1983), in two studies mentioned earlier, examined the effects of voice on judgments of the fairness of performance evaluation and posting procedures in the Canadian armed forces. In the first study, he examined reactions to an existing procedure for evaluating the performance of enlisted personnel and reactions to an innovative performance evaluation procedure being tested on a random sample of enlisted personnel. The innovative procedure differed from the standard procedure in that it allowed the person being evaluated to contribute a statement concerning his or her work during the period under consideration—essentially providing an opportunity for voice prior to the evaluation. Lissak found that people exposed to the voice procedure gave higher procedural justice ratings than did people exposed to the no-voice procedure. In a second study, Lissak capitalized on a naturally occurring variation in posting (transfer) procedures in the Canadian Forces. Some enlisted personnel serve under what is termed a regimental system: they are always in the same unit and are posted wherever their unit is posted. Other enlisted personnel serve under a nonregimental system: these men and women can serve in more than one unit in the course of their service, and they are transferred from one base to another as individuals. Personnel in the nonregimental system are given an opportunity to voice their preferences when posting decisions are made; personnel in the regimental system have no direct voice in their postings. Lissak selected samples of regimental and nonregimental personnel that were matched with respect to actual posting, rank, and specialty area. He found that subjects in the nonregimental, voice-available condition gave higher ratings of the fairness of the posting procedure than did subjects in the regimental, voice-unavailable condition. Table 8-5 shows the procedural justice ratings of subjects in both of Lissak's studies.

The studies just described demonstrate that the basic voice effect is seen in organizational settings, but they leave unanswered the question of whether the effect is due to instrumental or noninstrumental features of voice. As we noted in Chapters 5 and 7, voice could enhance procedural justice because voice is seen as leading to more equitable outcomes (as proposed by Thibaut & Walker, 1978) or because it provides some control over outcomes (as proposed by Brett, 1986). Alternatively,

TABLE 8-5. Procedural Justice and Voice in the Canadian Armed Forces

	Voice	Mute
Study 1: Performance evaluation procedure experiment		
Procedural justice index	11.42	8.64
Study 2: Posting procedure study		
Procedural justice index	10.18	8.18

Note. Higher values indicate greater perceived fairness. Study 2 values are unweighted marginal means averaging across three assignment bases. From Lissak (1983).

it could enhance procedural justice because it fulfills a desire to be heard and to have one's views considered, regardless of whether the expression influences the decision maker (as proposed by Tyler *et al.*, 1985). Our conclusion after reviewing voice effects in legal procedures was that at least some of the effect of voice on procedural justice is attributable to noninstrumental features of voice. Much the same picture appears to be emerging from research on organizational procedures.

The study by Earley (1984) shows a remarkable demonstration of a noninstrumental voice effect. Earley examined procedural fairness judgments in response to goal-setting procedures in a laboratory experiment. Some of Earley's subjects were allowed no voice in the goal-setting process, some were allowed (and encouraged) to express their preferences and views prior to the setting of a goal for their performance, and some were allowed to express their preferences and views *after* a goal had been set for their performance. If opinion expression *per se* has a positive effect on procedural justice judgments, one would expect subjects in both the predecision-voice and the postdecision-voice conditions to see the goal-setting procedure as more fair than those in the no-voice condition. On the other hand, if voice effects were due solely to instrumental control considerations, one would expect to see an enhancement of procedural justice in the predecision-voice condition, but not in the postdecision-voice condition.

Earley's results showed that subjects in the postdecision-voice condition showed gave higher ratings of the fairness of the procedure than did subjects in the no-voice condition; the procedural fairness ratings in the postdecision-voice condition were intermediate between the predecision-voice and the no-voice conditions. Earley's results were complicated somewhat by the fact that, notwithstanding a rather extensive effort to convince the subjects in the postdecision-voice condition that their input could not alter the already set goal, subjects in that condition sometimes saw themselves as having more control over the goal than did subjects in the no-voice condition. When the effects of this "illusion of control" response (cf. Langer, 1983) were eliminated statistically, however, there was still evidence of an enhancement of procedural fairness in the postdecision-voice condition. Thus Earley's experiment shows that purely expressive voice effects can occur in judgments of the fairness of organizational procedures.

As is the case with respect to procedures in other contexts, more research is needed to tell us when purely expressive voice effects occur in organizations. There is little doubt that such effects do occur, however, just as there is little doubt that instrumental voice effects also occur. Earley's finding that subjects in his postdecision-voice conditions showed an illusion of control response, together with similar findings in a recent study by Lind, Kanfer, Ambrose, and Conlon (1986), suggests that it may be difficult to disentangle instrumental and noninstrumental processes in the effect of voice on procedural justice. We believe that it is a matter of some theoretical importance that the two processes be disentangled and studied. Even if the effect arises from illusory control and purely expressive features, though, we have a good deal of evidence that the provision of voice enhances procedural justice, even in situations in which there is little objective reason to suspect that the exercise of voice will affect decisions. If organizational procedures are designed to provide voice (and if there is some assurance that the opinions expressed in the exercise of voice are given due consideration; cf. Tyler, 1987a), it is very likely indeed that the perceived fairness of the procedures will be high.

It is possible, using structural equation modeling methods, to test whether similar voice and control effects on judgments of procedural justice and judgments of personal control actually indicate that perceived control is causing the procedural justice differences. Earley and Lind (1987) used this method to test the role of perceptions of control in mediating procedural justice judgments. In both a laboratory experiment and a field experiment, they tested the effects of three levels of input in task assignment decisions: choice alone (that is, complete control over the decision in question) and choice plus voice (control over the decision plus an opportunity to express ideas about the choice), and no input at all. The experiments examined the effects of each level of input on task assignments and on the selection of procedures that would guide a later task assignment. On the basis of both instrumental and noninstrumental explanations of voice and control effects, Earley and Lind hypothesized that both procedural justice and control judgments would show stronger effects for voice, over and above choice, when the input concerned procedures for selecting tasks rather than the selection of tasks themselves.

Figure 8-2 shows the results for the laboratory experiment. The

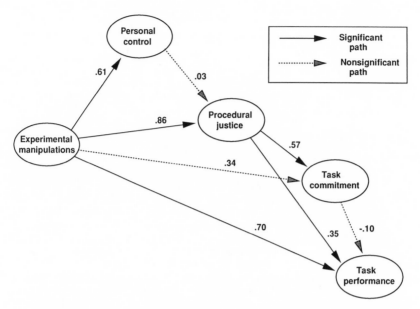

FIGURE 8-2. Causal model: Procedural justice, control, and performance.

structural equation analysis showed that, although the experimental manipulations produced similar effects on judgments of control and procedural justice, the control judgments did not *cause* the procedural justice judgments. The results of the field experiment also showed no significant causal link between control judgments and procedural justice judgments. Earley and Lind conclude that, at least in this experiment, the relationship between control and procedural justice is largely spurious: External variables have similar effects on control and procedural justice judgments, but the effects on procedural justice are causally independent of the effects on perceived control.

In organizational settings, as in other contexts, the enhancement of procedural justice by voice and control is *not* dependent on favorable outcomes; rather, it acts independently of outcome effects. A recent laboratory experiment by Paese (1985), mentioned above in our discussion of procedural justice effects on distributive fairness, provides a striking example of the independence of control and outcome effects on procedural justice judgments. Paese's procedural manipulation involved what he termed "criterion control," a form of participation similar to voice or process control in that it does not involve direct control over the outcome of the decision but rather input at an earlier stage in the decision-making process. Subjects in his study either were or were

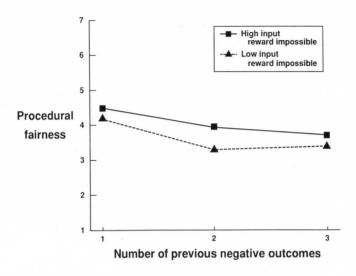

FIGURE 8-3. Effect of repeated failure on procedural fairness.

not allowed to choose the weight to be accorded each of two criteria in computing a score for their performance. The subjects in all conditions received three consecutive negative evaluations. The criterion control manipulation was crossed with a manipulation of the possibility that the subjects would receive any reward at all for their efforts—half of the subjects were given bogus feedback scores that were so low that after the second negative evaluation they knew they could not receive any monetary reward for their future work. Remarkably, the procedural justice advantage of the high criterion control procedure persisted even in the face of repeated negative outcome and the impossibility of improving outcomes. Figure 8-3 shows the procedural justice ratings of subjects in the conditions in which there was no possibility of reward.[4]

In summary, the picture that emerges in organizational settings of the role of control and expression in enhancing procedural justice is consistent with the general psychology of procedure that we have seen in other contexts. Procedures that provide for either control or expression are seen as fairer than those that limit control or expression. These effects are seen across a wide variety of procedures and they are seen in the face of negative outcomes, even repeated negative outcomes. The effects are so robust and so straightforward that we do not hesitate to

[4]The slight convergence of the two curves on ratings made after the third negative evaluation was due apparently to a "bottoming out" of subjects in the low input condition, not to any real erosion of the perceived fairness advantage of the high input procedure.

recommend the inclusion of opportunities for voice or for input or control in any organizational procedure wherein fairness is a major concern.

OTHER FAIRNESS STANDARDS

Research on organizational procedures has been influenced more by Leventhal's theoretical work on criteria for procedural justice than has research in other areas of procedural justice. One consequence of this is that organizational procedural justice research has avoided the preoccupation with voice that is seen in research on legal procedures. If the work described in this section had not been done, we might well imagine that most of the variation in peoples' procedural justice judgments was due to only two factors: voice and outcome. As we shall see in the following pages, it is apparent that many features of procedures contribute to fairness judgments.

Greenberg (1986b) reports an impressive field study of the factors that influence fairness in performance evaluations. He had middle managers in a variety of businesses think of a particularly fair or a particularly unfair performance evaluation that they had received. The respondents were then asked to report the single most important factor that made the experience fair or unfair. Another group of managers sorted the first group's responses using a Q-sort procedure. The Q-sort produced seven factors, which were cross-validated by a third group from the same sample. Finally, a fourth group rated the importance of each of the seven factors. Greenberg found that five of the seven factors were clearly based on procedural justice concerns; the remaining two factors were clearly based on distributive justice concerns. The procedural justice factors were: "soliciting input prior to evaluation and using it," "two-way communication during interview," "ability to challenge or rebut evaluation," "rater familiarity with ratees' work," and "consistent application of standards."[5] Greenberg points out that the first two of these procedural justice factors are closely related to issues of process control or voice, that the third procedural justice factor is closely related to Leventhal's correctability principle (Leventhal, 1980; Leventhal *et al.*, 1980), and that the fifth procedural justice factor is an example of Leventhal's consistency principle. It is arguable that the fourth factor—rater familiarity with ratees' work—is an example of Leventhal's accuracy of information principle; whether it fits Leventhal's theory or not, rater familiarity with ratee work is clearly an important factor in procedural justice in performance evaluations, as we will see below when we discuss another of Greenberg's studies.

[5]The distributive justice factors were "receipt of rating based on performance achieved" and "recommendation for salary or promotion based on rating."

Greenberg's findings are noteworthy in two respects. First, it is very encouraging that the voice variable accorded so much importance by Thibaut and Walker and two, or perhaps three, of Leventhal's six principles appeared when free-response methods were used to measure fairness concerns. Because most experimental studies vary the factors that the researcher believes to be important and because most closed-ended surveys ask only about factors that the researcher believes to be important, there is a danger that research will focus on matters that are accorded importance in current theories but have little to do with the day-to-day experience of procedural justice. Greenberg's findings show that this has not occurred. Second, it is encouraging that Greenberg found no difference in the importance accorded procedural and distributive factors when all of the fairness factors were rated for their importance. A frequent finding in studies of the role of procedural and distributive justice in determining overall fairness judgments is that procedural justice is at least as important as distributive justice, but these studies always bring procedural justice to the respondent's attention by asking about it. Greenberg's study offers another independent validation of the importance of procedural justice judgments.

Sheppard and Lewicki (1987) report a field study of managers' fairness experiences that confirms and extends the implications of Greenberg's study. They asked a sample of managers to give an instance in which they had been treated fairly and an instance in which they had been treated unfairly in each of seven major areas of managerial activity. The respondents were also asked to state the principle or rule that was obeyed or violated to make the experience fair or unfair. Sheppard and Lewicki found that more fairness rules were mentioned in managerial areas involving allocation and dispute management, and fewer rules were mentioned in areas such as staff development and managing daily routine. A content analysis of the rules showed that they included all six of Leventhal's procedural justice principles.

The Cornelius (1985) study examined two of Leventhal's six procedural justice criteria in the context of a laboratory experiment on performance evaluation procedures. In a manipulation of Leventhal's accuracy principle, half of the subjects in this experiment were told that their work would be judged on the basis of their entire output during the experimental session, and half were told that their work would be judged on the basis of a very small sample of their output. In a manipulation of Leventhal's consistency principle, half of the subjects were told that their performance evaluation would use a different, more strenuous index of their performance than would be used for other subjects, while the remaining subjects were told that the performance index would be the same for everyone. The subjects in the experiment rated the high accuracy procedure as more fair than the low accuracy procedure. There was, however, no difference in the procedural justice judgments resulting from the consistent and inconsistent procedures.

In a laboratory experiment, Greenberg (1987b) studied the procedural justice effects of the use of diaries in performance evaluations. The use of diaries to record workers' performance could be seen as assuring more accurate information and therefore would enhance procedural justice judgments by virtue of Leventhal's accuracy of information principle. Greenberg found that judgments of procedural fairness were substantially higher for an evaluation procedure that involved the use of performance diaries than for either a procedure that involved observation of performance without the use of a diary or no observation of performance. Observation without a diary was seen as a fairer procedure than no observation at all.

Thus there is growing evidence that at least in organizational procedures, and perhaps in all procedures, Leventhal's six principles of fairness are used to judge procedural justice. Several other factors that affect procedural justice judgments in organizations have received attention. One, of course, is the outcome of the procedure. As is the case in other contexts, outcomes seem sometimes to play a minor role in procedural justice judgments (e.g., Greenberg, 1987b) and sometimes a major role (e.g., Paese, 1985; see Figure 8-3 above) in determining whether people think a procedure is fair or unfair. A second additional factor is one that appears to us to address a rather basic principle of procedural justice—whether there is any *individualized* procedure allocating outcomes. For example, payment procedures that allocate rewards according to performance are seen as fairer than procedures that allocate rewards on a random basis (Greenberg, 1987a). Similarly, affirmative-action hiring procedures that use group quotas are viewed as unfair, but affirmative-action hiring procedures that incorporate minority hiring as one factor in a more individualized process are viewed as fair (Nacoste, 1985).

Another factor that has been seen in organizational contexts is the presence or absence of procedural explanations (Folger *et al.*, 1983) or acceptable accounts (Bies & Shapiro, 1987) for behavior that would otherwise violate established procedures. By procedural explanations we mean statements by a decision maker explaining, in terms of procedures or custom, why he or she behaved in a certain fashion. It appears that, although people are quite concerned with procedural justice and have definite ideas about the features that make procedures acceptable, the experience of procedural injustice can be moderated or eliminated if some account is given for the use of otherwise unfair procedures. The account need not be at a very high level of sophistication; it appears to be enough that the account is on its face reasonable.

DESIGNING ORGANIZATIONAL PROCEDURES

Two issues are of particular importance in deciding what procedural justice research has to say about how organizational procedures should be designed. First, we must distinguish between procedural justice findings that are sufficiently clear and widely replicated to be applied with little hesitation and those that are merely suggestive and should be applied with caution. Second, we must consider the possibility for abuse of our growing knowledge of procedural justice, especially the possibility that procedures that are fundamentally, objectively unfair can be made to look fair by skillful manipulation of perceptions that produce the experience of procedural justice.

On the basis of research on organizational procedures and the extent to which the findings of this research conform with our general knowledge of procedural justice, we are confident in advancing several practical recommendations. Primary among these recommendations is that those who study organizational psychology and organizational design should pay more attention to procedures, especially to the fairness of procedures. In organizational research, as in other behavioral and social sciences, the focus on outcomes and on social exchange processes has led, we believe, to the mistaken belief that attitudes and behavior are much more strongly determined by rewards and costs than is in fact the case. For example, outcome-oriented theories like that advanced by Naylor, Pritchard, and Ilgen (1981) seek to explain much of the psychology of the work place in terms of what are essentially social exchange processes. The Naylor, Pritchard, and Ilgen model is quite sophisticated and, like other social exchange models, it does explain a good portion of the attitudes and behavior it addresses. But we are convinced that such models omit critical features of the psychology of organizations. The research reviewed above on the consequences of procedural justice judgments shows that reactions to procedures are a strong factor in determining how people perceive, evaluate, and react to organizations.

As we noted above, we would recommend that organizational designers look to procedural justice research for effective means to enhance and maintain the quality of work life and the internal cohesiveness of organizations. The research we have examined shows that when procedures are fair the organization can expect to see greater employee

satisfaction, less conflict, and more obedience to procedures and decisions. These benefits can be realized at very little cost to the organization—in fact, it is quite likely that the investment of organizational resources in the achievement of procedural justice would produce much
greater benefit on these dimensions at less cost than would most other
changes in organizational policy or practice.

The next logical question is how the achievement of procedural
justice is to be accomplished. Among the findings that seem to us to be
so well established as to be ready for immediate application are the
incorporation of voice and the use of methods of gathering information
that are of obviously high accuracy. Both of these procedural features
have been found to be influential in a variety of procedures in organizations. The incorporation of voice is easily accomplished in most organizational procedures. The major barriers to wider use of voice procedures
seem to be not their cost but rather mistaken beliefs that (1) voice procedures lead to what we in procedural justice term "frustration effects"
or (2) workers would have little useful information to contribute to the
decisions affecting them. Both of these beliefs miss the point. As we
documented above, frustration effects are rare and appear to occur only
when there are other reasons to be suspicious of the procedure; we see
no reason for any organization to fear that allowing workers voice in
good faith would lead to problems when subsequent decisions are not
congruent with the positions advocated in the exercise of the voice. And
the conception that workers have little to contribute misses the point
that the workers *believe* that they have something to contribute. Similarly, the use of procedures that strive manifestly for accuracy takes
little effort and is likely to yield benefits for objective, as well as subjective, justice. Where information-gathering methods are known by management to be accurate but are not accepted as such by workers, there
may be problems, but in the absence of such conflict between objective
and subjective assessments of accuracy, there is little reason not to use
fair procedures.

We noted earlier that investment in fair procedures might well be
among the least costly methods for improving organizational attitudes,
cohesion, and compliance. This is a strong recommendation for the
application of procedural justice concepts, but it also offers temptation
for the abuse of procedural justice. This is an issue that we have touched
on before under the rubric of "false consciousness." For example, an
organization might introduce task-assignment procedures that appeared
to allow workers voice prior to the allocation of task assignments when
in fact the voiced preferences and values are never really considered.
Because the enhancement of procedural justice and its attendant benefits for attitudes and compliance depend on the *perception* of considera-

tion of voice rather than on the *reality* of consideration of voice, the organization can realize the benefits without offering real voice.

Such potential abuses are not a problem unique to organizations; we raised the issue in our discussions of courts and politics because the problem exists there as well. However, the problem has been raised most forcefully in the context of organizational procedures (Cohen, 1985), and the relative lack of restriction on organizational procedures might make such abuses more likely in this context.

We have no ready solution for the false consciousness problem, but we do note that some procedural justice research points to practical dangers in using sham procedures. As we noted earlier in this chapter, the situations that do produce frustration effects are generally those in which there was reason to doubt the honesty of the procedure. Further, the research on compliance and procedural justice has produced the happy finding that procedures that are seen as sham lead not only to lowered compliance but to clever noncompliance—a phenomenon that might give any Machiavellian executive pause in his or her scheme to use a procedural scam. We suspect that in many instances sham procedures carry the seeds of their own destruction and that they seldom accomplish the ends they seek to achieve.

This is not to say, however, that all abuses will be self-defeating. We must end this chapter with the warning that, excellent as we believe the benefits of ethical application of procedural justice to be, there is a potential for abuse.

Chapter 9

Conclusions and Hypotheses

We began this book with the intention of presenting a picture of the advances in the study of procedural justice that have occurred in the decade since Thibaut and Walker published their book on the topic. We have considered the work that Thibaut and Walker themselves drew upon, as well as more recent studies on the perceived fairness of legal, political, and organizational procedures. We will now move back from the trees, as it were, and contemplate the forest. In this chapter we consider two questions. First, what conclusions can we reach on the basis of the whole body of procedural justice research? And second, what hypotheses can we advance about topics or phenomena as yet unstudied?

THE VALIDITY OF PROCEDURAL JUSTICE PHENOMENA

Methodological Concerns

Logically and historically, the first challenge that procedural justice research had to meet concerned the validity of its basic phenomena. Are the procedural justice effects we have described "real" or are they artifacts of the research methods used to study them? As we noted in Chapters 2 and 3, virtually all of the early research on procedural justice used laboratory methods and undergraduate subjects. Almost as soon as the first procedural justice findings appeared there were criticisms of the methodology used in the research (e.g., Damaska, 1975; Hayden & Anderson, 1979). The underlying question in all these criticisms was whether procedural justice effects were artifacts of the laboratory settings used to study them and, if the effects did occur in the real world, whether they were as strong there as in the laboratory.

Tables 9-1a to 9-1d list the research to date supporting four of the

TABLE 9-1a. Studies Testing Process Control Enhancement of Procedural Justice Judgments

Laboratory and scenario studies	Field studies
Walker, LaTour, Lind, & Thibaut (1974)	Adler, Hensler, & Nelson (1983)
Thibaut, Walker, LaTour, & Houlden (1974)	Lissak (1983; Studies 2–5)
Folger (1977)*	Earley (1984; Study 3)
LaTour (1978)	Tyler, Rasinski, & Spodick (1985; Study 1)
Houlden, LaTour, Walker, & Thibaut (1978)	Tyler (1987a)
Lind, Erickson, Friedland, & Dicken- berger (1978)	Earley & Lind (1987; Study 2)
Walker, Lind, & Thibaut (1979)	
Lind, Kurtz, Musante, Walker & Thibaut (1980)	
*Austin, Williams, Worchel, Wentzel, & Siegel (1981)***	
Houlden (1980)	
Musante, Gilbert, & Thibaut (1983)	
Lind, Lissak, & Conlon (1983)	
Earley (1984; Study 1)	
Sheppard (1985)	
Tyler, Rasinski, & Spodick (1985; Studies 2 and 3)	
Leung & Lind (1986)	
Greenberg (1986b)	
Earley & Lind (1987; Study 1)	
Kanfer, Sawyer, Earley, & Lind (1987)	

Note. Citation in italics indicates direct disconfirmation of effect.
*Absence of the effect in some conditions; confirmation in other conditions.
**Reversal of effect.

most important procedural justice effects: the enhancement of pro- cedural justice judgments when those affected by the procedure are granted voice or process control, the enhancement of distributive justice judgments and satisfaction with outcomes by procedural justice judg- ments, the enhancement of attitudes toward authorities by judgments of procedural justice, and the instigation of various salutary behavioral effects by judgments of procedural justice. The process control and out- come fairness effects were among the first procedural justice phenome- na discovered by the Thibaut and Walker group. The leadership evalua- tion and behavior effects, although not discovered until after Thibaut and Walker had concluded their work on procedural justice, have re- ceived a great deal of attention in recent years.

The tables list the studies that have supported, partially supported,

TABLE 9-1b. Studies Testing Procedural Justice Enhancement of Satisfaction and Distributive Justice

Laboratory and scenario studies	Field studies
Walker, LaTour, Lind, & Thibaut (1974)	Tyler & Folger (1980)
Folger (1977)*	Adler, Hensler, & Nelson (1983)
Latour (1978)**	Lissak, Mendes, & Lind (1983)
Walker, Lind, & Thibaut (1979)**	Lissak (1983; Field Studies 1 and 2)
Folger, Rosenfield, Grove, & Corkran (1979; Studies 1 and 2)**	Tyler (1984)
Lind, Kurtz, Musante, Walker, & Thibaut (1980)	Tyler, Rasinski, & McGraw (1985)
Houlden (1980)	
Folger, Rosenfield, & Robinson (1983)	Bies (1986)
	Casper, Tyler, & Fisher (in press)
Cornelius (1985)	Alexander & Ruderman (1987)
Paese (1985)	Tyler (1987b)
Greenberg (1987a)	Rasinski & Tyler (in press)
Greenberg (1987b)	
Kanfer, Sawyer, Earley, & Lind (1987)	

Note. Citation in italics indicates direct disconfirmation of effect.
*Reversal of effect in some conditions; confirmation in other conditions.
**Absence of effect in some conditions; confirmation in other conditions.

and failed to support each of the four effects. As can be seen from the table, each effect has accumulated a large number of supportive studies and each has been observed in both laboratory and field studies. We have dealt in previous chapters with the few qualifications implied by the nonsupportive studies; the point of interest here is the fact that supportive findings are by no means restricted to studies using laboratory methods. Each of the effects has been validated repeatedly in field settings.

TABLE 9-1c. Studies Testing Procedural Justice Enhancement of Evaluations of Leaders, Authorities, and Institutions

Laboratory and scenario studies	Field studies
Folger, Rosenfield, Grove, & Corkran (1979)	Tyler & Caine (1981; Study 3)
Tyler & Caine (1981; Studies 1, 2, and 4)	Tyler (1984)
Folger & Martin (1986)	Tyler, Rasinski, & McGraw (1985)
Greenberg (1987b)	Tyler (1987b)
Kanfer, Sawyer, Earley, & Lind (1987)	Tyler, Casper, & Fisher (1987)
	Alexander & Ruderman (1987)

Note. The authors know of no study disconfirming this effect.

TABLE 9-1d. Studies Testing Procedural Justice Effects on Behavior

Laboratory and scenario studies	Field studies
Friedland, Thibaut, & Walker (1973)	Earley (1984; Study 3)
Thibaut, Friedland, & Walker (1974)	
Earley (1984; Study 1)	Tyler (1987b)
Cornelius (1985)**	
Earley & Lind (1987; Study 1)	Earley & Lind (1987; Study 2)***
Greenberg (1987a)	Rasinski & Tyler (in press)
Kanfer, Sawyer, Earley, & Lind (1987)	

Note. Citation in italics indicates direct disconfirmation of effect.
  *Reversal of the effect.
 **Absence of the effect in some conditions; confirmation in other conditions.
***Absence of the effect.

Indeed, as field studies of procedural justice have proliferated, it has become apparent that the laboratory and scenario methods used in early research may have caused us to underestimate the magnitude of procedural justice effects. Field research results have not only confirmed the findings of laboratory and scenario studies on procedural justice, but in fact have usually shown stronger procedural justice effects.

Tyler and Caine (1981) report a series of studies that permit one to compare the results of scenario studies and field studies on the consequences of procedural justice. The studies examined the effect of procedural justice in two contexts: student evaluations of teachers and citizen evaluations of political leaders. In the scenario studies, subjects were asked to place themselves within the context of a simulated decision and to respond as they felt they and others would to differing outcomes arrived at through different procedures. In the field studies, the participants were interviewed about actual outcomes that they had received and about the procedures used to reach those outcomes. Tyler and Caine found that in both contexts the effect of fair procedures on evaluations of authorities was stronger in the field setting than in the scenario setting.

Other procedural justice phenomena show similar robustness with respect to research methods. Indeed, we have seen not a single instance of a procedural justice effect that is bound to a particular method. We therefore have no hesitation at all is advancing our first conclusion:

Conclusion 1: Procedural justice effects are robust across methodologies.

SUBSTANTIVE CONCERNS

Arguably the most important findings of the Thibaut and Walker project were the discovery of three relations: (1) that perceptions of procedural justice result in increased satisfaction; (2) that procedural justice judgments are among the most important determinants of procedural preferences; and (3) that high process control procedures lead to higher procedural justice judgments. All three of these relations have been validated by research subsequent to that of Thibaut and Walker, although, as one might expect, all three relations have been found to have some exceptions and limitations.

As we noted in Chapters 2 and 4, one of the most striking contributions of the Thibaut and Walker work was the discovery that procedural variation could increase disputant satisfaction with the outcome and the experience of dispute resolution. This discovery offers a way to increase satisfaction even in situations in which there is no possibility for all parties to receive the outcomes they desire. Table 9-1b lists the numerous studies that have tested and, in the great majority of cases, confirmed this effect. As we have seen in Chapters 7 and 8, there is now clear evidence that the effect is not restricted to legal or dispute resolution contexts; it has been observed frequently in political and organizational contexts as well.

We have seen just two possible limitations on enhancement of satisfaction by procedural justice judgments, and both of these are in need of further research and analysis. First, a few studies have shown some attenuation of the effect under conditions of very favorable outcomes. It is not altogether clear whether this attenuation is due to measurement problems or whether it is a real phenomenon, but it may mean that the enhancement of satisfaction is stronger when outcomes are negative than when they are positive. The second possible limitation is what Folger has termed a "frustration effect," the occasional observation of very negative reactions to unfavorable outcomes from an apparently fair procedure. As we noted in Chapter 8, we believe that we can now specify the conditions that lead to the appearance of the frustration effect; in all other instances we would expect to see normal procedural justice effects. These considerations lead us to advance the following conclusion and hypothesis:

Conclusion 2: In most situations procedural justice judgments lead to enhanced satisfaction; this effect is especially strong when outcomes are negative.

Hypothesis 1: Frustration effects, negative reactions to apparently fair procedures, occur only when the procedure is weak; that is, when it is easy to suspect that the procedure is a sham.

Although it has been the subject of less research than has the procedural justice effect on satisfaction, the relation between procedural justice judgments and procedural preferences has been confirmed by several studies conducted since the conclusion of the Thibaut and Walker project. As we noted in Chapters 5, 6, and 8, quite a few studies have shown that procedural fairness is one of the major criteria for procedural choice, although there has also been recognition that procedural fairness is certainly not the only criterion. We summarize the current state of knowledge about the effect of procedural justice on procedural preferences as follows:

Conclusion 3: Procedural justice is one of the most important factors in determining which procedure will be preferred by those affected by a decision. Procedural justice is not, however, the only factor affecting procedural preference.

As can be seen from Table 9-1a, there have also been many positive replications of the process control effect. We will consider later the research on whether process control and voice effects are due to instrumental or expressive functions of voice. For the time being we simply note that the great bulk of the studies that have looked for process control or voice effects have found them. As we noted in Chapters 5 and 6, the recent cross-cultural work of Leung shows that, although other considerations can lead to the rejection of high process control procedures, the effect is seen even in non-Western societies. Our current knowledge of the effects of process control and voice can be summarized simply:

Conclusion 4: Procedures are viewed as fairer when they vest process control or voice in those affected by a decision.

GENERALIZATIONS OF PROCEDURAL JUSTICE

NEW RELATIONS

In the course of the past decade the study of procedural justice has expanded to include variables and social contexts far beyond those studied in the initial Thibaut and Walker work. We will consider first the generalization of procedural justice to the study of new relations among variables. Thibaut and Walker were concerned for the most part with the interrelationships among four variables: process control, procedural justice judgments, satisfaction with outcomes, and procedural preferences. Much of their research involved testing whether process control was a major cause of procedural justice judgments and whether these judgments in turn exerted substantial influence on satisfaction and preferences. More recent work has looked at new variables and sought to understand the role of procedural justice as a cause or a consequence of these other variables.

Evaluation of Authorities and Institutions

One area of expansion in the study of procedural justice has been the inclusion of evaluations of the authorities and institutions responsible for decision making. Although Thibaut and Walker recognized that an important function of fair procedures was to allow authorities to make unpopular decisions in a way that did not undermine their legitimacy as authorities, they focused their own research on litigant satisfaction with the decisions, not on their satisfaction with or evaluation of authorities.

As can be seen from Table 9-1c, quite a few studies have explored the effects of procedural justice judgments on reactions to authorities. In work settings, several studies have found procedural justice effects on the evaluation of supervisors and employers (Alexander and Ruderman, 1987; Bies, 1986; Kanfer et al., 1987). In legal settings, procedural justice effects have been found on the evaluations of judges, police officers, and the court system (Tyler, 1984; 1987b; Tyler & Folger, 1980). Finally, in the political arena procedural justice effects have been found on evaluations of political leaders and institutions (Tyler & Caine, 1981; Tyler, Rasinski, & McGraw, 1985). These studies have all found that procedural justice judgments affect the evaluation of authorities and institutions. With these studies in mind, we advance our next general conclusion:

Conclusion 5: Judgments of procedural justice enhance the evaluation of authorities and institutions.

While procedural justice judgments affect both the evaluation of authorities and personal satisfaction, direct comparisons of these two dependent variables show that procedural justice matters more when authorities or institutions are being evaluated (Tyler, 1986b, Tyler et al., 1987). We will offer in Chapter 10 two explanations of this close linkage between procedural justice judgments and evaluations of authorities and institutions. In brief, we argue there that whether one adopts a model of procedural justice based on self-interest or a model based on group identification, one would expect procedural justice judgments to have especially strong cognitive and affective links to the group mandating the procedure. This in turn suggests that attitudes about groups or institutions will be strongly affected by variation in procedural justice. We base our next hypothesis on this line of reasoning:

Hypothesis 2: Procedural justice enhances commitment and loyalty to groups and institutions.

Behavior

Research has also extended the study of procedural justice beyond the area of subjective feelings of satisfaction or dissatisfaction, which was considered in Thibaut and Walker's original work, to include the study of behavior. For example, Alexander and his associates have studied the relationship between procedural justice and turnover intention in work settings using both correlational (Alexander & Ruderman, 1987) and experimental designs (Alexander, Ruderman, & Russ, 1984; Alexander & Russ, 1985). These studies consistently find that workers who feel that evaluation procedures are unfair are more likely to intend to leave their jobs. Similarly, the Alexander and Ruderman study showed that perceptions of procedural justice were correlated with reports of greater interpersonal harmony and lower conflict and tension within organizations. In addition, as we saw in Chapter 8, a number of studies have shown that task performance is affected by the fairness of task assignment and performance evaluation procedures.

An experimental demonstration of the behavioral effects of unfair process in work settings is found in Greenberg (1987a), which is described in Chapter 8. In that study, student subjects in a work experiment were subjected to fair or unfair procedures of work evaluation. Following this experience, the subjects were placed in a room that had a poster with telephone numbers for reporting unfair treatment to the "ethical responsibility board." Greenberg found that having experienced unfair process led subjects to take slips of paper with the telephone number attached, suggesting an intention to report unfair procedure to the appropriate authorities.

In the legal arena, the influence of process fairness on behavior is suggested by the work of McEwen and Maiman (1984) on litigants in small claims courts and the work of Adler *et al.* (1983) on litigants in court-annexed arbitration cases, which we described in Chapter 4. McEwen and Maiman examined factors that were associated with compliance with judicial decisions. They found that the resolution of a dispute through mediation, as opposed to adjudication, enhanced compliance. This difference appeared to be linked, at least in part, to feelings of fair treatment. Similarly, Adler *et al.* found that the acceptance of nonbinding arbitration awards was linked to satisfaction with the award, which was in turn found to be closely linked to procedural justice judgments.

Using a sample of randomly chosen citizens in Chicago, Tyler (1987b) explored the effect of encounters with legal authorities on subsequent compliance with laws. He found that procedural fairness in such encounters influenced citizen views about the legitimacy of legal authority and, through that influence, affected citizen compliance with the law.

Procedural justice judgments have also been found to influence political behavior. Rasinski and Tyler (1986, see Chapter 7) conducted three studies exploring the influence of procedural justice judgments on political behavior. Two of the studies examined vote choice in the 1986 Presidential election. In each study it was found that citizens' vote choices were influenced by their judgments about the relative procedural fairness of the two presidential candidates (Reagan and Mondale). In the third study, citizens' behavioral reactions to public policies (writing a congressperson, attending political rallies) were examined. It was found that such activities were also influenced by feelings of procedural injustice.

On the basis of these findings, we offer another general conclusion:

Conclusion 6: Procedural justice affects behaviors, as well as attitudes and beliefs. Among the behaviors affected by procedural justice are disputing behavior, task performance, compliance with decisions and laws, voting, protest behavior, participation in institutional activities, and task performance.

Two caveats are in order with respect to this conclusion. First, although it is clear that all of these behaviors are affected by procedural justice, the magnitude of the procedural justice effect is sometimes less than that of distributive justice judgments or nonfairness factors. Alexander and Ruderman (1987) directly compared the influence of procedural concerns on job satisfaction, evaluation of authorities, and turnover intention within federal government agencies and found that turnover intention was less strongly related to procedural justice concerns than were satisfaction and evaluation. The second caveat is that procedural justice effects on performance, and perhaps on other behaviors, are often complex. We saw in Chapter 8 that there is some evidence that fairness in performance evaluation procedures can actually lead to decreased performance, a finding that is in sharp contrast to the positive relationship between procedural justice in task assignment procedures and performance. Our conclusion there was that performance, like other behaviors that might be affected by procedural justice, is multiply determined. In general, we believe that increases in procedural justice probably do often result in desirable changes in behavior, but salutary behavioral consequences are by no means so certain as are salutary attitudinal effects.

New Arenas

New Social Contexts

Procedural justice phenomena generalize to contexts other than the legal context of the original Thibaut and Walker research. As we saw in

Chapter 4, within the general area of law the study of procedural justice has not only continued to examine courtroom procedures, but has also extended to the consideration of less formal dispute resolution procedures, such as mediation and court-annexed arbitration. In addition, the procedural justice of legal contacts outside of courts has been explored. For example, a major topic of study has been the causes and consequences of procedural justice in citizen contacts with the police (e.g., Tyler, 1986b; Tyler & Folger, 1980).

Another new arena is political decision making, as we saw in Chapter 7. Recent studies have examined the basis of public policy evaluations and public judgments about the level of benefits received and taxes paid (Tyler, Rasinski, & McGraw, 1985), as well as the basis of public support for incumbent authorities and political institutions (Tyler & Caine, 1981; Tyler, Rasinski, & McGraw, 1985). In addition, a variety of kinds of political behavior have been considered, including voting, writing one's congressperson, and other similar actions (Rasinski & Tyler, 1986). This work indicates that procedural justice judgments are an important determinant of political evaluation and behavior.

In recent years the area of greatest growth in procedural justice research has been in the study of work organizations. One area of particularly strong research activity has been the study of procedures used in performance evaluation for promotions and raises. A large number of studies have been conducted in that area, and they have consistently found that employees react more favorably to evaluation procedures that they judge to be fair, irrespective of the outcome of those evaluations. Typical of such work is Greenberg's demonstration that workers perceive keeping a diary of their work for evaluation purposes as fairer and react more favorably to evaluations involving such performance procedures (Greenberg, 1987b).

We have little hesitation, therefore, in offering our next conclusion:

Conclusion 7: Procedural justice processes operate in arenas other than courtrooms. Procedural justice effects occur in much the same form in informal legal settings and in settings involving politics and work organizations.

Allocation Procedures

The initial work of Thibaut and Walker focused on issues of dispute resolution. This focus was natural because Thibaut and Walker were interested in the courts and in their function as institutions for resolving disputes. But this focus differed considerably from that of the then dominant theories of distributive justice, which emphasized allocation settings in their discussions of fairness (see, for example, Crosby, 1976). As we noted in Chapter 6, by positing that procedural justice was a major fairness concern in allocation contexts, Leventhal's theoretical work encouraged the study of procedural justice phenomena in a new procedural context, one more familiar to distributive justice researchers.

More recent research has broadened the scope of procedural justice work to include the study of allocation procedures. Some of these studies, such as that by Barrett-Howard and Tyler (1986), described in Chapter 6, have addressed generic allocation procedures in a wide variety of circumstances. Barrett-Howard and Tyler found that procedural justice concerns were as important as distributive justice concerns in the choice of allocation procedures and that both mattered more than did nonfairness issues. Other studies of procedural justice in allocation include the many studies of pay and promotion that have been conducted in work settings (Chapter 8), and studies of political allocations (Chapter 7). Such research has consistently shown that procedural concerns are important when allocation decisions are being made or when organizational policies are being determined.

Conclusion 8: Procedural justice matters in allocations as well as in dispute resolution.

The Ubiquity of Procedural Justice Concerns

We suspect that procedural justice effects generalize well beyond the procedures and social arenas studied to date. There are several areas that seem especially likely to benefit from the application of procedural justice concepts. In educational settings, perceptions that grading procedures are unfair may play an important role in student disillusionment and cheating. In health care, there are two potential areas in which procedural justice concerns might arise. First, in the context of normal doctor–patient interactions, patient judgments of unfair treatment by a doctor might contribute to dissatisfaction with medical care and, in extreme cases, to greater likelihood of formal complaints or malpractice suits. Second, procedural justice seems likely to be an important criterion for medical policy-making. When life and death decisions are being made, as is the case when scarce medical resources are being allocated, it is likely that procedural justice will be especially important to the legitimacy of medical institutions and the acceptability of their decisions. Another likely context for procedural justice effects is close interpersonal relationships, such as friendships, couples, and families. Feelings of unfair treatment are likely to have even more devastating consequences in a close personal relationship than in the more formal, institutional contexts that have been the setting of most procedural justice research. One might wonder to what extent the alienation that sometimes exists between children and parents or the strains that sometimes occur in sexual relationships, to cite just two examples, are linked to such things as feelings that one cannot voice one's opinions or that the other person does not respect one's interpersonal rights—in short, to judgments of procedural injustice.

In Chapter 6 we reviewed studies suggesting that procedural justice is an important concern in nearly all social contexts. Those studies showed that there are some differences between contexts in the absolute level of importance accorded procedural justice, but procedural justice was never seen as unimportant. There may be contexts in which little attention is given to the procedural justice concerns, but until they are discovered we advance the following hypothesis, at least for purposes of promoting future research:

Hypothesis 3: Procedural justice processes operate in all social settings.

Why do we believe that procedural justice effects are ubiquitous? Some of the most recent research in the area of justice judgments, including the Tyler (in press) study described in Chapter 5, show that procedural justice judgments are based in part on the perception that one's treatment by others shows politeness and respect and allows personal dignity (see also Messick, Bloom, Boldizar, & Samuelson, 1985; Mikula, 1986). For example, in the Tyler study one rather important determinant of procedural justice judgments in citizen contacts with authorities is the politeness of treatment. Given that the concern with how one is treated by authorities or by other individuals is an issue that is not unique to the decision-making context that was originally the focus of procedural justice research, it is quite reasonable to wonder whether other procedural justice effects are not universal features of social interactions. Might we not expect to see, for example, a value-expressive voice effect enhancing the perceived fairness of ordinary social interactions, and this in turn leading to higher evaluations of the other people involved in the interaction? As yet, there is far too little evidence to conclude definitively that procedural justice effects occur outside the general context of social decision making, but there is sufficient indication that this may be the case to prompt us to offer the following conclusion and hypothesis:

Conclusion 9: Procedural justice involves more than questions of how decisions are made. It also involves questions of how people are treated by authorities and other parties.

Hypothesis 4: Procedural justice processes and effects generalize beyond the decision-making context. Procedural justice effects occur in routine social interaction.

THE MEANING OF PROCEDURAL JUSTICE

PROCESS AND DECISION CONTROL

Thibaut and Walker focused on the perception of control as the key variable affecting procedural justice. They concluded that citizens preferred the adversary system because it allowed them to maintain the maximum amount of direct control over their case through control over the process of evidence presentation to the decision maker. As we noted in Chapters 5 and 8, this suggestion led to a series of studies on the influence of outcome and process control on procedural justice judgments.

We noted earlier in this chapter that most of the studies of process control have confirmed that procedures granting those affected a chance to present their evidence and arguments are seen as fairer than procedures that force those affected to be mute. The findings with respect to decision control have been more equivocal. Some studies (e.g., Lind *et al.*, 1983) have found that variations in decision control have no influence on satisfaction or judgments of procedural justice, whereas variations in process control have a large effect on such judgments. Other studies have not found a total absence of decision control effects, but rather that such effects are much smaller than are process control effects (e.g., Tyler, 1987a; Tyler, Rasinski, & Spodick, 1985).

As we noted in Chapters 5 and 8, the inconsistent effects of decision control raises the issue of whether process control and voice effects are mediated by instrumental concerns. The research evidence, which we reviewed in detail in those chapters, shows findings supportive of both instrumental and noninstrumental explanations of the process control effect. The initial Thibaut and Walker conception of the etiology of the process control effect held that process control enhances judgments of procedural fairness because it is instrumental in assuring fair outcomes. Because instrumental explanations of process control were where procedural justice began, as it were, the most striking advance has been the recognition that at least part of the process control effect is due to noninstrumental, expressive factors. We therefore express our conclusion on this point as follows:

Conclusion 10: Process control effects are based on more than the desire for fair outcomes. The opportunity to express one's views enhances procedural justice judgments in and of itself.

We note, however, that recent research suggests that the value of voice is not universal: the occurrence of process control effects may depend on the belief that the decision maker is considering what is said (Tyler, 1987a).

New Determinants of Procedural Justice

Because of the influential role of the Thibaut and Walker book in shaping procedural justice research, most studies on the antecedents of procedural justice have focused on process control and Folger's closely related concept of voice. As we noted in Chapter 6, however, beginning with Leventhal's work on procedural fairness in allocation, it has become apparent that there are other determinants of procedural justice judgments. Leventhal's theory suggests six rules that determine whether or not a procedure is seen as fair. Recent studies have confirmed that the study of procedural justice must expand beyond concerns with control if we are to understand fully the meaning of procedural justice.

We noted in Chapters 6 and 8 that generic studies of allocation situations and specific studies of organizational procedures have confirmed the importance, in at least some situations, of all of Leventhal's justice rules. An example is a study by Greenberg (1986b, see Chapter 8) in which managers described a recent instance of fair or unfair treatment and then explained the principle of justice that had been followed or violated. Greenberg found that seven justice principles accounted for most of the incidents. Five of the seven were procedural justice principles; the remaining two were distributive justice principles. The procedural justice principles included consistency, accuracy of information, and correctability, as well as voice and control-related principles. Similar results, showing that procedural justice is defined by a wide variety of criteria, are seen in other contexts (cf. Tyler, 1987b). As we noted earlier in this chapter, it now appears that procedural justice depends not only on how decisions are made but also on how people are treated generally in the social context in question.

Conclusion 11: Judgments of procedural justice involve more than control issues. Procedural justice is affected by other formal characteristics of procedures as well as by nuances of interpersonal behavior.

Because procedural justice judgments are affected by a variety of procedural characteristics, and because the importance of each characteristic varies from one situation to another, there is probably no single procedure that maximizes procedural justice in all situations. Perhaps in recognition of this, recent work has shown less concern with the fairness of particular procedures and more concern with psychological, judgmental processes in procedural justice. The complexity of trying to describe a single fairest procedure is emphasized by recent studies (e.g.,

Barrett-Howard & Tyler, 1986, Tyler, 1987b) showing that the situation in which a procedure is encountered can change the emphasis given to various criteria for procedural justice. Given this state of affairs, we can design procedures on the basis of what we know generally concerning the factors that contribute to procedural justice, but we must carefully evaluate procedural innovations to make sure we have not ignored situation-specific considerations.

IMPLICATIONS OF THE PROCEDURAL JUSTICE LITERATURE

Implications for the Social Sciences

Following the Second World War there were important developments in the field of economics. Those developments involved theories based on rational, outcome-oriented models of choice and decision making. The principal conceptual innovation was the articulation of the concept of expected utility calculations (Feather, 1964; Luce & Raiffa, 1957; Luce & Suppes, 1965; Savage, 1954; von Neumann & Morgenstern, 1947). Expected utility models allowed the conception of the individual as a personal utility maximizer to be used to account for social and economic behavior. Following these developments, "self-interested actor" conceptions of the person have expanded and come to dominate the analysis of political and social behavior. Increasingly it has been assumed that people are concerned primarily with the personal favorability of the outcomes they receive from employers, political institutions, or social groups and that they evaluate their personal happiness and their attachment to those groups in terms of their outcomes. The most important implication of the procedural justice literature is that such outcome-based conceptions of the person are incomplete—they ignore important concerns that people have. In particular, work in procedural justice shows a great concern with the processes of social life.

The view of the person as concerned with issues of process is not a new one. Past conceptions of the citizen have relied heavily on the idea that citizens evaluate the government in normative terms (Easton, 1965; Gamson, 1968; Sarat, 1975). Similarly, the importance of procedural concerns *per se* in politics has been widely noted in the past (Anton, 1967; Edelman, 1964; Engstrom & Giles, 1972; Murphy & Tanenhaus, 1969; Saphire, 1978; Scheingold, 1974; Wahlke, 1971). Hence we view the recent attention to procedural justice issues as a reemergence of a long-standing social science tradition rather than as the discovery of a new body of thought. This reemergence is important, however, since it counteracts the current dominance of outcome maximization perspectives.

Because people have been viewed as utility maximizers, much social science research and analysis has been directed at apparent violations of utility maximization principles. In political science, for example, considerable attention has been paid to understanding why citizens engage in such apparently nonutilitarian behaviors as voting. Research directed by models of social behavior that recognize the depth and strength of process concerns would focus on articulating the nature of the values that underlie attitudes and behavior, rather than cataloguing apparent irrationalities. This approach would be more likely to advance our understanding of all aspects of the social evaluation process.

Applications

The image of the person suggested by procedural justice research suggests a new way of looking at people's reactions to organizational, political, and legal decisions. In the area of organizational studies, for example, when conducting research on employee satisfaction we would include consideration of the procedures by which managers make decisions regarding pay and promotions, rather than focusing simply on the magnitude of increments in each employee's salary. In the legal arena, citizen reactions to court decisions would be seen as responsive to the experience of legal procedures, as well as to whether a litigant wins or loses his or her case. In the political arena, citizen reactions to political leaders would be recognized to be affected profoundly by the manner in which leaders make public policy.

In a partisan political atmosphere we would expect that various parties and leaders would compete for control of important symbols of fairness. Since members of the citizenry are socialized to give allegiance to principles of government, which include reference to process fairness, such as equal representation, leaders would be expected to use those symbols to justify their actions to the public. For example, competition over who holds the mandate to control the process of policy formation is an important theme in public presentations made by the President and by Congressional leaders, particularly those in the opposition party. After the President completes his state of the union address, for example, opposition Congressional leaders typically reply. Each seeks to generate a political mandate by appealing to symbols that suggest their representation of the citizenry.

An example of how officials seek to create a positive public climate depend on assumptions about the psychology of the person is found in Tyler (1984). Tyler found that traffic court judges sometimes obscured the fact that they were convicting a defendant by telling that person that they had to pay "court costs," without indicating that such costs implied that the person was being convicted of a crime. These efforts reflected the judge's implicit assumption that litigants would be annoyed by receiving poor outcomes. In fact, however, litigants were primarily concerned with having the opportunity to have their case heard by the judge. This opportunity was frequently thwarted by case pressures on the judges, leading to frustrated litigants. If judges recognized that litigants were primarily concerned with process issues, they would not obscure negative verdicts, an ineffective and potentially counterproductive tactic, but would instead focus on creating opportunities for voice.

In contrast to the lay psychology of self-interest, consider some of the practical implications of the procedural justice literature. Since those affected by decisions will evaluate them in procedural terms, decision makers can gain through designing and implementing policies in ways that accord with public views about what is fair. To the extent that policies or decisions are made in a fair way, their public acceptability will be enhanced. One clear implication of the procedural justice perspective is that leaders are freer than they commonly believe to follow painful policies that are sound in a long-term sense. Leaders often feel that their legitimacy and support are linked to their ability to deliver tangible outcomes to a constituency of self-interested citizens. Reflecting the assumptions of the economic model, they think that those members of the public affected by decisions will react to them in terms of the extent to which they personally gain or lose. The fact that people attend to matters of procedures and process gives leaders greater latitude to pursue policies that may be sound in the long term and to justify them to their constituents by stressing the fairness of the process through which decisions are being made.

But leaders should be wary of assuming that they know which procedures will be viewed as fair. The factors that drive lay judgments of procedural justice are sometimes quite different from those that are of greatest concern to scholars and policymakers. For example, the formal structure of American courts provides a number of procedural protections for those involved in dispute resolution. Practices such as plea bargaining are sometimes criticized as lacking in procedural fairness because they fail to provide these protections. However, when actual defendants are interviewed about their procedural concerns they are found to be little concerned with issues of procedural protection. This does not mean that citizens do not care about procedural justice. They clearly do, but they define justice in different terms than do legal scholars and policy makers. For example, in a study conducted by Casper *et al.* (1987) accused felons were found to be largely indifferent to whether their case was settled by plea bargaining or trial, but highly sensitive to issues of procedural justice. Their sense of procedural justice involved issues such as whether their attorney worked hard to present their case to the judge. Similarly Adler *et al.* (1983) found that litigants accepted arbitration hearings instead of trials if the arbitration hearings met their standards of fair process. To litigants fair process meant simply an opportunity to state their case to a neutral decision maker (cf. Perry, 1986). Citizens care about procedural fairness, but they often define it quite differently than do "experts."

We certainly do not advocate that the fairness judgments of the nonexpert should replace expert analysis of the desirability of procedures and objective measures of procedural efficacy. One potential difficulty with using public preferences as a basis for public policy is that the public may lack knowledge about the actual consequences of various decision-making procedures. Policy makers or experts may possess knowledge or experience that leads them rightly to prefer procedures that those affected by the procedures do not favor. In this case leaders face a conflict between procedures that they know to be desirable for objective reasons and procedures that would be more acceptable to their constituencies. The public typically has a limited awareness of how public policies are created, and there may be widespread ignorance of the compromises and trade-offs that interest-group politics usually requires. Therefore the public may desire procedures that are not feasible and may demand a more consistent set of policies than is politically realistic.

Another difficulty with placing too much emphasis on public views is that the public often shows a strong preference for the status quo. In survey research, for example, questions suggesting that a law is currently on the books generally lead to increased support for it. This general tendency to support the status quo may be important for system stability, but it may also lead members of the public to reject alternatives that might be preferred if they were actually experienced.

Chapter 10

Two Models of Procedural Justice

In this volume we have seen that procedural justice phenomena are reliable and robust and that they are ubiquitous features of social life. Chapter 9 summarizes the effects and processes that are observed regularly in procedural justice studies and offers hypotheses about how procedural justice might work in as yet untested contexts. Our goal in this chapter is to move beyond the generalization of research findings to a more analytic examination of the psychology of procedural justice. In particular, we consider here the implications of two models of procedural justice for our image of the person. It is through consideration of this issue that we believe we can say the most about how procedural justice works to produce the effects we have described throughout this book. Further, it is through consideration of this issue that we can see most clearly the importance of the psychology of procedural justice for fundamental concerns in social psychology and the other behavioral and social sciences.

We have not attempted to generate a unified theory of procedural justice. In our view, the body of research in procedural justice is, at this time, both too extensive and too limited to permit one to advance a broad and specific theory. There are many findings that must be accounted for, and at the same time there are too many holes in our knowledge to permit us to advance with confidence a single explanation of all the procedural justice effects and processes we know of now.

This does not mean that one must eschew theoretical analyses altogether. Although we cannot offer a unified theory of procedural justice, we can describe two fundamental models of procedural justice that between them explain nearly all of the basic procedural justice effects and that, we hope, will serve to push our understanding of the psychology of procedural justice further than has previous theoretical work. One of these models is the traditional model of informed self-interest used by Thibaut and Walker and Leventhal in their theories of procedural jus-

221

tice. The other model is based on group identification processes and on the view that procedural justice is a central cognition in perceptions of groups. By going some distance down each of these two paths, we can explore further some of the basic issues in procedural justice, even if we can also see that following either path to its logical conclusion would invite error. At the very least, we can organize our knowledge and offer alternative views of the processes we seek to understand, alternatives that can be tested in future research. At best, we may develop a foundation upon which a future unified theory of procedural justice can be built.

THE SELF-INTEREST MODEL

DESCRIPTION OF THE MODEL

We noted in Chapter 2 that one of the basic ideas in the Thibaut and Walker (1975, 1978) explanation of procedural justice effects was that individuals, finding themselves in conflict and having little success in negotiating a settlement, would have to turn to a third-party to resolve the dispute. In doing so, they would wish to assure themselves that the dispute would be resolved reasonably and in a fashion that permitted them to retain some form of control over their own outcomes. They would therefore be concerned with the procedure that governed the third-party intervention. Although Thibaut and Walker discuss procedural preferences in terms that focus on issues of control, what is most important about their theory is not control *per se*, but rather the underlying model of the person from which they derive their predictions about control preferences. That model suggests that people seek control over decisions because they are fundamentally concerned with their own outcomes. It is this concern that leads people to attend to issues of control and, in situations involving conflicts so difficult to resolve that disputants must forego decision control, to seek indirect control over decisions through process control.

The idea that people try to maximize their personal gain when interacting with others is a key feature of a number of social science and behavioral models of the person, including economic models (e.g., Laver, 1981), learning theories, and sociological and social psychological theories of social exchange and interdependence (Homans, 1961; Kelley & Thibaut, 1978; Thibaut & Kelley, 1959). As we noted in Chapter 7, such models also dominate the field of public policy analysis under the rubric of public choice theories. Self-interest models have widespread intuitive appeal and have proved to be an important starting point in many important studies in the behavioral and social sciences. They provide the underlying assumptions that shape the procedural justice theories of both Leventhal and Thibaut and Walker.

The Thibaut and Walker view of procedural justice is based on an egoistic conception of the person. They view procedural justice concerns as developing out of the operation of self-interest in the social arena. Basing concerns about fairness on a self-interested vision of the person is not unique to the study of procedural justice. Walster, Walster, and Berscheid (1978) similarly develop their theory of equity (that is, distributive justice) out of a self-interest model of the person. Theories of fairness can be concordant with images of the person as motivated to maximize personal gain in interactions with others. To include fairness concerns in self-interest models all that is needed is a recognition that individuals understand that they must curb their egoistic preferences in order to obtain outcomes that are available only through cooperation with others. One such social compromise, perhaps the fundamental one, is the acceptance of outcomes and procedures on the basis of their fairness, rather than on the basis of their favorability to one's own interests. If approached in this way, the importance of procedural justice does not argue that our conception of the person diverges from the model which underlies economic or learning theories. The major existing theories of procedural justice—those of Thibaut and Walker and Leventhal—assume an extended or informed self-interest model that includes this provision. In this section we explore how extensions and modifications of the self-interest model can explain some basic procedural justice processes.

Thibaut and Walker's original conception of the shift from concerns with decision control to concerns with process control posits a recognition by people that they cannot always maintain complete control over their outcomes when interacting with others. When people join and remain in groups they come to recognize that other people's outcomes or priorities must sometimes be accepted and their own desires must sometimes be delayed or foregone. This is the case because others will remain in the group only if their own concerns are also sometimes addressed.

Given these limits of social interaction, why would people choose to engage in it? In the long term, even with the compromises inherent in group interactions, people gain more through cooperation than they can gain alone. This logic of long-term gain applies to membership in small and informal groups as well as large and complex organizations. According to the informed self-interest model, whether we are speaking of a social group, a political system, or a work organization, people join and remain in that group because they believe that they gain in the long run.

But having decided to seek long-term gain from group membership, how can people assure that they actually will benefit in the long run from group membership? One way is to demand fairness in the procedures by which decisions are made. If procedures for decision making and dispute resolution are fair, then it is reasonable to expect long-term gains, even in the absence of short-term gains. Procedures also simplify decision making, since they eliminate the need for complex decisions that attempt to always satisfy everyone's interests and since they remove the necessity of renegotiating allocations each time a decision must be made. To the extent that all members of the group agree on a given procedure, conflict is averted and relations within the group become more harmonious (cf. Thibaut & Faucheux, 1965).

The implications of a long-term perspective on the value of membership in an organization is illustrated in Easton's theory of support for political organizations (Easton, 1965). Easton asks why citizens do not leave a political system or seek its overthrow when their own favored candidate does not win an election. He argues that they do not do so because they believe that, in the long run, their interests are served by the political system to which they belong. And why do they believe that their interests are served? Easton suggests that it is because people have "diffuse" support for the political system, that is, because they believe in the procedures and institutions of government. Given that the underlying processes of government are fair, citizens believe that, over time, they will receive reasonably high levels of outcomes from their political system. As a result the belief that decision-making procedures are fair promotes loyalty and good feeling toward the system.

The idea that a focus on procedural justice may be associated with a long-term view of self-interest is supported by a recent finding of Reis (1986) who showed that procedural justice concerns are associated with the delay of gratification. In his study Reis identified a wide variety of dispute resolution procedures and used multidimensional scaling techniques to identify the basic dimensions underlying those procedures. He found one dimension that was procedural in character, and variables loading on that dimension were related to views about the delay of gratification, that is, to viewing outcomes in a longer time frame. The idea that people focus on procedures when they are taking a long-term perspective on the personal value of a relationship or a group membership is also supported by the finding, reported in several previous chapters, that procedural justice affects leadership or institutional evaluations more strongly than it affects personal satisfaction. In making leadership or institutional evaluations people are taking a long-term perspective on membership within a group. With personal satisfaction they are reacting to a single decision.

Following this line of thought, we recognize that people must balance two potentially conflicting objectives: short-term personal gain and long-term relationship maintenance. In bargaining, this is called the "bargainer's dilemma." If one pushes harder to reach an agreement favorable to one's own interests, one may gain more, but this also increases the risk of disrupting the relationship and securing no agreement at all. With respect to procedural justice, this dilemma is partially resolved when people agree to let a procedure define how the decision will be made.[1] The Alexander and Ruderman (1987) study, described in Chapter 8, confirmed that procedural fairness is associated with lower levels of conflict and disharmony in organizations.

This line of reasoning led Leventhal to hypothesize that procedural justice judgments will be based on the balance of goals that the perceiver seeks in the relationship. Within organizations, goal trade-offs are always necessary. In long-term relationships within groups or organizations, goal trade-offs generally involve balancing the need to be productive and efficient, leading to high levels of outcome for the entire group, against the need to build group loyalties and commitment to the group, which lead to long-term group maintenance. In the distributive justice literature this trade-off has been thought to be reflected in a corresponding trade-off between equity in reward distribution, which is generally thought to foster efficiency and productivity in the short-term, and equality in reward distribution, which is thought to foster group harmony and commitment to the group (Okun, 1975; but see Deutsch, 1986).

Research examining the relationship between the goals sought in a given group and the importance attached to procedural justice consistently finds that concerns about group harmony increase the importance attached to using procedures believed by those involved to be fair (see Chapter 6). Concerns with productivity or efficiency, on the other hand, are not linked to issues of procedural justice. Group members believe that the extent to which procedures lead to short-term productivity or efficiency is unrelated to issues of fairness (Barrett-Howard and Tyler, 1986; Tyler, 1986b).

The finding that concerns about group harmony lead to an emphasis on procedural justice is consistent with the long-term self-interest perspective on procedural justice. We argue further that, when deciding the extent to which they will be loyal to a group or a relationship, people focus on the manner in which group decisions are made. If they believe that such decisions are made fairly, then group members are more in-

---

[1]The dilemma is not completely resolved because to some extent the problem is echoed in decisions about the design of procedures. There remain questions of how one can assure that the procedure used is as favorable as possible to one's own interests and how one can exercise outcome control within the procedure while at the same time making the procedure acceptable to others.

clined to accept a long-term commitment to the group. These findings suggest that procedural justice is crucial to the long-term maintenance of positive social relationships within groups. There has been relatively little research on the connection between procedural justice and group cohesiveness and solidarity, but we expect that procedural fairness will be found to have strong positive effects on commitment to organizations and institutions and on the reduction of conflict within groups, organizations, and societies.

PREDICTIONS FROM THE MODEL

Having described how procedural justice might be explained by a social psychology of informed self-interest, let us consider in greater detail some of the predictions of such a model for the topics we have been concerned with throughout this book. We are especially interested in the implications of the model for what variables affect judgments of procedural justice, how much overall importance or attention is accorded procedural justice concerns in various situations, and which variables are likely to be most strongly affected by procedural justice. After we have described the predictions that seem to us to flow from the self-interest model, we will consider some research findings relevant to these predictions.

Among the variables that would be expected most strongly to affect procedural justice judgments under this model are: (1) the favorability of the procedure to the perceiver, (2) the amount of control over outcomes afforded the perceiver, (3) the fairness of the outcomes provided by the procedure, and (4) the consistency with which the procedure is applied across people. The predictions that favorability and outcome control will affect procedural justice judgments follow rather directly from the basic assumption of the model, the provision that, absent some powerful reason for foregoing personal gain, people will view more favorably procedures that either directly advance their own interest or allow them to use the procedure to secure positive outcomes. The prediction that outcome fairness will be a strong determinant of procedural fairness rests on the supposition that, when the interests of others require that pure self-interest be compromised to secure long-term gain, distributive fairness will be demanded. If distributive justice has the importance that the informed self-interest model suggests it does, the production of fair outcomes is likely to be one of the prime desiderata of procedures and one of the essential elements of what is meant by a fair procedure. Finally, if the model is correct in assuming that procedures serve to increase harmony and decrease conflict, it seems reasonable to suppose that those procedures that are thought to be least likely to promote conflict about the procedure itself will be seen as most fair, and this in turn points to consistency across persons as a major determinant of procedural justice. Consistency across persons, like the equality rule in distributive justice, removes much of the basis for conflict and argument that might otherwise arise with respect to a given procedure. Because the model assumes that self-interest is a more basic, and thus more potent, factor than is the social compromise that raises concerns about distributive and procedural fairness, the model would predict that the relative importance of these four factors would be the order in which we have considered them here. Thus, for example, procedural favorability would be more powerful than consistency across persons in determining whether a particular procedure is seen as fair.

The informed self-interest model also makes predictions about when procedural justice will be an especially important feature of social life. In essence, the model views procedures as mechanisms for making difficult decisions in ways that permit the individual to continue to forego pure self-interest in the interest of long-term gain through social intercourse. To the extent that concern with procedural justice reflects this function of procedures, we would expect that the importance of procedural justice will be a function jointly of the importance accorded the decision and the extent to which interpersonal harmony is an important goal in the situation in question. As the importance of the decision increases, the importance of the mechanism for making the decision should increase, and the importance of assuring that the mechanism, which is to say the procedure, is fair should also increase. In addition, because fair procedures are thought to resolve or avoid conflict among group members, as the potential for conflict increases, the importance of procedural fairness will also increase.

What might the informed self-interest model predict to be the consequences of judgments of procedural fairness? First, as we noted above, the model would predict that procedural justice judgments will have stronger effects on general attitudes about the group or institution than on specific attitudes about a single experience. This is because procedural justice judgments have a level of generality with respect to time that matches general attitudes about groups or leaders but does not match specific attitudes about single experiences (cf. Fishbein & Ajzen, 1975). Thus a person's evaluation of leaders or institutions will be more strongly affected by procedural justice judgments than is his or her satisfaction with a particular outcome or experience. In addition, as also mentioned above, procedural justice judgments should have strong effects on group cohesiveness and group loyalty, because fair procedures will reassure members that their interests will be protected and advanced through group membership.

Strengths and Limitations of the Model

Procedural justice research shows that the informed self-interest model is a strong, but incomplete, explanation of how procedural justice works. Many of the predictions presented in the previous section have indeed been borne out empirically. For example, there is substantial evidence that favorability, outcome control, decision fairness, and consistency across persons are reasonably strong determinants of the perceived fairness of procedures. Procedural justice concerns have been found to be more influential when the decision is important and when there is concern about social harmony. And procedural justice has been found to exert more powerful effects on attitudes about groups and leaders than on satisfaction with specific outcomes.

Nonetheless, there are some reliable findings that pose problems for the self-interest model. Some of these findings are not entirely contrary to the model but instead involve effects that require so many assumptions or modifications of the model that the explanation strains the model. Consider for example the Paese (1985) finding, reported in Chapter 8, that repeated negative outcomes, even when they make it impossible for any positive outcome to be had, fail to negate the procedural justice advantage of high-input procedures. The informed self-interest model recognizes that procedures that produce negative outcomes can nonetheless be seen as fair because of the long-term perspective that social association requires. But how far does this tolerance for negative outcomes extend? In the case of the Paese experiment, the association was temporary and it was clear to subjects in the conditions of interest that no favorable outcomes would ever occur. It is difficult to see how one could account for an input effect on procedural justice in such circumstances, as long as the perceiver is assumed to be both self-interested and attentive to the implications of the negative outcomes.

There is a way the informed self-interest model could account for the Paese findings and other similar results (e.g., Lind et al., 1980) showing apparent resistance to negative outcomes in procedural evaluations. Drawing on work in social cognition, one might argue that once a procedure has been judged to be favorable, and therefore fair, disconfirmation of the favorability belief will not necessarily lead to abandonment of the fairness belief. Social cognition research shows, for example, that people do not revise their impressions of another when some of the facts upon which the impression was based are disproved (Srull & Wyer, 1979, 1980). Cognitions about procedural fairness might be similarly unaffected unless something specifically prompted a reevaluation of fairness beliefs about the procedure. This is the line of argument that Lind and Lissak (1985) used to explain why outcomes do not seem to affect procedural fairness judgments in the presence of an unflawed procedure but do affect fairness judgments when the procedure shows signs of being flawed. The problem that we face in knowing whether social cognition effects will allow a self-interest model to explain findings like Paese's is that we do not know how strong social cognition effects are relative to self-interest effects. If social cognition effects represent a minor complication of the predictions of the self-interest model, we have no difficulty in holding to the basic idea that procedural justice effects are due to informed self-interest. In this case we would expect findings like Paese's to hold only over the course of a few negative outcomes. If, on the other hand, resistance to reevaluation holds over many negative outcomes, the social cognition effects must be massive for the self-interest model to explain the empirical findings, and one would have to question whether it is not worthwhile to seek a more parsimonious general model.

A second threat to the informed self-interest model, and a much more serious one in our opinion, arises from findings that appear to be altogether outside the model. Two effects in particular fall in this category, the value-expressive enhancement of procedural justice and the effects of quality of treatment on procedural justice. We discussed value-expressive effects first in Chapter 5, where we noted that there is growing evidence that process control or voice enhances perceived fairness for reasons quite apart from any value it might have in affecting outcomes. In Chapters 7 and 8 we noted similar effects in the context of judgments of the fairness of political and organizational procedures. As we noted when we raised the issue of value-expressive effects as a finding contrary to outcome-based explanations of process control, it is difficult to see how such effects could be accounted for by explanations that suppose that people view procedures solely as instruments for generating either favorable or equitable rewards.[2]

There is also a small but growing number of studies that show other clearly noninstrumental effects. It is becoming increasingly clear that procedural justice judgments are strongly affected by concerns about how people are treated under the procedure. For example, Tyler (in press) examined this issue in the context of citizen experiences with the police and courts. He found that citizens were very concerned that their treatment by authorities be polite and show concern for their rights. This finding echoes an earlier similar finding by Tyler and Folger (1980). It appears that observing norms of politeness, showing respect for individuals, and generally following accepted social forms are part of what

[2]It might be argued that people so enjoy exercising voice that it is an outcome in and of itself. In our view, this position stretches the self-interest model to the point where it could account for virtually any finding and would therefore be of little value.

people mean by procedural justice (Bies, in press; Bies & Moag, 1986; Lane, 1986; Messick *et al.*, 1985; Mikula, 1986). It is difficult to see how the observation of social forms could play a major role in procedural justice judgments if people were mostly concerned with the outcome of the procedure, as assumed by the self-interest model.

A GROUP VALUE MODEL

To explain findings such as those just mentioned we need a model of procedural justice that does not depend on self-interest calculations of the sort described above. We are certainly not the first to seek an explanation for fairness phenomena that does not involve self-interest. Lerner's empathy-based theory of justice (Lerner, 1981), for example, argues that the outcome-based models are inadequate to explain people's concerns with justice. Lerner suggests that the most important step in developing an adequate theory of justice is to recognize that the traditional assumption that people are continually and centrally concerned with maximizing their outcomes must inevitably lead to a model that fails to capture the unique qualities associated with justice (1981, p. 22).

An alternative to the self-interest model for understanding procedural justice is to base our explanations of procedural justice effects on some type of group identification model. As is the case with the self-interest model, group identification models have a long history in social psychology. The work of Tajfel (e.g., 1969, 1978) on social categorization and intergroup bias is an early and powerful example of the usefulness of group identification models. More recently, work in the area of social dilemmas has produced additional evidence of the usefulness of such models. That research has suggested that people are strongly affected by identification with groups, even when that identification is based on minimal common circumstance (Brewer & Kramer, 1986; Kramer & Brewer, 1984; Messick & Brewer, 1983). Individuals in groups are more likely to put aside their own self-interest and act in a way that helps all group members than pure self-interest models would predict. In and of itself the occurrence of cooperative or altruistic effects does not show that self-interest is not operating. As we noted in the last section, one might assume that individuals are acting out of a concern for the long-term rewards or punishments that the group can deliver to them. However, Dawes (1986) has argued that some social dilemma effects are such that they cannot be explained by reference to expectations of personal gain. He suggests that there is some affective group identification process that influences behavior above and beyond questions of self-interest. Group identification concepts are also the subject of a small but growing body of theory and research in distributive justice (e.g., Messe, Hymes, & MacCoun, 1986; Reis, 1986).

PROCEDURES AS ELEMENTS OF GROUPS AND SOCIETIES

We call the particular group identification model presented here a "group value model" because we place special emphasis on the effects of values associated with group membership. The model begins by assuming that group membership is a powerful aspect of social life. Humans are by their very nature affiliative creatures, and they devote much of their energy to understanding the functioning of the various groups to which they belong and to participating in social processes within those groups. According to this model, affective relations within and between groups and cognitive constructions with respect to those relations are potent determinants of attitudes and behavior.

We begin our exploration of the application of the group value model to procedural justice concerns by arguing that there are two elements that govern much thought and behavior with respect to groups, organizations, or society. The first element is group identity, by which we mean the factors that distinguish the group in question from other social entities. The second is group procedure. Group procedures specify the authority relations and the formal and informal social processes that regulate much of the group's activity. Just as group identity defines the external features of the group, procedures define the internal features of the group. Given their role in regulating much of the interaction within groups, procedures and evaluations of them assume massive importance in our social life. Viewed in this way a new aspect of procedure is seen. Procedures specify authority relations, and we know from research such as that of Milgram (1965) that authority relations are very potent determinants of social behavior. Within the area of procedural justice we have seldom examined compliance with procedures, as opposed to compliance with outcomes. The present line of reasoning would suggest that mandating behavior in a procedure would be an especially powerful stimulus for occurrence of the behavior, a suggestion that has been borne out in at least one study (Lind, Park, & Ke, 1984). Similarly, explanations and justifications that appeal to people's sense of procedural propriety are especially likely to be accepted—a proposition that is confirmed by the study by Folger et al. (1983).

This model views the procedures we have been discussing as norms of treatment and decision making that regulate much of a group's social structure and process. When procedures are in accord with fundamental values of the group and the individual, a sense of procedural justice results.[3] Many of these fundamental values are the result of socialization. Of course, socialized values can vary from one group to another and from one person to another, but we believe that there are also some fundamental values that affect procedural justice in all groups. For example, all groups are concerned to some extent with solidarity and with maintaining authority relations. Similarly, members of any group would be expected to value status in the group and security about their group membership, as well as the opportunity to participate in the life of the group. Judgments of procedural justice depend on the extent to which a group's procedures are congruent both with these more or less universal values and with idiosyncratic values of the group or individual in question.

Because procedures are very important aspects of the perception of groups, evaluations of procedures, in the form of procedural justice judgments, would be expected to have strong effects on other group-relevant attitudes. It is hardly surprising, then, that procedural justice judgments affect evaluations of leaders and institutions. Indeed, according to the group value model, overall attitudes toward the group itself would be expected to be shaped in substantial part by procedural justice judgments. To the extent to which group procedures are seen as unjust, which is to say that the procedures are contrary to basic group or individual values, evaluation of the group and commitment to it will suffer. To the extent that group procedures are fair, evaluation of the group and commitment and loyalty to the group will increase.

Because psychological reactions to group membership are the major force behind procedural justice processes, attitudes toward the group might well affect procedural justice judgments, just as procedural justice judgments affect evaluations of the group. Thus a member who held the group in high esteem might see that group's procedures as fairer simply because the group endorses these particular procedures. John Thibaut once pointed out to one of the authors a literary example of an interesting procedural justice situation that one could interpret in this fashion. Arthur Koestler's novel *Darkness at Noon* is an account of a Soviet official who has been arrested and is being interrogated for trumped-up crimes against the state. The protagonist knows that any apparent justice in the procedure is a sham; he himself has in the past used similarly corrupt procedures in the service of the state. Ultimately, however, the protagonist convinces himself that he is being treated fairly, largely because he believes in the Soviet system of government and concludes that treatment such as that involved in his own downfall is necessary for the state to survive in a hostile world.

[3]An early finding of the Thibaut and Walker research group was that ratings of the propriety of procedures correlated highly with ratings of the fairness of and satisfaction with procedures.

Because this model views commitment to a society or organization as affected strongly by procedural justice, we might expect that authorities within organized societies would emphasize issues of procedural justice when communicating with members. This hypothesis has not been systematically tested but has received some indirect support. In the area of industrial organizations, Martin, Feldman, Hatch, and Sitkin (1983) found that organizational culture was dominated by stories about how allocation or decision-making conflicts were resolved (see also Tyler, 1986b).

The group value model assumes that many procedural justice values and beliefs are instilled through socialization. New members of groups learn procedural values and beliefs from older members. An account of how socialization can affect views about government procedures is available from Easton and Dennis (1969), in a second part of the theory of system support we mentioned above. As we noted, Easton's theory argues for the separation of diffuse system support from immediate concerns of self-interest. The aspect of the theory of interest here is the suggestion that children acquire support for the political system as part of the childhood socialization process. During socialization attachment to the system develops affectively, that is, without some rational evaluation of the potential personal gain or loss that would accrue from such support. Once established support is a long-term affectively tinged predisposition that is only loosely coupled to issues of short-term self-interest. Easton acknowledges the long-term gain perspective that we previously outlined when he suggests that repeated failures by the political system to solve problems and deliver positive outcomes would eventually lead to loss of diffuse support for the system. The socialization perspective is shown by the cushioning role of early affective attachment in the maintenance of diffuse support (Easton & Dennis, 1969). Individuals develop an affective loyalty to their social group before they make calculations about the utility of short- or long-term allegiance and this affective loyalty affects their reactions to later outcomes from the social system.

Psychological theories of socialization also emphasize the development of attachments as an important basis for value acceptance. Because they are members of a culture with common values, children accept social values and develop habits of behavioral compliance with them (Tyler & McGraw, 1986). Although following rules can clearly be in the individual's self-interest, such compliance does not necessarily flow from a thoughtful consideration of issues of self-interest on the part of the child. Rather, socialization instills the value of following rules for their own sake.

The extent to which rule obedience emerges as an important value in itself can be seen in the work of Kohlberg (e.g., 1969). Kohlberg distinguishes several potential motivations for rule obedience: self-interest (preconventional morality), belief in the intrinsic value of rule obedience (conventional morality), and agreement with the principles embodied in the rules (postconventional morality). Kohlberg finds that the majority of adults express a strong belief that obeying rules has value in itself.

An interesting question raised by the group value model is the procedural content of socialization. This issue has not been addressed in research, but we can suggest several areas in which socialization might occur. Socialization may determine which goals a group member views as valuable. For example, when procedures differ in the goals they will achieve, how is it decided which goals are of most value? The MacCoun and Tyler (in press) study reported in Chapter 4 provides an example from judgments of the procedural justice of juries. Larger juries lower the likelihood of convicting an innocent person, but they are also more costly in terms of societal resources invested. Some balance must be reached between social costs and costs to people who would suffer through wrongful conviction. How this balance is reached depends on the relative value citizens place on saving societal resources and protecting citizens. These values have a socialization component.

Socialization may also communicate beliefs about which goals are served by which procedures. The Leung (1985) study described in Chapter 6 showed that procedural preferences differ across cultures because of differences in beliefs about what values are served by one procedure or another. For example, it is part of our cultural heritage to believe that the goal of attaining truth in legal proceedings is best achieved through use of adversary trial procedures. As we noted in Chapter 5, there is growing evidence from studies of objective justice that this is not the case. Whether actually true or not, however, the belief is acquired through socialization, and it affects choices. Few citizens attend trials or have direct experience with them, and hence their knowledge of the courts is indirect. Even in the face of contrary evidence, preferences based on belief in the accuracy of adversary procedures may persevere. Austin and Tobiasen (1984) showed people that the inquisitorial system could produce verdicts that were of equal quality to those produced by the adversary system. Although their subjects acknowledged that they had been shown that the adversary system was no more accurate, they continued to prefer it.[4] This finding suggests that adversary procedures are not preferred because they are more accurate.

---

[4]We suspect that the psychology involved in this finding is similar to that raised in our previous discussion of social cognition and the resistance of procedural justice judgments to reevaluation in the face of negative outcomes. People might form fairness judgments

Procedural preferences are not unique in their independence from facts. Policy-related preferences are often publicly justified by reference to beliefs about social "facts" that do not really explain the preference. Another example of policy preferences that seem to be socialized to the point of being resistant to change is found in the case of support for the death penalty. If asked, most people indicate that they support the death penalty because it deters crime. When confronted with evidence that no such deterrence effect occurs, however, few people change their minds and cease to support the death penalty (Tyler & Weber, 1982). An examination of this seeming paradox suggests that preferences for or against the death penalty are linked closely to basic value orientations learned early in life and are not simply cognitive judgments about the utility of the death penalty.

The socialization perspective raised by the group value model suggests that at least some procedural preferences can be viewed as socialized attitudes. Like other such attitudes, for example, liberalism, racism, or authoritarianism, procedural preferences might be acquired during the childhood socialization process and come to acquire their own affective base. To state the point differently, because they are learned early and are linked to well-respected groups, some procedures are not only preferred but are liked for their own sake. They become general predispositions toward or against particular ways of solving problems that are only loosely linked to particular instances of those procedures.

Before accepting a socialization perspective, we need some evidence of socialization effects. One type of evidence for such effects is the finding that people who are involved in a procedure that they think is fair do not change their assessments of that procedure's fairness if it produces a poor or unfair outcome (e.g., Greenberg, 1987b; Lind et al., 1980). Another type of evidence supporting socialization effects is finding that judgments about the meaning of procedural justice are consistent across members of the same culture. Tyler (in press) looked for constancies in the meaning of procedural justice across citizen judgments of procedural fairness in encounters with the police and courts in Chicago. He found that, within the context of any particular type of experience, there was substantial agreement about the meaning of procedural justice. For example, people generally agreed that, in the context of dispute resolution procedures, representation was an important criterion for assessing whether one had received fair treatment. The Tyler (in press)

---

and procedural preferences on the basis of the accuracy belief, but they do not undertake a full reexamination of their fairness judgments and procedural preferences every time a linked belief is disconfirmed.

results reinforce the implication of the studies by Greenberg (1987b) and ⁓
Lind *et al.* (1980) that people have beliefs about procedural fairness
which are prior to and at least to some extent independent of personal
experiences. These beliefs are often shared by members of the same
culture. There is frequently a clear consensus among members of a given
culture about what procedural justice means.

While our discussion of socialization emphasizes the imposition of
group values about procedural fairness on members, the group value
model also recognizes that there are some values so basic to life in
groups that they will occur in all group settings. Consider, for example,
how the model might account for the procedural justice effects involved
in the value-expressive function of procedure-mandated voice. The
model assumes that in general people value participation in the life of
their group and that they value their status as group members. Procedures that allow voice are seen as fair because they provide opportunities for participation in group process and because the opportunity
to exercise voice constitutes a visible marker of group membership. In
contrast, mute procedures are seen as improper and therefore unjust
because they frustrate the desire to participate in group process and
because they appear to deny full membership rights to those denied
voice. The model can explain the finding that the voice effect does not
require that voice be effective in producing favorable outcomes but does
require that the decision maker appear to be giving due consideration to
the expressed values and arguments. If it is group participation and
status affirmation that are important, these are obtained as soon as it is
obvious that one's views are expressed and considered; there is no need
for a positive outcome to confirm these values.

An interesting implication of this line of reasoning is that the perception of control over outcomes might be correlated with perceptions of
procedural justice for spurious reasons. Procedures that allow participation and affirm membership status might have two effects: they enhance
perceived fairness by being in accord with basic values and they induce
feelings of control because they encourage the inference that one is an
active and full-fledged member of the group. The perception of control
is simply a by-product of the procedure, occurring in part because people are predisposed, given the slightest encouragement, to make attributions that they have control (cf. Langer, 1983) and in part because the
perception that one is a full-fledged member of a group leads to feelings
of effectiveness and control over one's environment. According to this
line of thought, control is not a link in the causal sequence leading to the
procedural justice judgment: that sequence involves only assessment of
whether the procedure is congruent with values of participation and
membership affirmation. As we noted in Chapter 8, there is some evi-

dence that illusory perceptions of control can be engendered by voice procedures, and we know from a number of studies that there are links between the provision of voice and procedural justice judgments that are not mediated by control. Recent studies by Earley and Lind (1987) show that in some instances some or all of the correlation between control and procedural justice is spurious to the causal relationship between voice and procedural justice.

The group value model would use similar reasoning to account for the procedural justice effects of politeness and other apparently minor aspects of treatment by authorities. When viewed from the perspective of what it says about one's status as a member of a group or society, impolite or undignified treatment is far more important than it might appear to be if judged purely in terms of the outcomes involved. Procedures and procedural behavior that violate basic norms of politeness will be seen as unfair both because the basic normative rules that are violated are valued in their own right and because impolite behavior denies the recipient's dignity as a full-status member of the group.

PREDICTIONS FROM THE MODEL

Having sketched some of the reasoning underlying the group value model, we can proceed to a consideration of what predictions the model might make with regard to some of the basic issues in the psychology of procedural justice. We must ask, as we did with the informed self-interest model, what predictions this model makes concerning what variables affect judgments of procedural justice, how much overall importance or attention is accorded procedural justice concerns in various situations, and which variables are most likely to be affected by procedural justice.

The group value model makes standards of procedural justice dependent upon the values endorsed by the particular group or society in question as well as the values of the individual perceiver. For this reason, the model would predict that the factors covered by Leventhal's ethicality justice rule will be potent determinants of procedural justice judgments. The particular procedural features that are included in the general category of ethicality will depend on the basic values of the group, but once these values are specified the model can predict how any given feature will affect the fairness of the procedure. The socialization argument suggests that there will also be a strong tendency for traditional procedures to be viewed as more just, simply because they have come to be part of the group's value system.

As we noted above, the group value model also predicts that there are some factors that will affect procedural justice regardless of the idiosyncratic values of the group or the perceiver. The extent to which the procedure provides for value expression (and consideration of the expressed ideas) and the extent to which people are treated politely and with dignity are two such factors. Because these factors are closely linked to what is seen in this model as one of the fundamental values underlying procedural justice—that is, recognition of one's status as a member of the group or society in question—they would be expected to be rather potent factors in procedural justice.

The group value model makes several predictions about the importance accorded procedural justice. First, because procedures are viewed in this model as being among the most important features of social life, rather than simply as mechanisms for obtaining long-term favorable outcomes, this model would accord procedural justice more importance generally than would the informed self-interest model. For this reason, procedural justifications and arguments are likely to be especially influential in changing attitudes, a point that is probably well known to astute politicians advocating or resisting social change. In addition, because procedures are viewed as linked very closely in the perceiver's perception to the group that mandates the procedure, the importance of procedural justice is likely to be a function of the importance of the group to the individual in question. Further, because procedures are manifestations of group values, it would be expected that group members who hold most strongly to the traditional values would judge procedures to be most important.

The group value model also predicts that procedural justice will assume special importance for individuals who are uncertain about their status within the group. To the extent that procedures carry the sort of implications we posited in our discussion above of the effects of value expression and politeness, those who are uncertain about how the group views them will be especially sensitive to whether procedures recognize their position within the group. When persons of insecure status see a procedure as being unjust because their status is ignored or rejected, they will react especially strongly to the procedural injustice, and the perception of injustice will have strong negative effects on a wide variety of attitudes, beliefs, and behavior. On the other hand, when such persons view the procedure as affirming their status in the group or society, they will react in a strongly positive fashion.

Turning to the question of what consequences might be expected of procedural justice under the group value model, we find predictions that are similar to those derived from the informed self-interest model, although the arguments leading to the predictions are quite different. The group value model suggests that attitudes about the group and about authorities within the group will be strongly affected by procedural justice judgments. According to the group value model, these effects are due to the close cognitive linking of procedural justice and other characteristics of groups, which arises because procedures are seen as one of the major defining features of groups. For the same reason, group loyalty and commitment will be strongly affected by procedural justice judgments.

The group value model suggests also that procedural justice will have the capacity to engender considerable affect on the part of the perceiver. We know from studies on other aspects of the psychology of group membership that groups have tremendous power to engender affect (e.g., Tajfel, 1969, 1978). Given that, according to this model, violations of procedural justice are viewed as violations of basic group or individual values, we would expect procedural injustice to be a potent source of anger and dislike with respect to whoever is seen as producing the injustice.

STRENGTHS AND LIMITATIONS OF THE MODEL

The group value model provides a credible explanation for many of the effects that are not explained by the informed self-interest model, but it runs afoul of the very effects that are most easily accounted for by that model. The group value model is at its best in accounting for such effects as the value-expressive function of voice and the importance of politeness and dignity as factors in procedural justice. The model's socialization component goes a long way toward explaining the growing evidence that, contrary to some of the earlier procedural justice findings, there are cultural differences in some procedural justice effects.

The model appears to be on solid ground with respect to many of its basic predictions. The finding that procedural justice effects are generally stronger in field studies than in laboratory studies is in accord with the prediction that the importance of procedural justice grows with increases in the importance of the group. Ethicality does appear to be a strong determinant of procedural justice judgments, as are voice and polite treatment. There is evidence from a recent study by Tyler (1986a), described in Chapter 4, that procedural justice does indeed have strong affective consequences. And, as we noted in our discussion of the strengths of the informed self-interest model, there is considerable evidence that procedural justice judgments are strongly linked to such group-oriented attitudes as evaluations of authorities and institutions; both models predict this. The model's prediction that those who most fervently hold traditional group values will also be the most concerned with procedural justice is borne out by research showing stronger procedural justice effects for political conservatives than for political liberals (Rasinski, 1987; Tyler & McGraw, 1986).

Problems arise for the group value model with respect to such simple effects as the lowering of procedural justice judgments following a negative outcome. Just as the self-interest model has difficulty explaining why such effects are not more powerful than they are, the group value model, because it makes no reference to outcomes, has difficulty explaining why such effects should occur at all.[5]

RECONCILIATION OF THE TWO MODELS

As we noted at the outset of this chapter, trying to develop a single theory of procedural justice poses some major problems. Among the most serious of these are the fact that the research evidence offers both some support and some disconfirmation of both of the models we have described and the fact that there is no readily apparent alternative to these two views of procedural justice. Further, the two models are so different with respect to the processes they hypothesize and the predictions they make that there does not seem to be any straightforward way to synthesize them into a single unified theory.

The most profitable short-term resolution of this dilemma, we believe, is to recognize that both models are reasonably accurate, if incomplete, descriptions of important aspects of the psychology of procedural justice. We therefore advocate accepting both models as good explanations of part of the psychology of procedural justice, in much the same way that physics, lacking a unified theory of electromagnetic phenomena, came to view light as both a particle or a wave, depending on which model accounted for the phenomenon in question. We think it is apparent from the procedural justice literature that people react to procedures in ways that clearly reflect both self-interest *and* cognitive and attitudinal reactions to group membership. In addition, the two models together explain most of the basic effects seen in procedural justice research. Our reading of the procedural justice literature has convinced us that people evidence both self-interest processes and group value processes at the same time. It is not a question of some situations prompting reactions that fit one model and other situations prompting reactions that fit another. Often, one can find evidence for both models in the same studies, as when we see a strong outcome effect side-by-side with a strong effect for expressive voice. The two sets of psychological processes seem to be functioning at the same time, in parallel, with each set having its effects on the beliefs, attitudes, and behavior that ultimately appear.

[5]The model has less trouble explaining why inequitable (as opposed to unfavorable) outcomes would decrease procedural justice. To the extent that equity is one of the fundamental values of the group, it would be expected to be a criterion for procedural justice.

A long-term solution to the dilemma posed by the two models must find some way to either explain how the processes posited by these models work together or to replace both models with some other description of procedural justice that explains all of the phenomena that have been observed. Whichever of these approaches ultimately yields a general theory of procedural justice, we see value in exploring the field with both models in mind. If future research finds effects that appear to be due to a combination of self-interest and group value processes, perhaps these effects will provide a reliable basis for positing and describing an interface between these two apparently distinct sets of procedural justice processes. If, on the other hand, future studies find effects that cannot be explained by either model, we will know to look elsewhere for a theory of procedural justice.

IMPLICATIONS OF PROCEDURAL JUSTICE FOR SOCIAL PSYCHOLOGY

We noted in our description of each of the two models that they are by no means unique to procedural justice; one can see many influential applications of each approach in other areas of social psychology as well as in the other social and behavioral sciences. Because of this wider use of both models, the procedural justice findings that support or disconfirm each model have implications for that entire approach to explaining social behavior. Thus the value-expressive and politeness effects seen in procedural justice studies not only pose problems for an informed self-interest model within procedural justice or even within the general study of justice but also pose problems for social exchange and public choice theories. Similarly, the outcome and outcome control effects seen in procedural justice offer encouragement for these theories and pose problems for group identification theories generally.

The field of procedural justice, situated as it is at the interface of the individual and the group, is a good vantage point from which to study fundamental social psychological phenomena and processes. One could argue that procedural justice, focusing as it does on how the individual views the social processes of groups, is a field of study that is quintessentially social psychological. With this in mind, it is reasonable to ask what procedural justice research can tell us about basic social psychological processes.

The major contribution of the procedural justice literature to our understanding of general social psychology is its support for a shift in emphasis from the outcome to the process of social interaction. The message of procedural justice for social psychology and, indeed, for the behavioral and social sciences generally is that people are far more concerned with social process than most of us would have imagined. There is a corresponding message in how modest is the influence of social outcomes. We do not wish to overdraw this implication; as we saw above, one cannot abandon altogether models that posit that people are concerned with outcomes. It is clear, though, that some important features of social attitudes and behavior can be explained only by reference to noninstrumental concerns, only through understanding that people pay a great deal of attention to the way things are done and the nuances of their treatment by others. In social psychology generally, as in procedural justice, we must change our image of the person to reflect this greater concern with, and sensitivity to, matters of social process.

* * * * * * * * * * *

In the years since Thibaut and Walker brought procedural justice to our attention, our knowledge and sophistication about this intriguing aspect of social psychology have grown remarkably. The field has shown itself to be the source of both interesting theoretical issues and useful applications. But there is much left to do; we have just begun to see some of the most intriguing aspects of procedural justice. We hope that this book will serve as a signpost along a much longer road to greater understanding of this intriguing topic.

Measurement of Procedural Justice Beliefs

The bulk of research on procedural justice has dealt with attitudes and beliefs about procedures, outcomes, leaders, and institutions. To understand fully the research and its implications, one might wish to consider the interview and rating questions used to measure some of the central concepts in the literature. In this appendix we present some of the questions used in recent studies of procedural justice.

Table A-1 presents the questions used to assess perceived procedural fairness in seven recent studies. This table includes items that directly assess evaluations of a specific procedure or experience; we present in a later table more global questions that address a variety of procedures at once. The studies included in the table were chosen to include a variety of methods and a variety of target procedures. All of the studies included the simplest assessment of procedural fairness—a question asking how fair the procedure is. Some of the studies asked other, closely related questions, such as how satisfied the respondent is with the procedure or how much the respondent would trust the procedure in a future dispute. In the studies that use multiple questions to tap procedural justice judgments, it is common practice to sum or average the ratings from the several scales or to use factor scores to produce a single, more reliable, index of procedural justice. The reliability statistics reported in studies that use multiple-question indices appear to support the practice of using summative measures (e.g., Kanfer *et al.*, 1987, report a Cronbach's alpha of .92 for their three-item index).

For social psychologists, the term *satisfaction*, perhaps because it is used frequently in social exchange theories, carries an outcome-oriented connotation, whereas the term *fairness* is seen as connoting reactions that are more strongly conditioned by distributional or procedural complexities. There is no evidence that survey respondents and experimental subjects draw any such distinctions; ratings of satisfaction with a procedure appear to tap much the same feelings as do ratings of the fairness of the procedure. Several studies (e.g., Lind *et al.*, 1980; Walker *et al.*, 1974; Walker *et al.*, 1979) report factor analyses of a variety of items

TABLE A-1. Assessing Procedural Justice: Survey and Questionnaire Items
I. Evaluations of Experience with a Procedure

Study and topic	Questions
Tyler & Folger (1980)	
Evaluating citizen–police encounters	How fairly were you treated by the police?
Tyler & Caine (1981)	
Evaluating local political decisions	How fair were the procedures used by Councilman Jones to reach his decision?
Evaluating grading procedures	How fair were the grading procedures used in the class?
Tyler (1984)	
Evaluating court experiences	How just and impartial were the procedures used by the judge in trying your case?
Adler, Hensler, & Nelson (1983)	
Evaluating arbitration hearing experiences	Now, thinking about the arbitration hearing itself—do you think the way it was conducted was very fair, somewhat fair, somewhat unfair, or very unfair?
Lind, Kurtz, Musante, Walker, & Thibaut (1980)	How satisfied are you with the trial procedure?
Evaluating laboratory adjudication experience	How much would you trust this procedure in a future dispute?
	How fair was the procedure used in this trial?
Lind & Lissak (1985)	How fair was the dispute resolution procedure in which you participated?
Evaluating laboratory dispute resolution	How satisfied are you with the procedure used in the dispute resolution?
	To what extent would you trust the dispute resolution procedure used in the trial if you were involved in a future dispute?
Kanfer, Sawyer, Earley & Lind (1987)	How fair is the procedure used to determine which company will receive the contract?
Evaluating performance evaluation procedure	How satisfied are you with the procedure used to determine which company will receive the contract?
	How satisfied are you with the procedure used to evaluate your company's performance?

designed to assess evaluative reactions to procedures. Among the rating and survey items that have been found to load highly on procedural justice factors are items asking about satisfaction with a procedure, items asking about the fairness and the propriety of a procedure or "the way [something] was done," and items asking about trust in the procedure. Items asking about satisfaction with outcomes, the fairness of outcomes, and the extent to which the outcomes reflect the true situation upon which the distribution is based all load strongly on distributive fairness factors. It is worthwhile to remember that procedural and distributive fairness can, and frequently are, measured by a variety of evaluative items other than simply questions about fairness *per se*. The results of many procedural fairness studies can be best understood if we remember that the variable of interest is in fact a general evaluative response to the procedure or social process in question.

Having mentioned the factor analyses conducted in some studies of procedural justice, we should warn about one use of such analyses that is probably suspect. We refer to the use of factor scores based on orthogonal rotations in factor analyses of distributive and procedural justice items. Distributive and procedural justice appear be naturally correlated because they share causal precursors and because each form of fairness judgment probably influences the other. Given this natural relation, orthogonal rotations can lead to ambiguous results or erroneous judgments. For example, Lind *et al.* (1980) note that the absence of effects for a manipulation of the outcome of a trial on perceptions of procedural justice may have resulted from the use of an orthogonal rotation in the generation of their factor score variables. More valid practices include using oblique rotations in generating factor scores, using summed indices that do not force orthogonality among variables, and using multivariate analysis of variance on univariate measures.

Table A-2 reports the questions used in several studies that investigated general evaluations of fairness in political decision making. The table includes both studies that asked specifically about procedural fairness and studies that generated measures of procedural justice from items asking about obviously unfair features of procedures and then combining responses.

Table A-3 presents questions used to assess perceptions of two features of procedures that are closely linked to procedural fairness: process control and decision control. An appreciation of the distinction between process and decision control can be gained from comparison of the items used to measure each of these two control concepts.

In closing we should note that the measurement of procedural justice variables has reached a level of sophistication that supports the development of increasingly fine-etched theories, but much needs to be done. Here, as in many other areas of social psychology, there is too little attention devoted to constancy of measurement across studies. One of our intentions in including this section is to provide researchers with some of the common measures used in past studies. We hope also to spur researchers to undertake careful studies of the measurement of such variables as procedural justice, distributive justice, and process and decision control. Such studies would benefit all of us who work in this area by providing finer instruments for the future investigation of procedural justice phenomena.

TABLE A-2. Assessing Procedural Justice: Survey and Questionnaire Items
II. General Evaluations of Procedures

Study and topic	Questions
Direct Assessment	

Tyler & Caine (1981)
  Evaluating national govern-
  ment procedures
	How fair are the procedures by which government benefits are distributed?
	How fair are the procedures used by the government to decide the benefits to which each citizen is entitled?
	How fair are the procedures by which government policies are determined?

Tyler, Rasinski, & McGraw (1985)
  Evaluating national govern-
  ment procedures
	The government provides citizens with many types of services and benefits, such as social security, medicare and medicaid, housing mortgage subsidies, veterans' benefits, student loans, and unemployment and workmen's compensation. How fair are the procedures by which the government decides who will receive government benefits?
	Now a few questions about the federal taxes the government collects to fund government programs: How fair are the procedures by which the federal government decides the level of taxes each citizen will pay?

Indirect Assessment	

Tyler, Rasinski, & McGraw (1985)
  Evaluating national govern-
  ment procedures
	In deciding what national policies to implement do you think that President Reagan usually, sometimes, or seldom considers the views of all sides before making decisions?
	Do you think that he usually, sometimes, or seldom takes enough time to consider his policy decisions carefully?
	Does he usually, sometimes, or seldom have enough time to make good policy decisions?
	Is he usually, sometimes, or seldom unbiased and impartial in making policy decisions?

Rasinski & Tyler (in press)
  Evaluating candidates' deci-
  sion-making procedures
	In deciding what social benefit policies to support or oppose do you think that Mr. Reagan (Mr. Mondale) will usually, sometimes, or seldom consider the views of all sides before making decisions?
	How much of an opportunity will Mr. Reagan (Mr. Mondale) give citizens to express their views before making policy decisions? Will citizens have a great deal of opportunity, some opportunity, a little opportunity, or not much opportunity at all to express their views before policy decisions are made?

(*continued*)

Study and topic	Questions
Rasinski & Tyler (*cont.*)	In deciding what social benefit policies to support or oppose will Mr. Reagan (Mr. Mondale) be equally influenced by the views of all citizens or groups of citizens, or will he favor some citizens over others?
	In appointing people to advise him and to run the agencies of the federal government will Mr. Reagan (Mr. Mondale) generally choose people who give equal weight to the interests of all citizens or will he choose people who favor the interests of some citizens over those of others?

TABLE A-3. Assessing Process and Decision Control: Survey and Questionnaire Items

Study and topic	Questions
Process Control	
Tyler, Rasinski, & Spodick (1985) Evaluating court experiences	How much opportunity did you have to present evidence in your case?
	How much control did you have over the way evidence was presented in your case?
Evaluating grading experiences	How much opportunity did you have to demonstrate your knowledge in the material that was graded?
Evaluating budget allocations	How much opportunity did those involved have to present evidence before budget allocation decisions were made?
Lind, Kurtz, Musante, Walker, & Thibaut (1980) Evaluating laboratory adjudication experience	To what extent were you able to control what happened in the trial?
	How much opportunity did each side have to present its facts?
Lind, Lissak, & Conlon (1983) Evaluating laboratory dispute resolution	To what extent do you feel you were able to control what happened to you under the procedure used in the dispute resolution?
Decision Control	
Tyler, Rasinski, & Spodick (1985) Evaluating court experiences	How much control did you have over the decision that was made in your case?
Evaluating grading experiences	To what extent could you influence that grade you received?
Evaluating budget allocations	How much control did those involved have over the budget allocations made?
Lind, Lissak, & Conlon (1983) Evaluating laboratory dispute resolution	How much influence did you have in determining the final outcome of the dispute resolution?

References

Adams, J. S. (1963). Toward an understanding of inequity. *Journal of Abnormal and Social Psychology, 67,* 422–436.

Adams, J. S. (1965). Inequity in social exchange. In L. Berkowitz (Ed.), *Advances in experimental social psychology,* (Vol. 2, pp. 267–299). New York: Academic Press.

Adler, J. W., Hensler, D. R., & Nelson, C. E. (1983). *Simple justice: How litigants fare in the Pittsburgh Court Arbitration Program.* Santa Monica, CA: RAND Corporation.

Alexander, S., & Ruderman, M. (1987). The role of procedural and distributive justice in organizational behavior. *Social Justice Research, 1,* 117–198.

Alexander, S., Ruderman, M., & Russ, T. L. (1984, August). *The nature of procedural justice and its influence on organizational behavior.* Paper presented at the meeting of the American Psychological Association, Toronto.

Alexander, S., & Russ, T. L. (1985, August). *Procedural and distributive justice effects: The role of social context.* Paper presented at the meeting of the American Psychological Association, Los Angeles.

Anton, T. J. (1967). Roles and symbols in the determination of state expenditures. *Midwest Journal of Political Science, 11,* 27–43.

Austin, W., Friedman, J. S., Martz, R. A., Hooe, G. S., & Ball, K. P. (1978). Responses to favorable sex discrimination. *Law and Human Behavior, 1,* 283–298.

Austin, W., & Tobiasen, J. M. (1984). Legal justice and the psychology of conflict resolution. In R. Folger (Ed.), *The sense of injustice* (pp. 227–274). New York: Plenum Press.

Austin, W., Williams, T. A., Worchel, S., Wentzel, A. A., & Siegel, D. (1981). Effect of mode of adjudication, presence of defense counsel, and favorability of verdict on observers' evaluations of a criminal trial. *Journal of Applied Social Psychology, 11,* 281–300.

Barrett-Howard, E., & Lamm, H. (1986). *Procedural and distributive justice: Definitions and beliefs of West German university students.* Unpublished manuscript, Northwestern University.

Barrett-Howard, E., & Tyler, T. R. (1986). Procedural justice as a criterion in allocation decisions. *Journal of Personality and Social Psychology, 50,* 296–304.

Bavelas, A. (1950). Communication patterns in task-oriented groups. *Journal of the Acoustical Society of America, 22,* 725–730.

Berkowitz, L., & Walster, E. (Eds.) (1976). *Equity theory: Toward a general theory of social interaction. Advances in experimental social psychology* (Vol. 9). New York: Academic Press.

Bies, R. J. (1986, August). *Identifying principles of interactional justice: The case of corporate recruiting.* Paper presented at the meeting of the National Academy of Management, Chicago.

Bies, R. J. (In press). The predicament of injustice: The management of moral outrage. In L. L. Cummings and B. M. Staw (Eds.), *Research in organizational behavior* (Vol. 9). Greenwich, CT: JAI Press.

Bies, R. J., & Moag, J. S. (1986). Interactional justice: Communications criteria of fairness. In R. Lewicki, M. Bazerman, & B. Sheppard (Eds.), *Research on negotiation in organizations* (Vol. 1, pp. 43–55). Greenwich, CT: JAI Press.

Bies, R. J., & Shapiro, D. L. (1987). Interaction fairness judgments: The influence of causal accounts. *Social Justice Research, 1,* 199–218.

Blau, P. M. (1968). Social exchange. In D. L. Sills (Ed.), *International encyclopedia of the social sciences* (Vol. 7). New York: MacMillan.

Blumberg, P. (1968). *Inequality in an age of decline.* New York: Oxford University Press.

Brett, J. M. (1986). Commentary on procedural justice papers. In R. Lewicki, M. Bazerman, & B. Sheppard (Eds.), *Research on negotiation in organizations* (Vol. 1, pp. 81–90). Greenwich, CT: JAI Press.

Brett, J. M., & Goldberg, S. B. (1983). Mediator–advisors: A new third-party role. In M. Bazerman & R. Lewicki (Eds.), *Negotiating in organizations* (pp.20165–176). Beverly Hills, CA: Sage.

Brewer, M. B., & Kramer, R. K. (1986). Choice behavior in social dilemmas: Effects of social identity, group size, and decision framing. *Journal of Personality and Social Psychology, 50,* 543–549.

Burger, W. E. (1982). Isn't there a better way? *American Bar Association Journal, 68,* 274–277.

Caddell, P. H. (1979). Crisis of confidence: Trapped in a downward spiral. *Public Opinion, 5,* 2–8.

Campbell, J. P., & Pritchard, R. D. (1976). Motivation theory in industrial and organizational psychology. In M. D. Dunnette (Ed.), *Handbook of industrial and organizational psychology* (pp. 63–130). New York: Wiley.

Casper, J. D., Tyler, T. R., & Fisher, B. (in press). Procedural justice in felony cases. *Law and Society Review.*

Citrin, J. (1974). Comment: The political relevance of trust in government. *American Political Science Review, 68,* 973–988.

Cohen, R. L. (1985). Procedural justice and participation. *Human Relations, 38,* 643–663.

Conlon, D. E., Lind, E. A., & Lissak, R. I. (1987). *Nonlinear and nonmonotonic effects of outcome on procedural and distributive fairness judgments.* Unpublished manuscript, University of Illinois, Champaign.

Cook, F. L. (1979). *Who should be helped?* Beverly Hills: CA. Sage.

Cook, T. D., & Campbell. D. T. (1979). *Quasiexperimentation.* Chicago: Rand-McNally.

Cornelius, G. W. (1985). *Evaluation fairness and work motivation.* Unpublished masters thesis, University of Illinois, Champaign.

Crosby, F. (1976). A model of egoistical relative deprivation. *Psychological Review, 83,* 85–113.

Crosby, F. (1982). *Relative deprivation and working women.* New York: Oxford University Press.

Damaska, M. (1975). Presentation of evidence and factfinding precision. *University of Pennsylvania Law Review, 123,* 1083–1106.

Davis, J. H. (1980). Group decision and procedural justice. In M. Fishbein (Ed.), *Progress in social psychology* (pp. 157–229). Hillsdale, NJ: Erlbaum.

Davis, J. H., Spitzer, C. E., Nagao, D., & Stasser, G. T. (1978). Bias in social decision by individuals and groups: An example from mock juries. In H. Brandstatter, J. Davis, & H. Schuler (Eds.), *Dynamics of group decisions* (pp. 33–52). Beverly Hills, CA: Sage.

Dawes, R. (1986). *Group identification and collective action.* Paper delivered at the Nag's Head Conference on Social Dilemmas. Nag's Head, NC.

deCarufel, A. (1981). The allocation and acquisition of resources in times of scarcity. In M.

J. Lerner & S. C. Lerner (Eds.), *The justice motive in social behavior* (pp. 317–342). New York: Plenum Press.

Deutsch, M. (1975). Equity, equality, and need: What determines which value will be used for distributive justice? *Journal of Social Issues, 31,* 137–150.

Deutsch, M. (1981). Justice in "the crunch." In M. J. Lerner & S. C. Lerner (Eds.), *The justice motive in social behavior.* New York: Plenum Press.

Deutsch, M. (1986). Cooperation, conflict, and justice. In H. W. Bierhoff, R. L. Cohen, & J. Greenberg (Eds.), *Justice in social relations* (pp. 3–18). New York: Plenum Press.

Earley, P. C. (1984). *Informational mechanisms of participation influencing goal acceptance, satisfaction and performance.* Unpublished doctoral dissertation, University of Illinois, Champaign.

Earley, P. C., & Lind, E. A. (1987). Procedural justice and participation in task selection: The role of control in mediating justice judgments. *Journal of Personality and Social Psychology, 52,* 1148–1160.

Easton, D. (1965). *A systems analysis of political life.* Chicago: University of Chicago Press.

Easton, D., & Dennis, J. (1969). *Children in the political system: The origins of political legitimacy.* Chicago: University of Chicago Press.

Ebreo, A. (1985, August). *Structural versus non-structural variations in process control: The effect of procedure, outcome, and lawyer interactional style on procedural fairness judgments.* Paper presented at the meeting of the American Psychological Association, Los Angeles.

Edelman, M. (1964). *The symbolic uses of politics.* Urbana: University of Illinois Press.

Engstrom, R. L., & Giles, M. W. (1972). Expectations and images: A note on diffuse system support for legal authorities. *Law & Society Review, 6,* 631–636.

Erickson, B., Holmes, J., Frey, R., Walker, L., & Thibaut, J. (1974). Functions of a third party in the resolution of conflict: The role of the judge in pretrial conferences. *Journal of Personality and Social Psychology, 30,* 293–306.

Feather, N. T. (1964). Subjective probability and decisions under uncertainty. In W. J. Gore & J. W. Dyson (Eds.), *The making of decisions* (pp. 339–355). New York: Macmillan.

Festinger, L. (1957). *A theory of cognitive dissonance.* Evanston, IL: Row, Peterson.

Fishbein, M., & Ajzen, I. (1975). *Belief, attitude, intention, and behavior: An introduction to theory and research.* Reading, MA: Addison-Wesley.

Fiss, O. M. (1984). Against settlement. *Yale Law Journal, 93,* 1073–1090.

Folger, R. (1977). Distributive and procedural justice: Combined impact of "voice" and improvement on experienced inequity. *Journal of Personality and Social Psychology, 35,* 108–119.

Folger, R. (1986a). Voice and decision control. In R. Lewicki, M. Bazerman, & B. Sheppard (Eds.), *Research on negotiation in organizations* (Vol. 1). Greenwich, CT: JAI Press.

Folger, R. (1986b). Rethinking equity theory: A referent cognitions model. In H. W. Bierhoff, R. L. Cohen, & J. Greenberg (Eds.), *Justice in social relations,* (pp. 145–164). New York: Plenum Press.

Folger, R., & Greenberg, J. (1985). Procedural justice: An interpretative analysis of personnel systems. In K. Rowland & G. Ferris (Eds.), *Research in personnel and human resources management,* Vol. 3 (pp. 141–183). Greenwich, CT: JAI Press

Folger, R., Rosenfield, D., Grove, J., & Corkran, L. (1979). Effects of "voice" and peer opinions on responses to inequity. *Journal of Personality and Social Psychology, 37,* 2253–2261.

Folger, R., Rosenfield, D., & Robinson, T. (1983). Relative deprivation and procedural justifications. *Journal of Personality and Social Psychology, 45,* 268–273.

Friedland, N., Thibaut, J., & Walker, L. (1973). Some determinants of the violation of rules. *Journal of Applied Social Psychology, 3,* 103–118.

Friedman, L. M. (1985). *A history of American law* (2nd ed.). New York: Simon and Schuster.

Fry, W. R., & Cheney, G. (1981, May). *Perceptions of procedural fairness as a function of distributive preferences.* Paper presented at the annual meeting of the Midwestern Psychological Association, Detroit.

Fry, W. R., & Leventhal, G. S. (1979, March). *Cross-situational procedural preferences: A comparison of allocation preferences and equity across different social settings.* Paper presented at the annual meeting of the Southeastern Psychological Association, Washington, DC.

Gamson, W. (1968). *Power and discontent.* Homewood, IL: Dorsey.

Gluckman, M. (1969). *Ideas and procedures in African customary law.* London: Oxford University Press.

Greenberg, J. (1981). The justice of distributing scarce and abundant resources. In M. J. Lerner & S. C. Lerner (Eds.), *The justice motive in social behavior.* New York: Plenum Press.

Greenberg, J. (1982). Approaching equity and avoiding inequity in groups and organizations. In J. Greenberg & R. L. Cohen (Eds.), *Equity and justice in social behavior* (pp. 389–435). New York: Academic Press.

Greenberg, J. (1984). On the apocryphal nature of inequity distress. In R. Folger (Ed.), *The sense of injustice* (pp. 167–188). New York: Plenum Press.

Greenberg, J. (1986a). The distributive justice of organizational performance appraisals. In H. W. Bierhoff, R. L. Cohen, & J. Greenberg (Eds.), *Justice in social relations* (pp. 337–352) New York: Plenum Press.

Greenberg, J. (1986b). Determinants of perceived fairness of performance evaluations. *Journal of Applied Psychology, 71,* 340–342.

Greenberg, J. (1987a). Reactions to procedural injustice in payment distributions: Do the ends justify the means. *Journal of Applied Psychology, 72,* 55–61.

Greenberg, J. (1987b). Using diaries to promote procedural justice in performance appraisals. *Social Justice Research, 1,* 219–234.

Greenberg, J., & Folger, R. (1983). Procedural justice, participation, and the fair process effect in groups and organizations. In P. Paulus (Ed.), *Basic group process* (pp. 235–256). New York: Springer-Verlag.

Hammond, K. R., & Adelman, L. (1976). Science, values, and human judgment. *Science, 194,* 389–396.

Hans, V., & Vidmar, N. (1986). *Judging the jury.* New York: Plenum Press.

Hansen, R. D., & Lowe, C. A. (1976). Distinctiveness and consensus: The influence of behavioral information on actors' and observers' attributions. *Journal of Personality and Social Psychology, 34,* 425–438.

Hayden, R. M., & Anderson, J. K. (1979). On the evaluation of procedural systems in laboratory experiments: A critique of Thibaut and Walker. *Law and Human Behavior, 3,* 21–38.

Heinz, A. M. (1985a). Procedure v. consequences. In S. Talarico (Ed.), *Courts and criminal justice.* Beverly Hills, CA: Sage.

Heinz, A. M. (1985b, June). *Plea bargaining, participant satisfaction, and system support.* Paper presented at the Law and Society Association. San Diego.

Henshel, R. L. (1980). The purposes of laboratory experimentation and the virtues of artificiality. *Journal of Experimental Social Psychology, 16,* 466–478.

Heuer, L. B., & Penrod, S. (1986). Procedural preference as a function of conflict intensity. *Journal of Personality and Social Psychology, 51,* 700–710.

Hochschild, J. (1981). *What's fair?: American beliefs about distributive justice.* Cambridge, MA: Harvard.

Hollander, E. P. (1985). Leadership and power. In G. Lindzey & E. Aronson (Eds.), *Handbook of social psychology* (pp. 485–538, Vol. 1, 3rd ed.). New York: Random House.

Homans, G. C. (1961). *Social behaviour: Its elementary forms.* London: Routledge and Kegan Paul.

Houlden, P. (1980). Plea bargaining. *Law & Society Review, 15,* 267–291.

Houlden, P., LaTour, S., Walker, L., & Thibaut, J. (1978). Preferences for modes of dispute resolution as a function of process and decision control. *Journal of Experimental Social Psychology, 14,* 13–30.

House, J. S., & Mason, W. M. (1975). Political alienation in America, 1952–1968. *American Sociological Review, 40,* 123–147.

Hutcheson, F. (1728). *An essay on the nature and conduct of the passions and affections, with illustrations on the moral sense.* London.

Insko, C. A., Thibaut, J. W., Moehle, D., Wilson, M., Diamond, W. D., Gilmore, R., Solomon, M. R., & Lipsitz, A. (1980). Social evolution and the emergence of leadership. *Journal of Personality and Social Psychology, 39,* 431–448.

James, F., Jr. (1965). *Civil procedure.* Boston: Little, Brown.

Jones, E. E., & Nisbett, R. E. (1971). *The actor and the observer: Divergent perceptions of the causes of behavior.* Morristown, NJ: General Learning Press.

Jöreskog, K. J., & Sörbom, D. (1981). *LISREL.* Morresville, IN: Scientific Software.

Kanfer, R., Sawyer, J., Earley, P. C., & Lind, E. A. (1987). Participation in task evaluation procedures: The effects of influential opinion expression and knowledge of evaluative criteria on attitudes and performance. *Social Justice Research, 1,* 235–249.

Kaplan, M. (Ed.) (1986). *The impact of social psychology on procedural justice.* Springfield, IL: Charles C. Thomas.

Kassin, S., & Wrightsman L.(Eds.), (1985). *The psychology of evidence and courtroom procedure.* Beverly Hills, CA: Sage Publications.

Katz, D. (1960). The functional approach to the study of attitudes. *Public Opinion Quarterly, 24,* 163–204.

Katz, D., Gutek, B. A., Kahn, R. L., & Barton, E. (1975). *Bureaucratic encounters.* Ann Arbor, MI: Survey Research Center, Institute for Social Research.

Kelley, H. H., & Thibaut, J. W. (1978). *Interpersonal relations: A theory of interdependence.* New York: Wiley.

Kerr, N. L., & Bray, R. M. (Eds.) (1982). *The psychology of the courtroom.* New York, NY: Academic Press.

Kinder, D. R., & Sears, D. O. (1985). Political psychology. In G. Lindzey & E. Aronson (Eds.), *The handbook of social psychology* (3rd ed.). Reading, MA: Addison-Wesley.

Kohlberg, L. (1969). Stage and sequence: The cognitive-developmental approach to socialization. In D. A. Goslin (Ed.), *Handbook of socialization theory and research.* New York: Rand McNally.

Kramer, R. M., & Brewer, M. B. (1984). Effects of group identity on resource use in a simulated commons dilemma. *Journal of Personality and Social Psychology, 46,* 1044–1057.

Kurtz, S. T., & Houlden, P. (1981). Determinants of procedural preferences of post court-martial military personnel. *Basic and Applied Social Psychology, 2,* 27–43.

Landis, J. M., & Goodstein, L. (1986). When is justice fair? *American Bar Foundation Research Journal, 1986,* 675–708.

Lane, R. E. (1962). *Political ideology.* New York: Free Press.

Lane, R. E. (1986). *Procedural justice: How one is treated versus what one gets.* Unpublished manuscript, Yale University.

Langer, E. J. (1983). *The psychology of control.* Beverly Hills, CA: Sage.

LaTour, S. (1978). Determinants of participant and observer satisfaction with adversary and inquisitorial modes of adjudication. *Journal of Personality and Social Psychology, 36,* 1531–1545.

LaTour, S., Houlden, P., Walker, L., & Thibaut, J. (1976). Procedure: Transnational perspectives and preferences. *Yale Law Review, 86,* 258–290.

Laver, M. (1981). *The politics of private desires.* New York: Penguin.

Lea, M., & Walker, L. (1979). Efficient procedure. *North Carolina Law Review, 57,* 363–378.

Leavitt, H. J. (1951). Some effects of certain communication patterns on group performance. *Journal of Abnormal and Social Psychology, 46,* 38–50.

Lerner, M. J. (1970). The desire for justice and reactions to victims. In J. Macaulay & L. Berkowitz (Eds.), *Altruism and helping behavior: Social psychological studies of some antecedents and consequences.* New York: Academic Press.

Lerner, M. J. (1974). The justice motive: "Equity" and "parity" among children. *Journal of Personality and Social Psychology, 29,* 1–52.

Lerner, M. (1986, July). *Some thoughts about the social psychology of justice.* Paper presented at the International Conference on Social Justice in Human Relations, Leiden.

Lerner, M., & Whitehead, L. A. (1980). Procedural justice viewed in the context of justice motive theory. In G. Mikula (Ed.), *Justice and social interaction* (pp. 219–256). New York: Springer-Verlag.

Lerner, S. C. (1981). Adapting to scarcity and change (I): Stating the problem. In M. J. Lerner & S. C. Lerner (Eds.), *The justice motive in social behavior.* New York: Plenum Press.

Leung, K. (1985). *Cross-cultural study of procedural fairness and disputing behavior.* Unpublished doctoral dissertation, University of Illinois.

Leung, K., & Lind, E. A. (1986). Procedural justice and culture: Effects of culture, gender, and investigator status on procedural preferences. *Journal of Personality and Social Psychology, 50,* 1134–1140.

Leventhal, G. S. (1976). Fairness in social relationships. In J. W. Thibaut, J. T. Spence, & R. C. Carson (Eds.), *Contemporary topics in social psychology* (pp. 211–240). Morristown, NJ: General Learning Press.

Leventhal, G. S. (1980). What should be done with equity theory? New approaches to the study of fairness in social relationships. In K. Gergen, M. Greenberg, & R. Willis (Eds.), *Social exchange: Advances in theory and research* (27–55). New York: Plenum Press.

Leventhal, G. S., Karuza, J., & Fry, W. R. (1980). Beyond fairness: A theory of allocation preferences. In G. Mikula (Ed.), *Justice and social interaction* (pp. 167–218). New York: Springer-Verlag.

Lewin, K., Lippitt, R., & White, R. K. (1939). Patterns of aggressive behavior in experimentally created "social climates." *Journal of Social Psychology, 10,* 271–299.

Lind, E. A. (1974). *Reactions of participants to adjudicated conflict resolution: A cross-cultural, experimental study.* Unpublished doctoral dissertation, University of North Carolina, Chapel Hill.

Lind, E. A. (1975). The exercise of information influence in legal advocacy. *Journal of Applied Social Psychology, 5,* 127–143.

Lind, E. A., Erickson, B. E., Friedland, N., & Dickenberger, M. (1978). Reactions to procedural models for adjudicative conflict resolution: A cross-national study. *Journal of Conflict Resolution, 22,* 318–341.

Lind, E. A., Kanfer, R., Ambrose, M., & Conlon, D. (1986). *Voice and the illusion of control.* Unpublished manuscript, RAND Corporation, Santa Monica, CA.

Lind, E. A., Kurtz, S., Musante, L., Walker, L., & Thibaut, J. W. (1980). Procedure and outcome effects on reactions to adjudicated resolution of conflicts of interests. *Journal of Personality and Social Psychology, 39,* 643–653.

Lind, E. A., & Lissak, R. I. (1985). Apparent impropriety and procedural fairness judgments. *Journal of Experimental Social Psychology, 21,* 19–29.

Lind, E. A., Lissak, R. I., & Conlon, D. E. (1983). Decision control and process control effects on procedural fairness judgments. *Journal of Applied Social Psychology, 13,* 338–350.

Lind, E. A., Park, S., & Ke, G. Y. (1984, August). *Procedures and practices: Formality and obedience to instructions.* Paper presented at the meeting of the American Psychological Association, Toronto.

Lind, E. A., Shapard, J. E., & Cecil, J. S. (1981). *Methods for empirical evaluation of innovations in the justice system.* Washington, DC: Federal Judicial Center.

Lind, E. A., Thibaut, J., & Walker, L. (1973). Discovery and presentation of evidence in adversary and nonadversary proceedings. *Michigan Law Review, 71,* 1129–1144.

Lind, E. A., Thibaut, J., & Walker, L. (1976). A cross-cultural comparison of the effect of adversary and nonadversary processes on bias in legal decision making. *Virginia Law Review, 62,* 271–283.

Lipset, S., & Schneider, W. (1983). *The confidence gap: Business, labor, and government in the public mind.* New York: Free Press.

Lissak, R. I. (1983). *Procedural fairness: How employees evaluate procedures.* Unpublished doctoral dissertation, University of Illinois, Champaign.

Lissak, R. I., Mendes, H., & Lind, E. A. (1983). *Organizational and non-organizational influences on attitudes towards work.* Unpublished manuscript, University of Illinois, Champaign.

Lissak, R. I., & Sheppard, B. H. (1983). Beyond fairness: The criterion problem in research on dispute intervention. *Journal of Applied Social Psychology, 13,* 45–65.

Locke, E. A. (1976). The nature and causes of job satisfaction. In M. D. Dunnette (Ed.), *Handbook of industrial and organizational psychology* (pp. 1297–1350). New York: Wiley.

Locke, E. A., & Schweiger, D. M. (1979). Participation in decision-making: One more look. In B. M. Staw (Ed.), *Research in organizational behavior* (Vol. 1) Greenwich, CT: JAI Press.

Luce, R. D., & Raiffa, H. (1957). *Games and decisions: Introduction and critical survey.* New York: Wiley.

Luce, R. D., & Suppes, P. (1965). Preference, utility, and subjective probability. In R. D. Luce, R. R. Bush, & E. Galanter (Eds.), *The handbook of mathematical psychology* (Vol. 3). New York: Wiley.

MacCoun, R. J., & Tyler, T. R. (In press) The basis of citizens' preferences for different forms of criminal jury: Procedural justice, accuracy, and efficiency. *Law and Human Behavior.*

Martin, J., Feldman, M. S., Hatch, M. J., & Sitkin, S. B. (1983). The uniqueness paradox in organizational stories. *Administrative Sciences Quarterly, 28,* 438–453.

McClosky, H. (1964). Consensus and ideology in American politics. *American Political Science Review, 58,* 361–382.

McClosky, H., & Brill, A. (1983). *Dimensions of tolerance: What Americans believe about civil liberties.* New York: Russell Sage.

McEwen, C. A., & Maiman, R. J. (1984). Mediation in small claims court: Achieving compliance through consent. *Law & Society Review, 18,* 1984, 11–49.

Merton, R. K., & Rossi, A. S. (1957). Contributions to the theory of reference group behavior. In R. K. Merton (Ed.), *Social theory and social structure,* (rev. ed., pp. 225–280). New York: Free Press.

Messe, L. A., Hymes, R. W., & MacCoun, R. J. (1986). Group categorization and distributive justice decisions. In H. W. Bierhoff, R. L. Cohen, & J. Greenberg (Eds.), *Justice in social relations* (pp. 227–248). New York: Plenum Press.

Messick, D. M., & Brewer, M. B. (1983). Solving social dilemmas: A review. In L. Wheeler & P. Shaver (Eds.), *Review of personality and social psychology* (Vol. 4, pp. 11–44). Beverly Hills, CA: Sage.

Messick, D. M., Bloom, S., Boldizar, J. P., & Samuelson, C. D. (1985). Why we are fairer than others. *Journal of Experimental Social Psychology, 21,* 480–500.

Mikula, G. (1986). The experience of injustice: Toward a better understanding of its phenomenology. In H. W. Bierhoff, R. L. Cohen, & J. Greenberg (Eds.), *Justice in social relations* (pp. 103–124). New York: Plenum Press.

Milgram, S. (1965). Some conditions of obedience and disobedience to authority. *Human Relations, 18,* 57–76.

Miller, A. (1979). *The institutional focus of political distrust.* Paper delivered at the American Political Science Association.

Miller, A. (1983). Is confidence rebounding? *Public Opinion, 6,* 16–20.

Moore, B. (1978). *Injustice: The social bases of obedience and revolt.* White Plains, NY: Sharpe.

Muller, E. N. (1979). *Aggressive political participation.* Princeton, NJ: Princeton University Press.

Muller, E. N., & Jukam, T. O. (1977). On the meaning of political support. *American Journal of Political Science, 27,* 785–807.

Murphy, W. F., & Tanenhaus, J. (1969). Public opinion and the United States Supreme Court: A preliminary mapping of some prerequisites for court legitimization of regime changes. In J. B. Grossman & J. Tanenhaus (Eds.), *Frontiers in judicial research.* New York: Wiley.

Musante, L., Gilbert, M. A., & Thibaut, J. (1983). The effects of control on perceived fairness of procedures and outcomes. *Journal of Experimental Social Psychology, 19,* 223–238.

Nacoste, R. W. (1985). Selection procedure and responses to affirmative action: The case of favorable treatment. *Law and Human Behavior, 9,* 225–242.

Nader, L. (1969). Styles of court procedure: To make the balance. In L. Nader (Ed.), *Law in culture and society.* Chicago: Aldine.

Naylor, J. C., Pritchard, R. D., & Ilgen, D. R. (1980). *A theory of behavior in organizations.* New York: Academic Press.

Neumann, J. von, & Morgenstern, O. (1947). *Theory of games and economic behavior* (2nd ed.). Princeton: Princeton University Press.

O'Barr, W. M., & Conley, J. M. (1985). Litigant satisfaction versus legal adequacy in small claims court narratives. *Law and Society Review, 19,* 661–701.

O'Barr, W. M., & Lind, E. A. (1981). Ethnography and experimentation— Partners in legal research. In B. D. Sales (Ed.), *Perspectives in law and psychology: The trial process* (pp. 181–208). New York, NY: Plenum Press.

Okun, A. M. (1975). *Equality and efficiency: The big tradeoff.* Washington, DC: Brookings.

Ophuls, W. (1977). *Ecology and the politics of scarcity.* San Francisco: Freeman.

Paese, P. (1985). *Procedural fairness and work group responses to performance evaluation procedures.* Unpublished masters thesis, University of Illinois, Champaign.

Perry, J. L. (1986, May). *The "crisis" in the courts: Critical change in the role of the judge.* Paper presented at the annual meeting of the Law and Society Association, Chicago.

Popper, K. R. (1959). *The logic of scientific discovery.* New York: Basic Books.

Prothro, J. W., & Grigg, C. M. (1960). Fundamental principles of democracy: Bases of agreement and disagreement. *Journal of Politics, 22,* 276–294.

Rasinski, K. A. (1986). *The influence of concerns about economic outcomes versus concerns about economic justice on political behavior.* Unpublished manuscript, University of Chicago.

Rasinski, K. A. (1987). What's fair is fair . . . or is it? Value differences underlying public views about social justice. *Journal of Personality and Social Psychology, 53,* 201–211.

Rasinski, K. A., & Tyler, T. R. (in press). Fairness and vote choice in the 1986 Presidential election. *American Politics Quarterly.*

Rasinski, K. A., Tyler, T. R., & Fridkin, K. (1985). Exploring dimensions of legitimacy: The mediating effects of personal and nonpersonal legitimacy on leadership endorsement and system support. *Journal of Personality and Social Psychology, 49,* 386–394.

Rawls, J. (1971). *A theory of justice.* Cambridge, MA: Harvard University Press.

Reis, H. T. (1986). Levels of interest in the study of interpersonal justice. In H. W. Bierhoff, R. L. Cohen, & J. Greenberg (Eds.), *Justice in social relations* (pp. 187–210). New York: Plenum Press.

Resnik, J. (1982). Managerial judges. *Harvard Law Review, 96,* 374–458.

Resnik, J. (1984). Tiers. *Southern California Law Review, 57,* 837–1011.

Saphire, R. B. (1978). Specifying due process values. *University of Pennsylvania Law Review, 127,* 111–195.

Sarat, A. (1975). Support for the legal system. *American Politics Quarterly, 3,* 3–24.

Sarat, A. (1976). Alternatives in dispute processing: Litigation in a small claims court. *Law & Society Review, 11,* 1976, 339–375.

Sarat, A. (1977). Studying American legal culture: An assessment of survey evidence. *Law & Society Review, 11,* 427–488.

Savage, L. J. (1954). *The foundations of statistics.* New York: Wiley.

Scheingold, S. A. (1974). *The politics of rights.* New Haven: Yale.

Shaftesbury, A. A. C. (1710). *Soliloquy, or advice to an author.* London.

Shaver, P. (1980, October). The public distrust. *Psychology Today.*

Shaw, M. E. (1954). Some effects of unequal distribution of information upon group performance in various communication nets. *Journal of Abnormal and Social Psychology, 49,* 547–553.

Sheppard, B. H. (1983). Managers as inquisitors: Some lessons from the law. In M. H. Bazerman & R. J. Lewicki (Eds.), *Negotiating in organizations* (pp. 193–213). Beverly Hills, CA: Sage.

Sheppard, B. H. (1984). Third-party conflict intervention: A procedural framework. In B. M. Staw & L. L. Cummings (Eds.), *Research in organizational behavior* (Vol. 6, pp. 20141–190). Greenwich, CT: JAI Press.

Sheppard, B. H. (1985). Justice is no simple matter: Case for elaborating our model of procedural fairness. *Journal of Personality and Social Psychology, 49,* 953–962.

Sheppard, B. H., & Lewicki, R. J. (1987). Toward general principles of managerial fairness. *Social Justice Research, 1,* 161–176.

Sheppard, B. H., Saunders, D. M., & Minton, J. W. (1986). *Procedural justice from the third party perspective.* Unpublished manuscript, Duke University, Durham, NC.

Sheppard, B. H., & Vidmar, N. (1980). Adversary pretrial procedures and testimonial evidence: Effects of lawyer's role and machiavellianism. *Journal of Personality and Social Psychology, 39,* 320–332.

Srull, T. K., & Wyer, R. S. (1979). The role of category accessibility in the interpretation of information about persons: Some determinants and implications. *Journal of Personality and Social Psychology, 37,* 1660–1672.

Srull, T. K., & Wyer, R. S. (1980). Category accessibility and social perception: Some implications for the study of person memory and interpersonal judgments. *Journal of Personality and Social Psychology, 38,* 841–856.

Storms, M. D. (1973). Videotape and the attribution process: Reversing actors' and observers' points of view. *Journal of Personality and Social Psychology, 27,* 165–175.

Stouffer, S. A. (1955). *Communism, conformity, and civil liberties.* New York: Wiley.

Sullivan, J. L., Piereson, J., & Marcus, G. E. (1982). *Political tolerance and American democracy.* Chicago: University of Chicago Press.

Tajfel, H. (1969). Cognitive aspects of prejudice. *Journal of Social Issues, 25,* 79–97.

Tajfel, H. (1978). *Differentiation between social groups: Studies in the social psychology of intergroup relations.* New York: Academic Press.

Thibaut, J. (1968). The development of contractual norms in bargaining: Replication and variation. *Journal of Conflict Resolution, 12,* 102–112.

Thibaut, J., & Faucheux, C. (1965). The development of contractual norms in a bargaining situation under two types of stress. *Journal of Experimental Social Psychology, 1,* 89–102.

Thibaut, J., Friedland, N., & Walker, L. (1974). Compliance with rules: Some social determinants. *Journal of Personality and Social Psychology, 30,* 792–801.

Thibaut, J., & Gruder, C. L. (1969). Formation of contractual agreements between parties of unequal power. *Journal of Personality and Social Psychology, 11,* 59–65.

Thibaut, J., & Kelley, H. H. (1959). *The social psychology of groups.* New York: Wiley.

Thibaut, J., & Walker, L. (1975). *Procedural justice: A psychological analysis.* Hillsdale, NJ: Erlbaum.

Thibaut, J., & Walker, L. (1978). A theory of procedure. *California Law Review, 66,* 541–566.

Thibaut, J., Walker, L., LaTour, S., & Houlden, P. (1974). Procedural justice as fairness. *Stanford Law Review, 26,* 1271–1289.

Thibaut, J., Walker, L., & Lind, E. A. (1972). Adversary presentation and bias in legal decision making. *Harvard Law Review, 86,* 386–401.

Tyler, T. R. (1984). The role of perceived injustice in defendant's evaluations of their courtroom experience. *Law & Society Review, 18,* 51–74.

Tyler, T. R. (1986a). Justice and leadership endorsement. In R. R. Lau & D. O. Sears (Eds.), *Political cognition* (pp. 257–278). Hillsdale, NJ: Erlbaum.

Tyler, T. R. (1986b). Procedural justice in organizations. In R. Lewicki, M. Bazerman, & B. Sheppard (Eds.), *Research on negotiation in organizations* (Vol. 1, pp. 7–23). Greenwich, CT: JAI Press.

Tyler, T. R. (1987a). Conditions leading to value expressive effects in judgments of procedural justice: A test of four models. *Journal of Personality and Social Psychology, 52,* 333–344.

Tyler, T. R. (1987b). *Why citizens follow the law: Procedural justice, legitimacy and compliance.* Unpublished manuscript, Northwestern University.

Tyler, T. R. (in press). *What is procedural justice? Criteria used by citizens to assess the fairness of legal procedures. Law and Society Review.*

Tyler, T. R., & Caine, A. (1981). The influence of outcomes and procedures on satisfaction with formal leaders. *Journal of Personality and Social Psychology, 41,* 642–655.

Tyler, T. R., Casper, J. D., & Fisher, B. (1987). *Maintaining allegiance toward political authorities.* Unpublished manuscript, American Bar Foundation.

Tyler, T. R., & Folger, R. (1980). Distributional and procedural aspects of satisfaction with citizen–police encounters. *Basic and Applied Social Psychology, 1,* 281–292.

Tyler, T. R., & McGraw, K. (1986). Ideology and the interpretation of personal experience: Procedural justice and political quiescence. *Journal of Social Issues, 42,* 115–128.

Tyler, T. R., Rasinski, K., & Griffin, E. (1986). Alternative images of the citizen: Implications for public policy. *American Psychologist, 41,* 970–978.

Tyler, T. R., Rasinski, K., & McGraw, K. (1985). The influence of perceived injustice on support for political authorities. *Journal of Applied Social Psychology, 15,* 700–725.

Tyler, T. R., Rasinski, K., & Spodick, N. (1985). The influence of voice on satisfaction with leaders: Exploring the meaning of process control. *Journal of Personality and Social Psychology, 48,* 72–81.

Tyler, T. R., & Weber, R. (1982). Support for the death penalty: Instrumental response to crime, or symbolic attitude? *Law & Society Review, 17,* 21–45.

Vidmar, N., & Laird, N. M. (1983). Adversary social roles: Their effects on witnesses' communication of evidence and the assessment of adjudicators. *Journal of Personality and Social Psychology, 44,* 888–898.

Wahlke, J. (1971). Policy demands and system support: The role of the represented. *British Journal of Political Science, 1,* 271–290.

Walker, L., LaTour, S., Lind, E. A., & Thibaut, J. (1974). Reactions of participants and observers to modes of adjudication. *Journal of Applied Social Psychology, 4,* 295–310.

Walker, L., Lind, E. A., & Thibaut, J. (1979). The relation between procedural and distributive justice. *Virginia Law Review, 65,* 1401–1420.

Walker, L., & Thibaut, J. (1971). An experimental examination of pretrial conference techniques. *Minnesota Law Review, 55,* 1113–1137.

Walker, L., Thibaut, J., & Andreoli, V. (1972). Order of presentation at trial. *Yale Law Journal, 82,* 216–226.

Walster, E., Berscheid, E., & Walster, G. W. (1973). New directions in equity research. *Journal of Personality and Social Psychology, 25,* 151–176.

Walster, E., Walster, G. W., & Berscheid, E. (1978). *Equity: Theory and research.* Boston: Allyn and Bacon.

White, R., & Lippitt, R. (1960). *Autocracy and democracy.* New York: Harper.

Wilson, J. Q., & Banfield, E. C. (1964). Public-regardingness as a value premise in voting behavior. *American Political Science Review, 50,* 491–505.

Wong, P. T. B., & Weiner, B. (1981). When people ask "why" questions, and the heuristics of attributional search. *Journal of Personality and Social Psychology, 40,* 650–663.

Wright, J. (1981). Political disaffection. In S. Long (Ed.), *Handbook of political behavior.* New York: Plenum Press.

Author Index

Adams, J. S., 1, 10, 11, 29, 37, 130, 176
Adelman, L., 37
Adler, J. W., 72, 81, 102, 210, 220
Ajzen, I., 227
Alexander, S., 82, 177, 178, 179, 209, 210, 211, 225
Ambrose, M., 194
Anderson, J. K., 41, 121, 203
Andreoli, V., 22
Anton, T. J., 153, 217
Austin, W., 69, 165, 234

Ball, K. P., 165
Banfield, E. C., 154
Barrett-Howard, E., 138, 139, 140, 141, 142, 145, 165, 213, 217, 225
Barton, E., 154
Bavelas, A., 9
Berkowitz, L., 129
Berscheid, E., 1, 11, 154, 223
Bies, R. J., 100, 165, 199, 209, 230
Blau, P. M., 10
Bloom, S., 214
Blumberg, P., 151
Boldizar, J. P., 214
Bray, R. M., 4, 89
Brett, J. M., 16, 95, 96, 97, 99, 192
Brewer, M. B., 230
Brill, A., 149, 171
Burger, W. E., 119

Caddell, P. H., 150
Caine, A., 46, 48, 162, 206, 209, 212
Campbell. D. T., 49, 50
Campbell, J. P., 176
Casper, J. D., 73, 78, 219
Cecil, J. S., 49
Cheney, G., 136, 138
Citrin, J., 153
Cohen, R. L., 26, 69, 181, 182, 183, 202
Conley, J. M., 106
Conlon, D. E., 97, 104, 111, 112, 194
Cook, F. L., 154
Cook, T. D., 49, 50
Corkran, L., 9, 69
Cornelius, G. W., 184, 190, 198
Crosby, F., 12, 154, 212

Damaska, M., 41, 61, 203
Davis, J. H., 7, 9, 19
Dawes, R., 230
deCarufel, A., 151
Dennis, J., 233
Deutsch, M., 7, 151, 225
Diamond, W. D., ii
Dickenberger, M., 9

Earley, P. C., 49, 59, 179, 185, 188, 189, 193, 194, 195, 237
Easton, D., 149, 217, 224, 233
Ebreo, A., 99
Edelman, M., 153, 171, 217

Engstrom, R. L., 153, 217
Erickson, B. E., 9, 13

Faucheux, C. i, 139, 224
Feather, N. T., 152, 217
Feldman, M. S., 233
Festinger, L., 11
Fishbein, M., 227
Fisher, B., 73, 95
Fiss, O. M., 122
Folger, R., 9, 12, 69, 74, 76, 165, 177, 179, 180, 181, 182, 183, 184, 185, 199, 207, 209, 212, 216, 229, 231
Frey, R., 13
Fridkin, K., 150
Friedland, N., 9, 79, 187
Friedman, J. S., 165
Friedman, L. M., 147
Fry, W. R., 130, 136, 137, 138, 141

Gamson, W., 217
Gilbert, M. A., 102
Giles, M. W., 153, 217
Gilmore, R., ii
Gluckman, M., 121
Goldberg, S. B., 16, 96, 99
Goodstein, L., 73
Greenberg, J., 57, 129, 151, 176, 177, 179, 185, 186, 187, 188, 197, 198, 199, 212, 216, 219, 235, 236
Griffin, E., 152
Grigg, C. M., 148
Grove, J., 9, 69

Gruder, C. L., i
Gutek, B. A., 154

Hammond, K. R., 37
Hans, V., 4, 89
Hansen, R. D., 38
Hatch, M. J., 233
Hayden, R. M., 41, 121, 203
Heinz, A. M., 73
Henshel, R. L., 45
Hensler, D. R., 72, 81, 102, 210, 220
Heuer, L. B., 88
Hochschild, J., 171
Hollander, E. P., 8
Holmes, J., 13
Homans, G. C., 10, 222
Hooe, G. S., 165
Houlden, P., 7, 9, 14, 16, 31, 35, 84, 85, 86, 99, 123
House, J. S., 153
Hutcheson, F., 154
Hymes, R. W., 231

Ilgen, D. R., 200
Insko, C. A., ii

James, F., 62, 63
Jones, E. E., 38
Jöreskog, K. J., 56, 189
Jukam, T. O., 169

Kahn, R. L., 154
Kanfer, R., 179, 185, 187, 190, 191, 192, 194, 209
Kaplan, M., 4
Karuza, J., 130
Kassin, S., 4, 89
Katz, D., 102, 154
Ke, G. Y., 231
Kelley, H. H., i, 1, 13, 14, 29, 152, 180, 222
Kerr, N. L., 4, 89
Kinder, D. R., 150, 168
Kohlberg, L., 233, 234
Kramer, R., 230
Kurtz, S. T., 67, 84, 85

Laird, N. M., 114, 115, 116, 118
Lamm, H., 142, 145

Landis, J. M., 73
Lane, R. E., 171, 172, 230
Langer, E. J., 194, 236
LaTour, S., 7, 9, 14, 27, 29, 30, 31, 35, 66, 67, 97, 98, 123, 186
Laver, M., 1, 152, 222
Lea, M., 120
Leavitt, H. J., 9
Lerner, M. J., 3, 7, 11, 230
Lerner, S. C., 151, 230
Leung, K., 88, 144, 145, 208, 234
Leventhal, G. S., 6, 7, 11, 107, 129, 130, 131, 132, 133, 134, 135, 136, 137, 138, 139, 140, 155, 175, 197, 198, 199, 213, 216, 221, 223, 225, 237
Lewicki, R. J., 57, 173, 198
Lewin, K., 8
Lind, E. A., 9, 18, 20, 21, 22, 25, 27, 33, 41, 44, 46, 49, 58, 59, 67, 69, 74, 76, 84, 85, 88, 94, 97, 98, 104, 111, 112, 113, 114, 116, 144, 179, 183, 185, 188, 189, 194, 195, 215, 228, 231, 235, 236, 237
Lippitt, R., 8
Lipset, S., 150
Lipsitz, A., ii
Lissak, R. I., 50, 51, 59, 74, 76, 87, 88, 97, 104, 111, 112, 174, 179, 183, 185, 186, 187, 191, 192, 228
Locke, E. A., 177, 188
Lowe, C. A., 38
Luce, R. D., 152, 217

MacCoun, R. J., 89, 91, 231, 234
Maiman, R. J., 64, 81, 99, 210
Marcus, G. E., 149
Martin, J., 233
Martz, R. A., 165
Mason, W. M., 153
McClosky, H., 148, 149, 171
McEwen, C. A., 64, 81, 99, 210

McGraw, K., 155, 160, 162, 170, 171, 209, 212, 233, 239
Mendes, H., 179
Merton, R. K., 11
Messe, L. A., 231
Messick, D. M., 214, 230
Mikula, G., 214, 230
Milgram, S., 231
Miller, A., 150, 153
Minton, J. W., 123
Moag, J. S., 100, 230
Moehle, D., ii
Moore, B., 12, 154
Morgenstern, O., 152, 217
Muller, E. N., 12, 150, 162, 169
Murphy, W. F., 64, 153, 217
Musante, L., 67, 102, 103, 104

Nacoste, R. W., 165, 199
Nader, L., 121
Nagao, D., 19
Naylor, J. C., 200
Nelson, C. E., 72, 81, 102, 210, 220
Neumann, J. von, 152, 217
Nisbett, R. E., 38

O'Barr, W. M., 46, 106
Okun, A. M., 225
Ophuls, W., 151

Paese, P., 184, 195, 199, 228, 229
Park, S., 231
Penrod, S., 88
Perry. J. L., 121, 220
Piereson, J., 149
Popper, K. R., 43, 44, 45
Pritchard, R. D., 176, 200
Prothro, J. W., 148

Raiffa, H., 152, 217
Rasinski, K. A., 59, 96, 98, 101, 102, 103, 150, 152, 154, 155, 160, 162, 166, 168, 170, 209, 210, 212, 215, 239
Rawls, J., 4, 30, 31, 32

Reis, H. T., 224, 231
Resnik, J., 122
Robinson, T., 165, 184
Rosenfield, D., 9, 69, 165, 184
Rossi, A. S., 11
Ruderman, M., 82, 177, 178, 209, 210, 211, 225
Russ, T. L., 210

Samuelson, C. D., 214
Saphire, R. B., 217
Sarat, A., 84, 121, 154, 217
Saunders, D. M., 123
Savage, L. J., 152, 217
Sawyer, J., 179, 185
Scheingold, S. A., 153, 171, 217
Schneider, W., 150
Schweiger, D. M., 177
Sears, D. O., 150, 168
Shaftesbury, A. A. C., 154
Shapard, J. E., 49
Shapiro, D. L., 165, 199
Shaver, P., 150
Shaw, M. E., 9
Sheppard, B. H., 57, 85, 86, 87, 88, 100, 101, 114, 115, 116, 117, 118, 123, 173, 198
Siegel, D., 69
Sitkin, S. B., 233
Solomon, M. R., ii
Sörbom, D., 56, 189
Spitzer, C. E., 19
Spodick, N., 59, 96, 98, 101, 102, 103, 215
Srull, T. K., 228

Stasser, G. T., 19
Storms, M. D., 38
Stouffer, S. A., 149
Sullivan, J. L., 149, 171
Suppes, P., 152, 217

Tajfel, H., 230, 239
Tanenhaus, J., 64, 153, 217
Thibaut, J. W., i, ii, 1, 4, 5, 6, 7, 8, 9, 10, 11, 12, 13, 14, 15, 16, 17, 18, 19, 20, 21, 22, 23, 24, 25, 26, 27, 28, 29, 30, 31, 32, 33, 34, 35, 36, 37, 38, 39, 40, 41, 42, 44, 52, 66, 67, 69, 76, 79, 83, 84, 87, 89, 94, 95, 96, 97, 100, 102, 109, 113, 114, 115, 116, 117, 118, 119, 121, 131, 132, 135, 139, 151, 152, 154, 180, 187, 192, 198, 203, 204, 206, 207, 208, 210, 211, 212, 215, 216, 221, 222, 223, 224, 232, 242
Tobiasen, J. M., 234
Tyler, T. R., 2, 46, 48, 51, 53, 56, 59, 65, 69, 70, 73, 74, 76, 78, 80, 81, 89, 91, 96, 98, 99, 101, 102, 103, 104, 105, 107, 109, 110, 132, 134, 138, 139, 140, 141, 142, 150, 152, 155, 160, 162, 163, 165, 168, 170, 171, 193, 194, 206, 209, 210, 212, 213, 214, 215, 216, 217, 218, 225, 229, 233, 234, 235, 239

Vidmar, N., 4, 89, 114, 115, 116, 117, 118

Wahlke, J., 153, 217
Walker, L., 4, 5, 6, 7, 8, 9, 10, 11, 12, 13, 14, 15, 16, 17, 18, 19, 20, 21, 22, 23, 24, 25, 26, 27, 28, 29, 30, 31, 32, 33, 34, 35, 36, 37, 38, 39, 40, 41, 42, 44, 52, 58, 59, 66, 67, 69, 76, 79, 83, 87, 89, 94, 95, 96, 97, 98, 100, 104, 109, 111, 113, 114, 115, 116, 117, 118, 119, 120, 121, 123, 131, 132, 135, 154, 187, 192, 198, 203, 204, 206, 207, 208, 209, 211, 212, 215, 216, 221, 222, 223, 242
Walster, E., 1, 11, 37, 129, 154, 223
Walster, G. W., 1, 11, 37, 129, 154, 223
Weber, R., 235
Weiner, B., 112
Wentzel, A. A., 69
White, R. K., 8
Whitehead, L. A., 7
Williams, T. A., 69
Wilson, J. Q., 154
Wilson, M., ii
Wong, P. T. B., 112
Worchel, S., 69
Wright, J., 150, 153
Wrightsman L., 4, 89
Wyer, R. S., 228

Subject Index

Accuracy of information, 19, 22–25, 28, 36–38, 63, 76, 107, 113, 114, 120, 132–134, 184, 185, 190, 197–199, 201, 216, 234

Adjudication, 12–15, 17, 21, 27, 31–35, 38, 45, 47, 58, 81, 84, 88, 94–99, 102, 104, 111, 119, 121, 122, 144, 145, 210

Adversary legal procedures, 12, 13, 15–25, 27–36, 38, 44, 45, 47, 58, 67, 69, 83, 84, 86, 88, 89, 94, 95, 98, 104, 111, 113–122, 124, 127, 129, 144, 145, 215, 234

(*See also* Process control)

Affirmative action, 149, 164, 165, 199

Allocation, 1, 3, 5, 6, 10, 11, 30, 62, 69, 74, 99, 107, 129–136, 138, 139, 142, 148, 151, 173–176, 179–182, 190, 198, 201, 212, 213, 216, 224, 233

Arbitration, 12, 14–17, 72, 81, 99, 102, 106, 124–127, 210, 212, 220

Authorities, evaluations of, 6, 56, 57, 64, 65, 71, 72, 76–80, 83, 105, 107, 109, 135, 147–151, 154, 179, 204, 206, 209–212, 214, 229, 238, 239

Authority, obedience to, 64, 231

Bargainer's dilemma, 225

Bargaining, 12, 14, 15, 31, 73, 78, 86, 120, 144, 219, 225

Bias suppression, 3, 19–26, 36–38, 44, 47, 113–117, 127, 131, 136, 137, 156, 181, 182

Cognitive conflict, 37–39

Cognitive dissonance, 11

Communication networks, 8, 9, 27

Comparable worth, 164, 165

Competitive relationships, 14–16, 138, 180, 181

Compliance
with decisions, 46, 64, 65, 76, 81–83, 93, 95, 99, 125, 187, 201, 202, 210, 211
with laws, 6, 63–65, 76, 79–81, 83, 84, 93, 95, 175, 211

Conflict of interests, 5, 12, 14, 16, 26, 27, 29, 37–39, 58, 82, 126, 152, 164, 186, 195, 196, 213, 214, 223, 235, 237, 239, 240, 246

Consistency, 63, 107, 109, 126, 131, 147, 149–151, 153–155, 178, 197, 198, 203, 210, 211, 229, 239–241

Context, effects of, 122, 124, 135–145, 211–216, 221

Control
by request, 100
content, 100
decision. *See* Decision control.
process. *See* Process control.

Cooperative relationships, 138

Correctability, 107, 126, 132, 140–142, 216

Correlational design, 46, 48, 50–52, 56, 59, 210

Cost of procedures, 63, 88, 90–92, 113, 118–121, 127, 201, 234

Court-annexed arbitration. *See* Arbitration.

Cross-national studies, 33,35, 47, 48, 58, 88

(*See also* Culture)

Culture, 3, 88, 135, 136, 141–145, 233–236

Cushion of support, 64, 67, 68, 71, 72, 150, 163, 233

Decision control, 35, 36, 85, 88, 96–100, 102, 103, 107–110, 121, 122, 132, 171, 215, 222, 223

Decision quality, 19, 107, 110, 119, 125, 127, 162, 163, 229, 234

Distributive justice, 4, 7, 10–12, 30, 37, 39, 46, 53, 55, 62, 65–70, 74, 81, 94, 96, 102, 103, 105, 111, 121, 129–135, 138, 139, 154–156, 158, 160, 161, 163–166, 168, 170–172, 175–187, 197, 198, 204, 211–213, 216, 223, 225–227, 231
  (*See also* Equity; Outcome fairness)

Equity, 10–12, 29, 30, 37, 96, 101, 130, 154, 168, 175–177, 182, 223, 225, 240

Ethicality, 107, 109, 110, 125–127, 132, 134, 142, 237, 239

Expectancy bias, 20–22, 25, 38, 117

False consciousness, 4, 76, 163, 201, 202

Field experiments, 41, 42, 48–50, 56, 59, 188, 189, 194, 195

Field studies, 41, 42, 47, 50, 51, 59, 72, 81, 102, 174, 184, 185, 187, 189, 197, 198, 205, 206, 239

Formal relationships, 138, 139

Frustration effect, 69, 180–184, 201, 202, 207

Goal-setting procedures, 189, 193

Group value model, 230–241

Hybrid legal procedures, 86, 87, 101, 117

Impartiality, 106, 107, 125–127

Informal relationships, 138, 139, 214, 216, 223

Inquisitorial legal procedures, 12, 13, 15–25, 27, 29–31, 33–35, 38, 44, 58, 67, 69, 86, 88, 94, 113–121, 129, 144, 234

Institutions, evaluations of, 1, 4, 6, 46, 53, 61, 63–66, 70, 76, 79, 84, 129, 135, 149, 150, 160, 190, 196, 226, 229, 230, 241, 243, 244, 249, 256

Interaction goals, 130, 132, 134, 242, 251

Interdependence theory, 239
  (*See also* Social exchange)

Job satisfaction, 195, 196, 228

Jury procedures, 9, 10, 19, 89–92

Laboratory experiments, 6, 10, 14, 19, 20, 27, 41–46, 48, 52, 58, 59, 68, 79, 98, 99, 104, 121, 155, 179, 180, 184–191, 193–195, 198, 199, 203, 205, 206, 239

Leadership, 8, 66, 148, 149, 151–153, 160, 166, 171, 172, 179, 204, 206, 209, 218–220, 224, 227

Legitimacy, 8, 64, 65, 76–81, 92, 119, 153, 209, 210, 213, 219

Mediation, 12–16, 64, 81, 88, 96, 99, 100, 121–123, 134, 144–145, 210, 212

Objective justice, 3–5, 9, 12, 18–22, 26, 36, 37, 47, 63, 76, 89, 92, 95, 108, 113, 117, 127, 162, 200, 201, 220, 234

Order effects, 19, 22, 36, 113

Organizational attitudes, 66, 174, 177–179, 200, 201

Outcome fairness, 3, 7, 10, 26, 51, 53, 62, 65–67, 69, 70, 81, 130, 157, 158, 172, 176, 179, 180, 184, 186, 192, 204

Outcome-oriented theories, 1, 2, 39, 95–100, 152–154, 192, 215, 217, 222–230
  (*See also* Self-interest model)

Outcome versus process, 1, 2, 11, 28, 29, 39, 42, 55, 62, 65, 67, 73, 78, 92, 95, 100, 101–105, 110–112, 133, 135, 152–154, 161, 163–165, 171, 188–190, 195, 199, 200, 212, 215, 217, 219, 222–230, 239–242

Panel studies, 56, 78, 105

Participation, 8, 69, 70, 92, 102, 103, 176, 177, 181, 183, 195, 211, 236

Path diagrams, 55

Performance. *See* Task performance.

Post-conflict relations, 118, 121, 122

Power, 18, 101, 106, 138, 139, 142, 149, 150, 171, 187, 239

Procedural preferences, 13, 15, 31–34, 47, 48, 63, 64, 83–91, 93, 101, 114, 118, 122–125, 144, 145, 163, 222, 223, 235, 237, 249, 250

Process control, 9, 15, 17, 30, 35–40, 58, 59, 83, 85–88, 93–111, 117, 121, 122, 125, 129, 132, 134, 144, 145, 170, 176, 194, 197, 204, 207, 208, 215, 223, 229, 236
  (*See also* Voice)

Process-oriented theories, 1–3, 96–109, 153–158, 163, 191, 200, 217–220

Public choice theory, 1, 151–153, 222, 241
  (*See also* Outcome-oriented theories)

Relative deprivation, 11, 12, 154, 185
Representation, 107, 109, 110, 132, 134,
    136, 140, 235

Scenario studies, 33, 41, 46–49, 56, 59, 69,
    84, 86, 88, 89, 99, 100, 135, 138, 144,
    170, 206
Self-interest model, 22, 125, 222–230, 241
    (*See also* Outcome-oriented theories)
Social climate, 8, 27
Social cognition, 38, 112, 131, 209, 222,
    228, 229, 231, 234, 238, 240
Social dilemmas, 230
Social exchange, 12–14, 26, 27, 29, 96,
    152, 200, 222, 241
Social reform, 122
Socialization, 37, 232–237, 239
Subjective justice, 3–5, 12, 18, 19, 26, 30,
    31, 36, 39, 47, 63, 76, 89, 92, 108, 113,
    116, 127, 201, 209
Substantive law, 62
Supervisors, evaluations of, 178, 179, 209
Survey methods, 51–59, 65, 67, 73, 74, 80,
    82, 98, 104, 107, 150, 155, 166, 168,
    177, 220

System support
    diffuse, 149, 160–162, 212, 233
    specific, 149, 150, 160–162, 212

Task performance, 8, 9, 27, 28, 49, 175,
    176, 179, 188–191, 210, 211
Third-party dispute resolution, 12, 13–17,
    31, 34, 35, 85, 86, 97, 100, 101, 104,
    111, 120, 123, 173, 222
Trust in government. *See* System support,
    diffuse.
Turnover, 178, 210, 211

Usefulness analysis, 53, 65

Value-expressive effects. *See* Voice.
Veil of ignorance, 30–33, 114
Voice, 9, 49, 170–172, 174–177, 179–183,
    186, 189–198, 201, 202, 204, 208, 214–
    216, 219, 229, 236, 237, 239, 240
    (*See also* Process control)
Voting behavior, 152–154, 166, 168, 175,
    211, 218